Contents

General Editors' Preface

The outlines of contemporary critical theory are now often taught as a standard feature of a degree in literary studies. The development of particular theories has seen a thorough transformation of literary criticism. For example, Marxist and Foucauldian theories have revolutionized Shakespeare studies and 'deconstruction' has led to a complete reassessment of Romantic poetry. Feminist criticism has left scarcely any period of literature unaffected by its searching critiques. Teachers of literary studies can no longer fall back on a standardized, received methodology.

Lecturers and teachers are now urgently looking for guidance in a rapidly changing critical environment. They need help in understanding the latest revisions in literary theory, and especially in grasping the practical effects of the new theories in the form of theoretically sensitized new readings. A number of volumes in the series anthologize important essays on particular theories. However, in order to grasp the full implications and possible uses of particular theories it is essential to see them put to work. This series provides substantial volumes of new readings, presented in an accessible form and with a significant amount of editorial guidance.

Each volume includes a substantial introduction which explores the theoretical issues and conflicts embodied in the essays selected and locates areas of disagreement between positions. The pluralism of theories has to be put on the agenda of literary studies. We can no longer pretend that we all tacitly accept the same practices in literary studies. Neither is a *laissez-faire* attitude any longer tenable. Literature departments need to go beyond the mere toleration of theoretical differences: it is not enough merely to agree to differ; they need actually to 'stage' the differences openly. The volumes in this series all attempt to dramatize the differences, not necessarily with a view to resolving them but in order to foreground the choices presented by different theories or to argue for a particular route through the impasses the differences present.

The theory 'revolution' has had real effects. It has loosened the grip of traditional empiricist and Romantic assumptions about language and literature. It is not always clear what is being proposed as the new agenda for literary studies, and indeed the very notion of 'literature' is questioned by the post-structuralist strain in theory. However, the uncertainties and obscurities of contemporary theories appear much less worrying when we see what the best critics have been able to do with them in practice. This series aims to disseminate the best of recent criticism, and to show that it is possible to re-read the canonical texts of literature in new and challenging ways.

RAMAN SELDEN AND STAN SMITH

Acknowledgements

We are grateful to the following for permission to reproduce copyright material:

Columbia University Press for the chapter 'Reading Writing: Eliot' from *The Ethics of Reading* by J. Hillis Miller (1987), copyright © 1987 Columbia University Press; Heinemann Educational Books Ltd for the chapter '*Middlemarch* & the Classic Realist Text' by David Lodge from *Critical Essays and Documents* edited by Arnold Kettle (1981); Johns Hopkins University Press for the article 'Rhetoric & Realism in 19th Century Fiction' by Jonathan Arac from *English Literary History*, Vol. 46 (1979) & an extract from '*Romola*: Trauma, Memory, Repression' by Dianne F. Sadoff in *Monsters of Affection: Dickens, Eliot and Brontë on Fatherhood* (1982); the Editors of *Literature and History* for the article 'Power & Knowledge in "The Lifted Veil" ' by Terry Eagleton from *Literature and History*, Vol 9 (1983); Macmillan Accounts & Administration Ltd for extracts from *James Joyce and the Revolution of the Word* by Colin MacCabe (1978); Modern Language Association of America for the article 'The Decomposition of the Elephants: Double-Reading *Daniel Deronda*' by Cynthia Chase from *PMLA*, 93 (1978); Princeton University Press for extracts from *Narrative and Its Discontents* by David Miller, copyright © 1981 by Princeton University Press; University of California Press & the author, Catherine Gallagher, for the article 'The Failure of Realism: Felix Holt' from *Nineteenth-Century Fiction*, Vol. 35, No 3 (December 1980), © 1980 by the Regents of the University of California; The University of Chicago Press & the authors, Sandra M. Gilbert for the article 'Life's Empty Pack: Notes toward a Literary Daughteronomy' from *Critical Inquiry*, Vol. 11 (1985) & Mary Jacobus for the article 'The Question of Language: Men of Maxims and *The Mill on the Floss*' from *Critical Inquiry*, Vol. 8 (1981); Yale University Press for an extract from the chapter 'George Eliot as Angel of Destruction' by Susan Gubar from *The Madwoman in the Attic* by Sandra M. Gilbert & Susan Gubar (1979).

1 Introduction

George Eliot's reputation as a novelist of the first rank has never perhaps been entirely secure. Her literary status has been subject to great fluctuations, and even during those periods when her reputation has been at its highest level critical doubts have not been completely silenced. In some ways this has been responsible for making her a more rather than less significant literary figure, for it has made her works the focus of critical debate, a debate that has been productive at several important stages in the history of modern criticism. Critics who admire her fiction have felt that they had to defend her literary practice and often this has required the development of alternative critical approaches to counter the objections of those who have attacked her work.

Form and realism

The ascendancy of a theory of fiction largely founded on Jamesian principles formed the basis of the low critical regard in which her novels were held in the first half of this century, and defenders of her work between the 1940s and 1960s had to discredit the idea that such principles could be appropriately applied to her work if they were to reinstate her as a major novelist. Though an admirer of her, Henry James had been severely critical of certain aspects of her novels, primarily because they offended against his concept of form. James disapproved of novels with multiple plots and believed that the novel should aspire to be an organism in which nothing was extraneous, with narration restricted in scope by adopting a single point of view and moral or philosophical commentary by the narrator excluded as James attached particular artistic value to dramatic presentation.

The first major critic to question Jamesian objections to George Eliot's fictional practice was F. R. Leavis. In the section on her in *The Great Tradition* (first published in 1948), Leavis acknowledges James's critical intelligence but realizes that James's formalism and aestheticism need to be opposed if George Eliot is to be acknowledged as one of the greatest of English novelists. As Leavis points out, James had claimed that, for George Eliot, the novel 'was not primarily a picture of life, capable of deriving a high value from its form, but a moralized fable, the last word of a philosophy endeavouring to teach by example', and he also saw the 'absence of free aesthetic life' as a weakness in George Eliot's nature. For Leavis, however, form and aesthetic qualities cannot be seen as separate from moral concern and human interest: 'Is there any great novelist whose preoccupation with "form" is not a matter of his responsibility towards a rich human interest, or complexity of interests, profoundly realized? – a responsibility involving, of its very nature, imaginative sympathy, moral discrimination and judgement of relative human values?' Leavis also does not see George Eliot's absorption with abstract ideas as a problem, for 'it must not be concluded that the point about her is that her novels contain intellectual elements – patches, say, of tough or dryly abstract thinking undigested by her art. . . . At her best she has the impersonality of genius.'[1]

Later defenders of her work, notably Barbara Hardy in *The Novels of George Eliot* and W. J. Harvey in *The Art of George Eliot* (first published in 1959 and 1961 respectively), were more sympathetic to formalism and aestheticism, as traditionally understood, than was Leavis and attempted to show that though George Eliot did not adopt Jamesian methods, her fictional practice could nevertheless be defended in formalist terms. Hardy's book is subtitled 'A Study in Form' and its aim is to demonstrate that the realistic, moral and philosophical aspects of George Eliot's novels are almost always controlled by form, while Harvey defends techniques which had been seen as anti-formalist or inartistic, such as omniscient narration with its direct address to the reader, in formalistic terms. Hardy and Harvey in effect try to prove that George Eliot's fiction is not irreconcilable with the dominant Anglo-American formalist approach, the New Criticism, which, in its early phase in the late 1930s and 1940s, had shown little interest in the nineteenth-century novel and, by implication at least, held it in low critical esteem.

The New Critics had directed their attention mainly to lyric poetry and especially admired metaphysical poetry and the work of Modernists such as T. S. Eliot. Only those novels which could be discussed in the terms they applied to the kind of poetry they favoured – that is, which embodied irony, ambiguity, tension, paradox in their form – tended to find favour with them. This made them sympathetic to Jamesian principles and antagonistic to the kind of novels that could not be easily reconciled with them. However, the later New Criticism, which emerged towards the end of the 1950s and dominated the 1960s, particularly in America, did not place the same emphasis on the necessity for literary structures to incorporate irony or ambiguity and shifted the critical focus to thematic coherence. Since George Eliot's novels could be shown to exhibit a high degree of thematic coherence they therefore became appropriate subjects for the kind of analysis favoured by the later New Criticism. During the 1960s, therefore, George Eliot's literary status was high and she became one of the most critically discussed of writers.

It could be argued, however, that certain critical problems had not been faced. Critics like Barbara Hardy and the later New Critics had apparently demonstrated that there was no serious conflict between George Eliot's realism on the one hand and the moral dimension and didactic impulse of her novels on the other, even though on the surface the interests of moralism and didacticism could not be served without realistic criteria being compromised. By showing that both the realism and the moral aspect of the novels were under the control of formal organization or thematic structure this conflict seemed to be overcome. Thus Hardy argues that what she calls 'coincidence', which often appears to be used for moral or didactic purposes and which would seem to be at odds with realism, should be understood as a formal device,[2] and for the later New Critics as long as one could discern thematic patterning, the question of whether realism and moralism were in conflict could be ignored.

Certain critics, however, have raised troublesome objections. For example, Leo Bersani argues that 'The formal and psychological reticence of most realistic fiction makes for a secret complicity between the novelist and his society's illusions about its own order. Realistic fiction serves nineteenth-century society by providing it with strategies for containing (and repressing) its disorder within significantly structured stories about itself.' Though *Middlemarch* 'is a novel about connecting enterprises which fail', by the end of the novel George Eliot 'is making connections which the rest of the novel has trained us to see as naïve, unworkable novelistic connections. The subtle, almost indefinable influence of one life on other lives has been replaced by melodramatic connections of crime and rare coincidence.'[3] Carol Christ has also pointed out that throughout George Eliot's fiction her heroines are saved from difficult decisions or aggressive confrontations by the deaths of their husbands: 'Such a pattern of plot construction need not be notable in itself, but for the fact that it is so strangely inconsistent with Eliot's commitment to realism.' Though George Eliot 'defines herself as a tragic historian portraying a world under the direction of an indifferent providence', the fact that 'she allows that providence to rescue her more favored characters betrays a reluctance not only to abandon the idea of a benevolent providence but to confront the most tragic consequences of her own vision'. Thus form and pattern, instead of being regarded as the means by which realism and George Eliot's moral concern and didactic purpose are reconciled, can be interpreted as merely covering up a fundamental problem about her fiction.

But perhaps the most basic problem raised by realist fiction is that of language rather than form. Since form is unavoidable in any kind of writing – as Roland Barthes points out, 'the discourse, or the complex of words superior to the phrase, has its own forms of organization; it too is a classification and a classification which signifies'[5] – both defences of George Eliot's fiction and objections to it in formalistic terms are questionable. Even the most extreme type of realism that tries to create a world of total randomness will inevitably use formal means in order to represent that, and form itself can convey meaning. Thus any kind of realistic fiction must have a formal organization of some sort and this will be meaningful independent of the work's realism. One of the most significant developments in George Eliot's fiction is the move from a formal structure that does not call attention to itself – as in *Adam Bede* and *The Mill on the Floss* – to the highly organized structuring of the later fiction based on the use of a double plot which emphasizes connection and pattern. It is clear from her short essay 'Notes on Form in Art'[6] that George Eliot had thought about formal questions, and it seems likely that she concluded that since form was unavoidable, one might as well foreground it in fiction and thus exploit it aesthetically rather than trying to pretend that the realist novel could do without it. But this only highlights the more serious issue: the problem of language in the realist novel. Should literary language not acknowledge that it can never be totally mimetic? In apparently claiming to capture reality in language, was the realist novel not fundamentally flawed? Such questions have been central to debate within George Eliot criticism of the past twenty years.

The question of language

The work of Roland Barthes has been crucial in placing the question of language at the forefront of criticism, especially as applied to the novel. Barthes expresses hostility to the realist novel throughout his criticism. The reasons for this are perhaps most apparent in his essay 'Science versus Literature'. For science, he declares, 'language is simply an instrument, which it profits to make as transparent and neutral as possible', whereas 'Ethically, it is only by its passage through language that literature can continue to shake loose the essential concepts of our culture, one of the chief among which is the "real" '. The structuralist critic must 'turn himself into a "writer" . . . in order to rediscover the crucial problems involved in every utterance, once it is no longer wrapped in the beneficent cloud of strictly *realist* illusions, which see language simply as the medium of thought'. To believe in 'scientific discourse' is to accept 'that there exists a neutral state of language': 'Scientific discourse believes itself to be a superior code; writing aims at being a total code, including its own forces of destruction. It follows that writing alone can smash the theological idol set up by a paternalistic science.'[7]

Barthes here is contrasting *écriture* – writing in the literary sense – with *écrivance* – writing which, like scientific discourse, seeks to be merely instrumental and is thus transparent and neutral. His opposition to the realist novel is that it also is a form of 'écrivance', and thus complicit with the prevailing ideologies which he believes literature should aim to undermine. In his major work on the novel, *S/Z*, Barthes qualifies this view. Instead of the *écriture/écrivance* division, he formulates two new textual categories: *scriptible/lisible*, usually translated as 'writerly' and 'readerly'. The aim of the 'writerly' text 'is to make the reader no longer a consumer, but a producer of the text'. Its plurality of meaning cannot be controlled: 'this text is a galaxy of signifiers, not a structure of signifieds'. 'Readerly' texts – 'We call any readerly text a classic text' – 'are products (and not productions)',[8] but Barthes concedes that they have a limited plurality, and *S/Z* illustrates this by means of a commentary on *Sarrasine*, a short work by Balzac, an author identified with the realist novel. The limited plurality of the classic text is based on connotation, and *S/Z* is concerned to reveal the layers of connotation that make up the classic text.

Barthes's work has had a particularly powerful influence on certain British post-structuralist critics, who aim to create a materialist criticism that can combine structuralism, Lacanian psychoanalysis and Marxism. Thus Rosalind Coward and John Ellis see *S/Z* as seeking 'to demonstrate how language produces the realist text as natural', and the role of criticism in relation to realism is the 'liberating function' of showing 'the production of meaning at work in the realist text itself'. For Coward and Ellis 'realism stresses the product and not the production. It represses production in the same way that the mechanism of the market . . . represses production in capitalist society. . . . Realism naturalises the arbitrary nature of the sign; its philosophy is that of an identity between signifier and signified on the level of an entire text as much as that of a single word.' The identity between the signifier and the signified in realist writing

> is the precondition of its ability to represent a *vraisemblable*, an accepted natural view of the world. It does not mean that all writing is absolutely transparent, but rather that the narration, the dominant discourse, is able to establish itself as Truth. The narration does not appear to be the voice of an author; its source appears to be a true reality which speaks.

Such narration constructs the subject who reads it since the narrative is only intelligible if the reader adopts a fixed position in relation to the text: 'The subject of narration is a homogeneous subject, fixed in a relation of watching.' Coward and Ellis see little difference between the 'readerly' text and *écrivance:*

> The way of writing complementary to this mode of consumerist reading is that of *écrivance*, instrumental use of language. It is a use of language that calls up a vast reserve of echoes from similar texts, similar phrasings, remarks, situations, characters. The process is not one of pure repetition therefore, but, rather, a limited exploitation of the plurality of language, through a controlled process of echoing, re-calling. . . . Realism is 'a copy of a copy', supported by connotation, a 'perspective of citations'. It is silent quotation, without inverted commas, with no precise source.[9]

As the work of Balzac exemplified for Barthes the 'readerly' or classic text of French realism, George Eliot's work constituted 'classic realism' for these British critics. Peter Widdowson refers to her as 'the avatar of liberal realism' and goes on to write:

> For realism is not just a matter of literary form; it is the common-sense expression in aesthetic terms of an ideology in which the unified individual human subject 'makes sense' of his/her world by negotiation with external forces – Nature, Society, etc., which presupposes a universe that *can* be made sense of and an always potentially self-determining human subject.[10]

Stephen Heath draws a direct comparison between George Eliot and Balzac as realists:

> Realism then, as it has come to be understood in connection with the novel, is always grasped finally in terms of some notion of the representation of 'Reality', which is reflected in the literary work as in a mirror. . . . Thus George Eliot, for example, can offer her novels naturally as an attempt to 'give a faithful account of men and things as they have mirrored themselves in my mind'. This is the same kind of 'innocence' that was encountered in Balzac's description of the *Comédie Humaine* as a 'visual dictation': the idea of an *account* introduces a notion of selection but without in any way revealing a problem, without challenging the assumptions of the natural attitude; no problem is posed by saying that the account is to be a *realistic* account and, indeed, it is precisely this that prevents the recognition of any problem.

For Heath as for Widdowson 'the work that is realistic is that which repeats the received forms of "Reality". It is a question of reiterating the society's system of intelligibility.' The readability of the realist novel 'is relayed by a series of codes and conventions, by the text of the already known and written: that work is readable, therefore, which is cast within their horizon, which repeats them in their naturalized transparence. . . . The basis of this repetition . . . is an absence of writing; language is lost in a monologue of re-presentation.'[11]

These ideas are applied most fully to George Eliot by Colin MacCabe in the essay reprinted in this collection. While French criticism tended to use Balzac and the 'nouveau roman' to illustrate the differences between realism and a kind of writing that problematizes the representation of 'reality', MacCabe sets George Eliot and James Joyce in opposition for this purpose. The major difference between them, he argues, lies in the fact that George Eliot employs narration as a metalanguage whereas Joyce's texts 'refuse the very category of metalanguage' (pp. 156–7).[12] In using inverted commas to separate characters' speech from narration, a writer like George Eliot, MacCabe claims, creates a hierarchy of discourses in which the narrator's discourse is different in kind from all other discourses in the text. Narration is a metalanguage which 'refuses to acknowledge its own status as writing' and 'functions simply as a window on reality. This relationship between discourses can be taken as the defining feature of the *classic realist text*' (p. 158). MacCabe admits some qualification of this thesis in relation to George Eliot: 'It would be a distortion to consider George Eliot's texts as totally determined by that discursive organisation that I have defined as the classic realist text. Within her novels there are always images which counter the flat and univocal process which is the showing forth of the real' (p. 162), but his final position is that 'George Eliot's texts are devoted to repressing the operations of the signifier by positing a metalanguage which exists outside of materiality and production. The multitude of objects which appear in her texts do not bear witness to the activity of signification, to the constitutive reality of absence, but rather, in their massive identity, they deny the existence of such activity' (p. 168).

David Lodge is a British critic who combines several critical approaches: New Critical formalism, the practical-critical tradition of close analysis, structuralism, Bakhtinian dialogic criticism. In the essay of his which is included in this collection he employs all of these in presenting a critique of MacCabe's form of post-structuralism and its concept of the 'classic realist text'. In particular he argues that, in a novel like *Middlemarch*, the narration does not function as a metalanguage which ignores the materiality of language and invites the reader to become an observer of a transparent reality. Replacing MacCabe's distinction between object language and metalanguage by the Platonic distinction between mimesis – narrating by imitating another person's speech – and diegesis – narrating in one's own voice – he writes: 'Mimesis and diegesis, like metaphor and metonomy, are fundamental, and, on a certain level, all-inclusive categories of representation, and a typology of texts can be established by assessing the dominance of one over the other' (p. 175). He goes on to argue that the narration in *Middlemarch* cannot be simply categorized as metalanguage, that MacCabe especially fails to take account of 'the extensive use of free indirect speech, which obscures and complicates the distinction between the two types of discourse' (p. 176). Lodge also makes use of Bakhtin's characterization of the discourse of the novel as 'polyphonic' or 'polyglottal' to undermine MacCabe.[13]

Lodge's critique of MacCabe is successful up to a point but it perhaps only qualifies or modifies MacCabe's thesis rather than seriously undermining its theoretical assumptions. This would require a more fundamental rejection of the view that the language of her novels is reflective. Such a rejection is to be found in the work of certain American deconstructionist critics, particularly J. Hillis Miller.

The deconstructionist debate

American and British post-structuralist critics differ considerably in their attitude to George Eliot's fiction. Whereas Barthes's distinction between 'écriture' and 'écrivance' or 'scriptible' and 'lisible' texts has been very influential on British post-structuralist critics, the main American post-structuralist tradition – Derridean deconstruction as interpreted by such critics as Paul de Man and J. Hillis Miller – has been unsympathetic to such distinctions and their implied historicism. De Man, for example, asked in an interview about his attitude to the concept of postmodernity, replied: 'The notion of modernity is already very dubious; the notion of postmodernity becomes a parody of the notion of modernity. . . . It strikes me as a very unmodern, a very old-fashioned, conservative concept of history, where history is seen as succession', and he stated that he felt 'perfectly at ease writing on eighteenth- or seventeenth-century authors'.[14]

Barbara Johnson, a critic much influenced by de Man, in an essay on Barthes's *S/Z*, deconstructs the distinction between the 'writerly' and 'readerly' text. Johnson has formulated what is probably the most cited definition of deconstructive criticism: 'it proceeds by the careful teasing out of the warring forces of signification within the text itself'. Barthes's aim in *S/Z* had been to reveal the 'difference' at work within the text, a form of 'difference', as Johnson puts it, which is not 'between' entities but 'within' them in the sense that it subverts the text's claim to have a unified identity. She goes on to argue that what Barthes's analysis of Balzac's *Sarrasine* shows is that the distinction between the 'writerly' and the 'readerly' text – a difference between – collapses into a difference within since the characteristics Barthes identifies with the 'writerly' are apparent in this 'readerly' text: 'Like the readerly text, Sarrasine's deluded image of La Zambinella is a glorification of perfect unity and wholeness. . . . But like the writerly text, Zambinella is actually fragmented, unnatural and sexually undecidable.' Thus 'Balzac has already in a sense done Barthes's work for him. The readerly text is itself nothing other than a deconstruction of the readerly text.'[15]

J. Hillis Miller, in the various essays he has written on George Eliot, in effect argues that George Eliot has already done the work of critics like MacCabe who believe in the 'classic realist text' for them. As one might put it: the classic realist text, at least as written by George Eliot, is itself nothing other than a deconstruction of the classic realist text. Whereas such critics as MacCabe and Stephen Heath refer to passages in George Eliot's works that support their view that she sees the novel as reflecting reality like a mirror, Miller can point to passages that undermine that view, such as the comment in *The Mill on the Floss* that Aristotle should have lamented 'that intelligence so rarely shows itself in speech without metaphor – that we can so seldom declare what a thing is, except by saying it is something else' (Book 2, chapter 1), and her remark in 'Notes on Form in Art' that 'form is unlikeness . . . every difference is form.'[16] These and other passages in her work suggest that George Eliot can be seen as a deconstructionist *avant la lettre*.

Miller's first essay on George Eliot, after his conversion to deconstructionism, was published in 1974 and was entitled 'Narrative and History'. Unlike previous critics who had tried to defend George Eliot from James's criticism by arguing that her works could be accommodated to Jamesian principles if the latter were slightly modified, Miller goes on the attack against James by focusing on his claim that 'It is impossible to imagine what a novelist takes himself to be unless he regards himself as an historian and his narrative as history'. He sees James as part of that 'logocentric' tradition in Western thinking – one which includes both writers of historical and fictional narrative – which sees form in terms of unity and teleology: 'The end of the novel is the final exposing of the fates of the characters as well as of the formal unity of the text. The notions of narrative, of character, and of formal unity in fiction are all congruent with the system of concepts making up the Western idea of history.'[17]

Certain fictional narratives, however, have questioned this concept of form, and 'this putting in question of narrative form becomes also obliquely a putting in question of history or of the writing of history'. Miller's claim is that though *Middlemarch* is not an anti-novel like *Don Quixote* or *Tristram Shandy* but 'solidly within the tradition of realistic fiction', it is such a work. He sees history as one of a number of parallel themes – the others being religion, love, art, and superstition – which are related to a particular character who 'is shown to be mystified by a belief that all the details he confronts make a whole governed by a single center, origin, or end. In each case the narrator demystifies the illusion and shows it to be based on an error, the fundamental linguistic error of taking a figure of speech literally.' Further, 'the belief that history is progressive, teleological . . . is deconstructed along with the rest.' Thus

> the novel, so to speak, pulls the rug out from under itself and deprives itself of that solid ground without which, if Henry James is right, it is 'nowhere'. Her fiction deprives itself of its ground in history by demonstrating that ground to be a fiction too, a figure, a myth, a lie, like Dorothea's interpretation of Casaubon or Bulstrode's reading of his religious destiny.

Though history in the novel is governed by no metaphysical principle, it is not chaos: 'It is the result of the unordered energies of those who have made it, as well as of the interpretations these energies have imposed on history. History, for her, is stratified, always in movement, always in the middle of a march, always open to the reordering of those who come later.' There is no origin, only an 'act of interpretation . . . an act of the will to power imposed on a prior "text"', and 'in place of the concept of elaborate organic form, centered form, form organized around certain absolute generalizable themes, George Eliot presents a view of artistic form as inorganic, acentered, and discontinuous'.[18] Miller concludes by comparing George Eliot's view of history with those of Nietzsche and Walter Benjamin.

Miller's essay of 1975, 'Optic and Semiotic in *Middlemarch*', adopts a slightly different position. He recognizes the totalizing impulse that informs the work: 'a fragment is examined as a "sample" of the larger whole of which it is a part', and the behaviour of the characters 'manifests certain general and universal laws'. He also shows that one aspect of this totalizing impulse is 'the presentation by the narrator of certain all-encompassing metaphors which are proposed as models for Middlemarch society', each group of metaphors being 'related to the others, fulfilling them, but at the same time contradicting them, cancelling them out, or undermining their validity'. The order created by the totalizing metaphors is, however, contradicted by the implications of the pier-glass analogy which begins chapter 27 and which suggests that reality is without any intrinsic order. Further, all seeing 'is falsified by the limitations of point of view' and this must also apply to the point of view of the narrator. Miller's conclusion is that 'This incoherent, heterogeneous, "unreadable", or nonsynthesizable quality of the text of *Middlemarch* jeopardizes the narrator's effort at totalization. It suggests that one gets a different kind of totality depending on what metaphorical model is used.' It had been less certain in this essay that Miller believed that George Eliot as author was in control of the novel's deconstructive aspect – it had looked at first as if language and metaphor undermined the totalizing enterprise against the author's will – but by the end of the essay, in which he refers to 'George Eliot's insight into the dismaying dangers of metaphor' and 'her recognition of the deconstructive powers of figurative language',[19] it is clear that Miller still sees her as a collaborator in the novel's deconstruction.

Miller has continued to write on George Eliot and his most recent essay on her, which is reprinted in this collection, is on *Adam Bede*. Clearly the early works present a greater challenge to a critic like Miller, who sees her as deconstructing some of the basic assumptions and procedures that underlie realism in fiction. In this essay Miller focuses on chapter 17, a chapter much cited by those who have questioned realism in the novel, for here it seems clear that, as Miller puts it, 'For Eliot, a story is validated by its truth of correspondence to historical, social and human reality, a human reality assumed to exist outside language' (p. 36). Miller claims that it is a mistake to assume that the novel presents such a view. He argues that one of the novel's concerns is a search for 'the proper language of storytelling' (p. 45). At first it seems as if 'A measuring, hardheaded, literally naming, referential language, dramatized in the novel in Adam's profession of carpentry, seems to give the reader a model for the proper language of narration. But no, somewhat surprisingly, both the language of mathematics and the language of literal naming are dismissed as of no account, as ineffective' (p. 45). Having dismissed all possible alternatives, it turns out, claims Miller, that

> Realistic narration must depend, as this chapter of *Adam Bede* conspicuously does, on figurative language. Even more narrowly, it can be said to depend on a special form of figurative language: catachresis, the use of terms borrowed from another realm to name what has no literal language of its own. . . . The renaming of things by the figure called catachresis is genuinely performative. It brings something altogether new into the world, something not explicable by its causes. (p. 46)

Thus 'Even though chapter 17 is strongly committed, in its overt affirmations, to realism as exact reproduction, the covert argument is for a use of figurative language' (p. 47). What realist fiction does, therefore, is to bring 'groundless novelty into the social world' (p. 49), and for Miller, even in this early work, George Eliot is aware of this.

Miller is not the only critic who takes such a view of George Eliot. Jonathan Arac in his essay on *The Mill on the Floss,* reprinted here, also argues that the conventional view that the nineteenth-century novelist adheres to a naïve realism in which language is transparent is untenable.

Arac's strategy is to 'begin with a harmonious reading of *The Mill on the Floss* in relation to a center and then attend to the waywardnesses that undo the pattern the geometrical eye has defined' (p. 67). Though these 'waywardnesses' have no priority over the 'harmonious reading' they constitute a force in the novel that 'is different from it and incommensurable with it. One can see in this second pattern "romantic" excess contrasted to the "realistic" fine-grain of the first, or one may see the first as a compensatory, romantic myth of order, built up by the mind's attempt to defend itself against the real violence of the second. I call this second pattern the hyperbolic' (p. 69).

Arac then goes on to look at various manifestations of hyperbole, a figure which George Eliot herself introduces into the novel in relation to Bob Jakin: 'to throw one's pocket-knife after an implacable friend is clearly in every sense a hyperbole, or throwing beyond the mark' (Book I, chapter 6). The hyperbole figure is also related, Arac argues, to the discussion of metaphor in the novel since it implies that 'When we aim our words at a thing, we're always off the mark. All language contains a hyperbolic potential' (p. 71). The hyperbolic pattern in the novel 'escapes our analogies, which are rooted in the will for a natural continuity that this pattern denies, and which demonstrate the pattern in failing to master it' (p. 77). As with Miller, Arac sees George Eliot as in control of the novel's deconstruction of conventional realism, since he refers to her 'awareness' of the conflict between realism and rhetoric which 'makes her book an active clash between the hope of a fitting language and the recognition that language is never at one with reality, any more than the world is at one with itself' (p. 80).

This view of George Eliot is not shared by all American post-structuralist critics. Cynthia Chase, in her essay on *Daniel Deronda*, which is included in this collection, recognizes that there is a deconstructive element in the novel. Indeed, her analysis of Hans Meyrick's letter in chapter 52 is probably the most powerful demonstration of the existence of such an element in George Eliot's fiction. Meyrick, in playfully reversing causality so that effect precedes cause, performs an act often identified with deconstruction. Jonathan Culler, in his book *On Deconstruction*, discusses the reversal of causality as exemplifying deconstructive practice: 'Causality is a basic principle of our universe', but 'The causal scheme is produced by a metonymy or metalepsis (substitution of cause for effect): it is not an indubitable foundation but the product of a tropological operation.'[20] Chase believes Meyrick's letter 'functions as a deconstruction of the novel' (p. 199) and attempts to demonstrate this by applying Meyrick's deconstructive view of causality to the novel's plot:

In naming Deronda's revealed Jewish parentage as the 'present cause'

> of his demonstrated vocation for Jewishness, its 'past effects', Meyrick's letter is naming the cause as an effect of its effects, and the effects as the cause of their cause, and is therein identifying the contradictory relationship between the claims of the realistic fiction and the narrative strategy actually employed.
>
> (pp. 203–4)

She goes on to argue that the concepts of origin, identity, subject, and representation are also subject to deconstruction in Meyrick's letter, though this is not to refute such concepts since 'The deconstructive operation, while it consists in pointing out that the concept of causality amounts to an aberrant and arbitrary ordering of rhetorical elements, is itself no more than an equally aberrant reordering of these elements, the performance of another tropological operation' (p. 206).

In contrast to Hillis Miller or Arac, however, Chase takes the view that realism and conventional plot structure in this novel and by implication in George Eliot's fiction generally seek to defeat deconstruction. Though 'Meyrick's letter proposes an interpretation of the novel that is substantially and radically at odds with the explanations of its narrator . . . seriousness and idealism triumph over parody and the ironic spirit. Meyrick's letter functions to exemplify the spirit and the style that the hero transcends' (p. 199). Chase's position differs from that of British post-structuralists like MacCabe and Heath since she suggests that George Eliot's fiction incorporates an awareness of the problematics of realist representation, but she is closer to them than to Hillis Miller or Arac in that she believes that George Eliot's fundamental aim is to sustain rather than undermine 'classic realism'.

Central to Chase's position that the dominant narrative aims to discredit or undermine Meyrick's way of looking at things is her belief that the realistic narrative itself contains a fundamental contradiction which George Eliot either ignores or tries to cover up in the interests of sustaining a plot that is committed to the 'triumph of idealism over irony'. The contradiction centres around the question of circumcision. The plot hinges on Deronda discovering that he is a Jew and thus acquiring an identity that gives his life purpose and direction, but since he must have been circumcised and therefore known he was Jewish, the plot is unhinged. Thus plot and narrative structure operate in the interests of idealism since they show Deronda's discovery and acceptance of his Jewish identity but this cannot be reconciled with the requirements of realism which demand that he be circumcised. The narrative must disregard Deronda's circumcision but realism functions to draw attention to it.

In the essay of my own on *Daniel Deronda* which is reproduced here I argue against Chase's view of circumcision. I claim that though unmentioned and unmentionable circumcision is implicit in the novel and not, as Chase believes, an absence or gap in the text in a Machereyan sense.[21] Nor does it render the novel's realism incoherent since it is an ambiguous sign that cannot be identified only with Jewishness. For Chase's reading to work, circumcision must be a transparent sign of Jewishness but, I argue, historical evidence refutes this. Her reading is itself open to deconstruction since, contradicting post-structuralist theory, it identifies the signifier (circumcision) with the signified (Jewishness) while, in contrast, the novel thematizes the priority of the signifier over the signified. Whereas Chase sees the suppression of circumcision as an indication that idealism seeks to invalidate irony or deconstruction, I suggest that its indirect presence in the novel can be assimilated to Meyrick's irony since something so trivial and inherently ambiguous has such momentous consequences, thus creating a disequilibrium that mocks causality. Of course, discussing this subject is only to repeat that disequilibrium as circumcision is obviously a triviality in the context of a novel concerned with such major themes as identity, alienation, nationhood. But just as circumcision is of such great importance in the effect it has on Deronda's life it could have a similar effect on how George Eliot is perceived in critical terms, for if, as I claim, circumcision is included in the novel and alluded to indirectly then this destabilizes George Eliot's reputation as a heavy Victorian moralist and suggests that she is a more playful and self-conscious writer than most readers and critics have thought.

A critic who adopts a position somewhat intermediate between Hillis Miller's and Arac's position and that of Chase and British post-structuralists is D. A. Miller. In a long essay on *Middlemarch*, part of which is reprinted in this collection, he is concerned with 'a central tension in the traditional novelistic enterprise: namely, a discomfort with the processes and implications of narrative itself'. George Eliot, in *Middlemarch*, 'directs her text toward a state of all-encompassing transcendence from which it is continually drawn back by the dispersive and fragmentary logic of the narrative itself'. The scenes of closure in the novel, such as Mrs Bulstrode's meeting with her husband after his disgrace and Dorothea's recovery in chapter 80 from the crisis of having unexpectedly found Ladislaw and Rosamond together, are, he argues, 'in fact the site of radical ambiguities, so that it becomes doubtful whether transcendence has taken place, or merely a deluded transcendence effect'.[22] But he sees the deconstructive aspect of the novel as having less force than Hillis Miller attributes to it. Though it could be taken as destabilizing 'a traditional ground' (p. 188), it could also be a device to frighten one into returning to it. D. A. Miller's critical project is to 'explore the double valency of such a text' (p. 188). This position offers an attractive compromise since 'classic realism' and deconstructive forces in the text are held in balance without the one triumphing over the other.

Politics, ideology and the realist text

Whereas post-structuralist criticism has been predominantly concerned with the problem of language in George Eliot as a writer of realist fiction, Marxist critics, or critics strongly influenced by Marxism, have focused primarily on the associated question of the relation between realism and ideology. John Goode, for example, in an essay on *Adam Bede*, sees the novel 'as the first major exercise in programmatic literary realism in English literature', but believes 'it is necessary to discriminate between the mimesis and the ideology which frames it.' He argues that this ideology has strong similarities with that of Herbert Spencer, a writer whose 'ethic springs from class-interest'. Goode does not, however, unlike 'vulgar' Marxists for example, see this as necessarily a criticism: 'To see the novel as a process of transforming historical realities into ideological fable is not to underestimate its impressiveness. I am not arguing that *Adam Bede* is a fictional version of Herbert Spencer, but that the concrete realization of the empirical vision exists in tension with the historically specific ideology which shapes it.' The novel itself also offers, Goode argues, an implicit critique of that ideology by, for example, 'showing that reification is a psychological response to a particular situation'.[23]

Raymond Williams, in an essay mainly on *Adam Bede* in *The Country and the City*, states that 'Most novels are in some sense knowable communities' in that 'the novelist offers to show people and their relationships in essentially knowable and communicable ways.' But, he claims, 'what is knowable is not only a function of objects – of what is there to be known. It is also a function of subjects, of observers – of what is desired and what needs to be known.' For Williams, George Eliot's effort to represent rural communities realistically is compromised by her bourgeois consciousness and the tradition of the novel she inherits. He finds the characters in *Adam Bede* unconvincing as soon as they have to speak or act as individuals. This creates a conflict between 'an analytically conscious observer of conduct with a developed analytic vocabulary' and 'people represented as living and speaking in mainly customary ways'.[24] Her fictional discourse is designed to represent individuals in a bourgeois sense for a predominantly bourgeois readership and thus fails to depict convincingly a non-bourgeois world.

Williams does not mention *Silas Marner*, which perhaps poses some problems for his thesis. Though realistic in terms of its 'story' or the basic material that is constructed into the form of a novel, the 'discourse' of the work, or the means by which that material is organized artistically to serve the purposes of fiction, is a significant break from the conventions of realism in that it exploits the style and form of fairy-tale and myth. Thus, for example, Silas Marner at the level of 'story' is a weaver carrying his materials on his back, yet in terms of the novel's, discourse' he is also an alienated Ancient Mariner type of figure who is carrying a symbolic burden of guilt, and a fairy-tale-like feature of the narrative such as his mysterious loss of consciousness at significant moments is realistically accounted for by his suffering from catalepsy. It seems probable that the departure from conventional realist 'discourse' which is evident in *Silas Marner* is an attempt to overcome the kind of problems realist fiction has in depicting convincingly rural communities which have a high level of *Gemeinschaft*. Though George Eliot never departs from realism at the level of 'story' in her novels, critics have perhaps not sufficiently recognized her continual experimentation at the level of 'discourse'.

Terry Eagleton, however, in his essay on her work in his book *Criticism and Ideology* finds such variations in fictional discourse symptoms merely of the problem the bourgeois novelist has in reconciling realism and ideology. Nineteenth-century bourgeois ideology, he argues, had to face the problem that 'it was unable to produce a set of potently affective mythologies which might permeate the texture of lived experience of English society.' It therefore had to rely on the heritage of Romantic humanism or what Eagleton calls the 'Culture and Society' tradition: 'a tradition which offered an idealist critique of bourgeois social relations, coupled with a consecration of the rights of capital'. Thus George Eliot seeks to reconcile a modified Romantic individualism with 'certain "higher", corporate ideological modes' so that 'the Romantic individualist may submit to the social totality without sacrifice to personal self-fulfilment'.

What results from this is that 'a potentially tragic collision between "corporate" and "individualist" ideologies is consistently defused and repressed by the forms of Eliot's fiction'. The function of the use of pastoral or myth or moral fable or historical realism is 'to recast the historical contradictions at the heart of [her] fiction into ideologically resolvable terms'. Thus '*Middlemarch* projects back onto the past its sense of contemporary stalemate; and since the upshot of this is a radical distrust of "real" history, that history is effectively displaced into ethical, and so "timeless", terms'. *Daniel Deronda* 'is driven to the desperate recourse of adopting a mystical epistemology to resolve its problems, and so is effectively forced beyond the bounds of realism'. Eagleton explains the formal innovations of *Deronda* as 'a realism now buckling under ideological pressures it is unable to withstand'. He sees her novels as motivated by a drive to create ideological closure but their formal discontinuities, which testify to absences and dislocations in the text, 'lay bare the imprint of the ideological struggles which beset the texts'.[25] Such struggles, Eagleton suggests, are present despite the attempt by George Eliot as a bourgeois novelist to create seamless organic wholes in which liberal humanist ideology is totally integrated with the conventions of realism.

In *Criticism and Ideology* Eagleton sees Marxist criticism as aiming to create a 'science of the text', but there is a regressive 'vulgar' Marxist tendency to criticize the novels for their failure to recognize Marxist solutions. In a more recent essay on 'The Lifted Veil', which is reprinted here, one sees Eagleton revising the position he adopted in *Criticism and Ideology* by looking at this text from a significantly different Marxist position, one which has clearly felt the effect of post-structuralism.

A feature of George Eliot criticism of the past twenty years or so has been the high degree of interest in this short story, which earlier critics had tended to ignore. Eagleton's reading has a good deal in common with some of the deconstructionist readings of the fiction I have discussed above but with a greater emphasis on politics and ideology. He relates Latimer's aptitude for prevision to science since predictability is the basis of the power of science. Yet such predictability is in conflict with bourgeois history and capitalism, with their bases in such concepts as individual freedom and economic self-interest: 'Knowledge is power, but the more you have of it the more it threatens to rob you of your desire and render you impotent' (p. 55). Latimer is allegorized as 'a dreadful image of where, given a little extrapolation, the whole of bourgeois knowledge could land up' (p. 57). Eagleton also sees the story as an allegory of how realism deconstructs itself: 'Carrying on regardless, narrating as though you don't know the end, assuming an ignorance where you acknowledge a truth, is clearly a dilemma at the very heart of realist writing' (p. 61). He sees a connection between this contradiction within realist narrative and that within a society governed by market forces which also must work 'by fiction, speculative hypothesis, partial prevision, its insights as much the product of blindness as the visionary Latimer is the son of his benighted father' (p. 62). The story undermines the idea that the omniscience of the narrator in realist fiction can overcome these difficulties since it questions the disinterestedness of the narrator's knowledge. For Eagleton, this story anticipates the epistemological scepticism of a work like Henry James's *The Sacred Fount*.

The 1980s has seen the emergence of a political and social criticism which has clearly been influenced by Marxism (though Foucault is perhaps an even stronger influence) but which focuses much more directly on the specific historical context of the literary text than more straightforward forms of Marxist criticism which, as in Eagleton's *Criticism and Ideology* essay, tend to favour a broad approach to historical and ideological questions. Indeed these critics, generally known as 'new historicists', though British exponents are sometimes called 'cultural materialists', would reject the division between text and context. Louis Montrose, one of the leading new historicists, has stated that the new historicism's 'collective project is to resituate canonical literary texts among the multiple forms of writing, and in relation to the non-discursive practices and institutions of the social formation in which those texts have been produced'. The critic should also recognize that he or she is historically situated since 'the project of historical resituation is necessarily the textual construction of critics who are themselves historical subjects'. Montrose urges that the concept of literature 'as an autonomous aesthetic order that transcends the shifting pressure and particularity of material needs and interests' be rejected: 'By representing the world in discourse, texts are engaged in constructing the world and in accommodating their writers, performers, readers, and audiences to positions within it.'[26]

The new historicism has been associated primarily with the study of the English Renaissance, but Catherine Gallagher in her book, *The Industrial Reformation of English Fiction*, demonstrates its applicability to the nineteenth-century novel by analysing several texts, including *Felix Holt*, which is discussed at length. She relates both the politics and the realism of the novel to the question of representation in literature and debates about political representation involving such writers as James Mill, John Bright, John Stuart Mill and Matthew Arnold. In the essay included in this collection, which was later incorporated in her book, she is concerned with how the 'narrative method we now call metonymic realism' (p. 146), which assumes that fact and value are reconcilable, comes under stress. George Eliot's early novels, Gallagher argues, were metonymic in that 'they operate on the assumption that observable appearances bespeak deeper moral essences' (p. 146), but metonymic representation always needed to be supplemented by other forms of representation since appearances could be deceptive. Fact, or realism on its own, was not enough, and this created a discontinuity between fact and value which came to a head, Gallagher argues, in the 1860s and produced a crisis for the form of the realist novel since it was realized that 'Realistic fiction . . . invariably undermines, in practice, the ideology it purports to exemplify' (p. 147).

Felix Holt is a particularly significant work as it 'reflects the formal consequences for George Eliot's realism of the new need for a transcendent realm of values and ultimate meanings' (p. 148). Thus Felix as a character is a 'cultured' person in an Arnoldian sense who is not knowable in terms of metonymic realism. As with Chase on *Deronda*, Gallagher claims that the causality intrinsic to metonymic narrative is reversed since, instead of meanings finding expression in signs, Felix believes 'signs cause their meanings. In Felix's image, the sign literally becomes the meaning; the two are indistinguishable' (p. 151). For example, in the trial scene Felix's 'cultured nature' simply 'overwhelms the evidence, the facts', so that 'Felix and the plot that revolves around him contradict the inductive metonymic assumptions of the rest of the novel. What is explicitly recommended in the exemplary person of Felix Holt is implicitly denied in the book's dominant narrative method' (p. 153). Gallagher's work has affinities with Chase and especially with Eagleton's chapter on George Eliot in *Criticism and Ideology* in that she relates the formal discontinuities in the novel to the failure by George Eliot and other nineteenth-century intellectuals to find a way of overcoming the contradictions within liberalism as an ideology which, Gallagher suggests, had created a cultural crisis in the 1860s.

Feminism

The problem of language and the relation between realism and ideology, which I have discussed above as dominant critical concerns in George Eliot criticism of the past twenty years or so, are connected with the third major focus of recent critical debate on her work: whether or not her work is sympathetic to feminism. In all three areas discussion has centred around whether her fiction upholds traditional perspectives in relation to language, ideology or gender, or whether it subjects traditional perspectives to an indirect and subtle critique. Zelda Austen and Elaine Showalter in their articles, 'Why Feminist Critics Are Angry with George Eliot' and 'The Greening of Sister George' show how early feminist criticism was largely antagonistic to George Eliot. As Austen puts it:

> The conclusion one might draw from these fictions is that the heroine does better to accept her lot, submit to the yoke of marriage, and curb her desires rather than continue willful, aspiring, unconventional, and impatient of restraint. . . . The feminist critic calls for a literature that will show women active rather than docile, aggressive and ambitious rather than retiring and submissive, successful in forging their way through the world as heroes are, rather than content to be chosen by successful men.[27]

George Eliot, many feminists critics have believed, did not allow her heroines the kind of freedom she achieved in her own life. Contemporary feminist criticism, however, has found a way of reading her which calls into question the view that her work is anti- or non-feminist in perspective.

In their book, *The Madwoman in The Attic*, Sandra Gilbert and Susan Gubar read nineteenth-century women authors as reacting to both a literal confinement by men and a metaphorical confinement within male literary forms: 'We decided . . . that the striking coherence we noticed in literature by women could be explained by a common, female impulse to struggle free from social and literary confinement through strategic redefinitions of self, art, and society', and this desire for liberation is expressed through a need 'to act out male metaphors in their own texts, as if trying to understand their implications'.[28] In the interpretation of *Scenes of Clerical Life* (mainly written by Gubar), which is included in this collection, it is argued that beneath the surface of the stories there is feminine rage:

> While each heroine represses her anger and submits to the necessity for renunciation, the author as the goddess Nemesis acts 'for' her in much the same way that Frankenstein's monster acted 'for' his creator or Bertha Mason Rochester acted 'for' Jane Eyre. Thus . . . in *Scenes of Clerical Life*, it is the novelist – not as the male narrator, but as the female author behind the scenes – who plays the part of the madwoman.
>
> (p. 34)

Gillian Beer has published a feminist defence of George Eliot which is strongly historical in approach. She emphasizes George Eliot's connections with the Victorian feminists Barbara Bodichon and Bessie Rayner Parkes, and provides persuasive evidence that Dorothea in *Middlemarch* was partly modelled on the latter. She also points out that George Eliot subscribed to a feminist journal edited by Parkes and suggests, though this could be interpreted as special pleading, that she may have avoided becoming an active supporter of the women's movement because her irregular personal life might have damaged its reputation. In reply to earlier feminist critics, who had particularly attacked *Middlemarch*, Beer asserts: 'George Eliot . . . did engage with issues vital in the life of the women's movement. . . . What is demonstrable is that she was intimately familiar with the current writing and actions of the women's movement and that in *Middlemarch* particularly, she brooded on the curtailment of women's lives in terms drawn from that movement and in sympathy with it.'[29]

An interesting recent development in feminist criticism has been the interaction between feminism and contemporary critical theory. Mary Jacobus, in her essay on *The Mill on the Floss*, reprinted here, like post-structuralist critics is concerned with the question of language, but from a feminist perspective. She argues, following the French feminist theorist Luce Irigaray, that the feminine is subordinated in discourse itself and that 'a "work of language" which undoes the repression of the feminine constitutes in itself an attack on the dominant ideology' (p. 84). Since women can 'have access to language only by recourse to systems of representation that are masculine', women, according to Irigaray, have to resort to 'mimeticism', that is, 'an acting out or role playing within the text which allows the woman writer to know better and hence to expose what it is she mimics' (p. 86). For Jacobus 'what pleases the feminist critic most . . . is to light on a text that seems to do her arguing, or some of it, for her – especially a text whose story is the same as hers' (p. 87). *The Mill on the Floss,* she believes, is such a text since it 'uncovers the divide between the language or maxims of the dominant culture and the language itself which undoes them' (p. 88).

Thus for Maggie Tulliver, and implicitly for George Eliot, Jacobus argues, Latin's role as a vehicle for a cultural imperialism that excludes women is deflected when she realizes that as a living language it had once been spoken by women who 'had not needed to learn it from Mr Stelling or the institutions he perpetuates' (p. 91). Yet the text cannot simply be read as a work of feminist deconstruction since the ending of the novel seems to suggest that difference can be overcome: 'What is striking about the novel's ending is its banishing not simply of division but of sexual difference as the origin of that division' (p. 94). For Jacobus this suggests that the Irigaray solution of 'mimeticism' may not be enough: in 'attempting to swallow or incorporate an alien language, [the woman writer] is swallowed up by it in turn. . . . Miming has become absorption into an alien order' (p. 95). Female desire finally proves uncontainable. Both Irigaray – for whom 'the price paid by the woman writer for attempting to inscribe the claims of women "within an order prescribed by the masculine" may ultimately be death' (p. 95) – and George Eliot 'kill off the woman engulfed by masculine logic and language. . . . What we may find in both Eliot and Irigaray is a critique which gestures beyond cultural boundaries, indicating the perimeters within which their writing is produced' (p. 96). Here one sees criticism clearly moving in the direction of politics and cultural critique.

The bringing together of literary criticism and cultural critique is most powerfully represented in this collection by Sandra Gilbert's essay, 'Life's Empty Pack: Notes toward a Literary Daughteronomy', which focuses predominantly on *Silas Marner*. Gilbert sees George Eliot's relation to feminism as ambivalent since in this novel she deconstructs patriarchal culture while at the same time being an apologist for it. Gilbert chooses George Eliot as her 'paradigm of the female precursor' (p. 100) because her acceptance in the Victorian period as one of the major writers and thinkers irrespective of gender endowed her with a power that 'disquieted' her female contemporaries and descendants. For Gilbert

> the terror of the female precursor [for women artists] is not that she is an emblem of power but, rather, that when she achieves her greatest strength, her power becomes self-subverting: in the moment of psychic

> transformation that is the moment of creativity, the literary mother, even more than the literal one, becomes the 'stern daughter of the voice of God' who paradoxically proclaims her 'allegiance to the law' she herself appears to have violated.
>
> (p. 101)

In *Silas Marner*, Gilbert argues, George Eliot creates a 'fictionalized "daughteronomy" [which] becomes a female myth of origin narrated by a severe literary mother who uses the vehicle of a half-allegorical family romance to urge acquiescence in the Law of the Father' (pp. 102–3). But in exploring the father–daughter relationship in this novel George Eliot 'clarifies for herself and and for her readers the key differences between sonship and daughterhood' (p. 105).

Gilbert makes use of various literary critical methods and theories – particularly psychoanalysis – in her analysis of the novel, and her essay exemplifies another strong tendency within contemporary criticism, namely, the refusal on the part of the critic to see him or herself as a mere commentator on the text. Criticism such as Gilbert's claims imaginative equality with the literature that it interprets. Thus she sees *Silas Marner* and works influenced by it, such as Edith Wharton's novella *Summer*, as revealing that 'father–daughter incest is a culturally constructed paradigm of human desire' (p. 116). What she has done in her readings of *Silas Marner* and *Summer* is to 'have extrapolated . . . the idea that the father needs the daughter because she is a suitably diminished "milk giver", a miniaturized version of the mother whom the patriarchal culture absolutely forbids him to desire' (p. 117). Her conclusion is that *Silas Marner* and the other related texts she considers offer readers 'a paradigm of the prescription for father–daughter incest that lies at the heart of female psychosexual development in patriarchal society' (p. 122).

Though Gilbert's essay exemplifies the imaginative power of the critic, she also seeks to persuade the reader that her interpretation has objective validity, as is clear from the number and length of her footnotes. Other feminist critics reject the concept of objectivity in criticism and argue that feminist literary interpretation should directly promote political aims. Catherine Belsey, for example, a feminist critic strongly influenced by British post-structuralism, chooses to read *Daniel Deronda* 'productively' since she believes that 'texts are plural, and that their meanings are *produced* by bringing to bear on the raw material of the work itself discourses pertinent to the twentieth century'. She contrasts her feminist reading with that of Leavis in *The Great Tradition*: 'instead of looking to *Daniel Deronda* for confirmation of a banal morality, it is more productive to read it, for instance, as challenging the sexual power relations of its society in ways which have an identifiable bearing on our own'.[30] Thus she sets out to produce a reading that is specifically designed to be politically relevant to readers in the last quarter of the twentieth century.

Though Belsey argues that, unlike Leavis, she is not claiming her reading of the novel as an attack on patriarchy is 'exhaustive or final', her approach is open to the objection that it leads to a 'monologic' way of reading a novel that seems to me to be deeply 'dialogic'.[31] Or, more exactly, for Belsey dialogism does not function within the text, or synchronically, but operates diachronically as a changing series of monologic readings which will emerge as the novel is interpreted in different social and political contexts. But Belsey – who sees English 'as a site of struggle'[32] between competing critical discourses – raises important questions about the politics of reading literary texts which contemporary criticism is increasingly having to confront, and the critical debate centred on George Eliot's works which I have tried to bring out in the essays chosen for this volume is clearly relevant to the discussion of such questions.

Psychoanalysis

Another contemporary critical mode that has played a significant role – though to a lesser degree than those which I have discussed above – in current George Eliot criticism has been psychoanalytic interpretation. The work of some of the critics I have already considered, for example, Colin MacCabe, Mary Jacobus and Sandra Gilbert, clearly reflects the influence of psychoanalysis, particularly in its Freudian and Lacanian forms, but several recent critics of George Eliot have attempted to apply a more thoroughgoing psychoanalytical critical approach to her novels. Her work offers more scope than most writers for such an approach since many early letters survive containing comments such as the following, written shortly after her father's death: 'What shall I become without my Father? It will seem as if a part of my moral nature were gone. I had a horrible vision of myself last night becoming earthly sensual and devilish for want of that purifying restoring influence.'[33]

Dianne F. Sadoff has perhaps produced the most interesting psychoanalytic criticism of George Eliot to date. She is one of the three novelists, the others being Dickens and Charlotte Brontë, whom Sadoff considers in her psychoanalytic study of the Victorian novel, *Monsters of Affection*. Sadoff argues that George Eliot uses one of Freud's 'primal scenes', the scene of seduction in which 'the child has been or imagines she has been seduced by her father or a figure of authority from the class of father', as 'metaphor' in her novels: 'Her heroine desires a "sort of father" yet defines him as a figure of law and authority: narrative structure seeks to undercut his authoritative word and so to usurp it textually as the discourse of a male narrator, the authority of a male author.' She goes on to argue that 'the scene of paternal seduction retroactively seeks to represent and solve a major enigma confronting the daughter: the origin or upsurge of her sexuality', and when narrated as story 'represents the beginning of a woman's history'.[34] It is obvious that there is a good deal of common ground between Sadoff's psychoanalytic criticism and deconstructive and feminist readings, though her more orthodox Freudian viewpoint leads to differences between her and Gilbert on the question of paternal seduction.

Sadoff believes her psychoanalytic approach is particularly applicable to *Romola*, a text that has returned to favour to a considerable extent in recent criticism, since she believes it is even more of a confessional novel than *The Mill on the Floss*. Since in writing *Romola* George Eliot had to draw upon her childhood history, Sadoff argues that the traumatic memory of the scene of seduction forced her 'to reinterpret the events of her experience and to repress those memories or to control and bind them in order to go forward in her life and career' (pp. 134–5). Romola 'binds herself to the law of fathers, discovers the inauthentic authority of each, and so proceeds to bind herself to her own law' (p. 135). But desire is seen as destructive and therefore must be controlled by Romola and all the characters in the novel, which leads to its repression. Thus Romola rebels against one father figure only to submit to the authority of another. For Sadoff this leads to a contradiction in the narrative since George Eliot fails 'to resolve her feelings about paternal authority and daughterly desire' (p. 140). Yet this controlling of memory and its traumatic effects through repression in *Romola* was ultimately to prove beneficial since, Sadoff suggests, such repressed material was reworked to powerful artistic effect in *Middlemarch* and *Daniel Deronda*.

Though Sadoff believes that *Romola* is George Eliot's most confessional novel, it can also be claimed, perhaps more persuasively, that it is her most philosophical novel. It seems inevitable that in focusing on the psychoanalytic aspect of the text, Sadoff must neglect its concern with moral, religious and political issues, and that therefore this is a severe limitation of her reading. However, Sadoff suggests that this division can theoretically be bridged when she states that her ultimate concern in her book is with 'the symbolic father, the concept of paternity in the dominant ideology of Victorian England in the arenas of politics, sexuality, and religion'.[35] But since, as she admits, she does not discuss these wider issues, it remains to be seen whether her psychoanalytical critical approach to the novel can persuasively lead on to an exploration of its philosophical or ideological dimensions.

One further aspect of recent George Eliot criticism needs to be mentioned, though this book is not the place to represent such criticism. The past twenty years has seen the publication of numerous studies of her intellectual and cultural context which have considerably modified traditional conceptions of her as a writer. Such contextual interpretation of her writing has been aided by the availability of such primary material as two further volumes of the Haight edition of her letters, several volumes of her notebooks, and information about the books she owned and read.[36] There has been new work on her connections with positivism and nineteenth-century social theory as well as studies of her relation to such areas and topics as science, Darwinism, Romanticism, German thought, Biblical criticism and hermeneutics, art, the 'information culture' of the nineteenth century.[37] A section of the guide to further reading is devoted to such contextual studies.

If one has to try, in conclusion, to express what has been the most important effect of criticism of the past twenty years on George Eliot's reputation and literary standing, the central point one should make, I think, is that she can no longer be convincingly regarded as a writer who is a product of a somewhat narrow and limited nineteenth-century English culture and thus as a less significant figure than such contemporaries as Flaubert, Dostoevsky, or Nietzsche, whose works continue to challenge modern readers at the deepest level. An example of the kind of assessment of her that seems to me to be now unsustainable can found in an article by Richard Rorty, a philosopher and writer who is held in highest respect but who is perhaps not familiar with recent George Eliot criticism. Rorty is concerned with Freud's major contribution to modern thought and he argues, to some extent reformulating Nietzsche's attack on her in *Twilight of the Idols*,[38] that morality as conceived by nineteenth-century intellectuals, which 'centered on replacing the love of God with the love of scientific truth', is called into question by Freud: 'What Freud did to this morality was to make *love itself* morally dubious – Huxley's and Freud's own love of truth as much as Gerard Hopkins's love of Mary, Achilles' of Patroclus, or Swift's of Stella and of human liberty.' Rorty asks the question: 'can literature retain its function as the organ of secular morality now that the love of humanity and truth which was central to that morality has been ironized by Freud? . . . Can anybody write as George Eliot or Henry James wrote once they have a Freudian vocabulary in the back of their minds?'[39]

Most of the essays in this collection suggest that Rorty's position on George Eliot lacks credibility. It is clearly contradicted by 'The Lifted Veil', which anticipates the idea that love is itself 'morally dubious', and it is significant that recent George Eliot criticism, unlike previous criticism of her work, views 'The Lifted Veil' as an integral part of her *oeuvre* and not as a strange anomaly.[40] In classic deconstructionist fashion, a text previously regarded as marginal has been shown to be central and has thus fundamentally altered how her fiction in general is read. Further, in showing how her work engages with issues central to such important areas of discussion as feminism and deconstruction – particularly the latter, which is as challenging to orthodox humanist assumptions as

Freud's insight into love – much recent criticism again refutes Rorty's belief that George Eliot's work is of its time in the most limited sense. In the light of the readings her fiction has received from modern criticism views such as Rorty's are clearly outdated.

In selecting the material for this reader, I have had two main aims: to show the centrality of George Eliot to contemporary literary theory and critical debate, as I hope I have demonstrated above, and also to provide critical coverage of the whole range of her fiction, with her most highly regarded novels having at least two essays devoted to them. I have, however, arranged the essays to follow the chronological order of publication of her work since I do not want to suggest that my discussion of their relation and significance in this Introduction is the only one possible. Though the essays exemplify various contemporary critical perspectives, and the differences within and between them, they should also be allowed some degree of autonomy and be read for their own particular merits.

Notes

1. F. R. LEAVIS, *The Great Tradition: George Eliot, Henry James, Joseph Conrad* (Harmondsworth: Penguin Books, 1966), pp. 40, 43–4.
2. See BARBARA HARDY, *The Novels of George Eliot: A Study in Form* (London: The Athlone Press, 1963), pp. 115ff.
3. LEO BERSANI, *A Future for Astyanax: Character and Desire in Literature* (London: Marion Boyars, 1978), pp. 62– 3, 63–4, 65–6.
4. CARAL CHRIST, 'Aggression and Providential Death in George Eliot's Fiction', *Novel*, 9 (1975–6), pp. 136, 140.
5. ROLAND BARTHES, 'Science versus Literature', *The Times Literary Supplement*, 28 September 1967, p. 897.
6. See *Essays of George Eliot*, ed. Thomas Pinney (London: Routledge & Kegan Paul, 1963), pp. 431–6.
7. BARTHES, 'Science versus Literature', pp. 897, 898.
8. BARTHES, *S/Z*, trans. Richard Miller (London: Jonathan Cape, 1975), pp. 4, 5.
9. ROSALIND COWARD and JOHN ELLIS, *Language and Materialism: Developments in Semiology and the Theory of the Subject* (London: Routledge & Kegan Paul, 1977), pp. 45, 46–7, 49, 50, 51–2.
10. PETER WIDDOWSON, 'Hardy and History: A Case Study in the Sociology of Literature', *Literature and History*, 9 (1983), p. 13.
11. STEPHEN HEATH, *The Nouveau Roman: A Study in the Practice of Writing* (London:

Elek, 1972), pp. 19–20, 21, 22. See also Catherine Belsey's discussion of 'classic realism' in relation to George Eliot in *Critical Practice* (London: Methuen, 1980), pp. 67–74.

12. All page numbers cited in the text refer to this collection.
13. Several recent critics have also discussed George Eliot's fiction in Bakhtinian terms. See, for example, the works by Rosemary Clark-Beattie and Peter K. Garrett in 'Further Reading'.
14. Paul de Man, *The Resistance to Theory* (Minneapolis: University of Minnesota Press, 1987), p. 120.
15. Barbara Johnson, *The Critical Difference: Essays in the Contemporary Rhetoric of Reading* (Baltimore: Johns Hopkins University Press, 1980), pp. 5, 8, 11.
16. *Essays of George Eliot*, pp. 432–3.
17. J. Hillis Miller, 'Narrative and History', *English Literary History*, 41 (1974), pp. 458, 461.
18. ibid., pp. 462, 464, 466, 467, 468.
19. J. Hillis Miller, 'Optic and Semiotic in *Middlemarch*', in *The Worlds of Victorian Fiction*, ed. Jerome Buckley (Cambridge, Mass.: Harvard University Press, 1975), pp. 126, 127, 128, 143, 144.
20. Jonathan Culler, *On Deconstruction: Theory and Criticism after Structuralism* (London: Routledge & Kegan Paul, 1983), pp. 86, 86–7.
21. See Pierre Macherey, *A Theory of Literary Production*, trans. Geoffrey Wall (London: Routledge & Kegan Paul, 1978).
22. D. A. Miller, *Narrative and Its Discontents: Problems of Closure in the Traditional Novel* (Princeton: Princeton University Press, 1981), pp. x, xiii.
23. John Goode, 'Adam Bede', in *Critical Essays on George Eliot*, ed. Barbara Hardy (London: Routledge & Kegan Paul, 1970), pp. 19, 33, 37, 36, 40.
24. Raymond Williams, *The Country and the City* (London: Chatto and Windus, 1973), pp. 165, 169, 173.
25. Terry Eagleton, *Criticism and Ideology: A Study in Marxist Literary Theory* (London: New Left Books, 1976), pp. 102, 111, 112, 121, 123, 124.
26. Louis Montrose, 'Renaissance Literary Studies and the Subject of History', *English Literary Renaissance*, 16 (1986), pp. 6, 8, 9.
27. Zelda Austen, 'Why Feminist Critics Are Angry with George Eliot', *College English*, 37 (1976), p. 551.
28. Sandra M. Gilbert and Susan Gubar, *The Madwoman in the Attic: The Woman Writer and the Nineteenth-Century Imagination* (New Haven: Yale University Press, 1979), pp. xi–xii, xii.
29. Gillian Beer, *George Eliot* (Brighton: Harvester Press, 1986), pp. 179–80
30. Catherine Belsey, 'Re-Reading the Great Tradition', in *Re-Reading English*, ed. Peter Widdowson (London: Methuen, 1982), p. 130.

31. John Goode brings out the dialogic quality of the novel particularly powerfully when he writes: 'Deronda is not only made to reject his mother for a higher concept of relationship, but also to reject her position without showing its inadequacy. . . . However much we explain Eliot's "realism" in terms of available ideologies her fiction remains a way of seeing – her affections clad with a knowledge that embraces Deronda's vision and Gwendolen's bewilderment.' See Goode, ' "The Affections Clad with Knowledge": Woman's Duty and the Public Life', *Literature and History*, 9 (1983), pp. 50, 51.

32. Belsey, pp. 134, 130.

33. *The George Eliot Letters: 9 Vols*, ed. Gordon S. Haight (New Haven: Yale University Press, 1954–78), I, p. 284.

34. Dianne F. Sadoff, *Monsters of Affection: Dickens, Eliot and Brontë on Fatherhood* (Baltimore: Johns Hopkins University Press, 1982), pp. 2, 3, 68.

35. Ibid., p. 4.

36. See *The George Eliot Letters*, ed. Haight; *Some George Eliot Notebooks: An Edition of the Carl H. Pforzheimer Holograph Notebooks: 4 Vols*, ed. William Baker (Salzburg: Universität Salzburg, 1976–85); *George Eliot's 'Middlemarch' Notebooks: A Transcription*, eds John Clark Pratt and Victor A. Neufeldt (Berkeley: University of California Press, 1979); George Eliot, *A Writer's Notebook, 1854–79, and Unpublished Writings*, ed. Joseph Wiesenfarth (Charlottesville: University of Virginia Press, 1981); William Baker, *The George Eliot–George Henry Lewes Library: An Annotated Catalogue of Their Books at the Dr Williams's Library, London* (New York: Garland, 1977); William Baker, *The Libraries of George Eliot and George Henry Lewes* (Victoria, BC: University of Victoria Press, 1981).

37. See books and articles listed in 'Further Reading' by the following: Rosemary Ashton, Gillian Beer, Mary Wilson Carpenter, Suzanne Graver, Robert A. Greenberg, George Levine, Michael York Mason, William Myers, K. M. Newton, E. S. Shaffer, Sally Shuttleworth, Donald D. Stone, Martha S. Vogeler, Alexander Welsh, Hugh Witemeyer, T. R. Wright.

38. See Friedrich Nietzsche, *Twilight of the Idols; The Anti-Christ*, trans. R. J. Hollingdale (Harmondsworth: Penguin Books, 1968), pp. 69–70.

39. Richard Rorty, 'Freud, Morality, and Hermeneutics', *New Literary History*, 12 (1980–1), pp. 178–9, 179–80.

40. In addition to the Eagleton article included in this collection, see, for example, Gillian Beer, 'Myth and the Single Consciousness: *Middlemarch* and "The Lifted Veil" ', in *This Particular Web: Essays on 'Middlemarch'*, ed. Ian Adam (Toronto: University of Toronto Press, 1975); Gilbert and Gubar, *The Madwoman in the Attic*, chapter 13; Mary Jacobus, *Reading Woman: Essays in Feminist Criticism* (London: Methuen, 1986), pp. 249–74; Charles Swann, ' "Déjà vu, Déjà lu": "The Lifted Veil" as an Experiment in Art', *Literature and History*, 5 (1979), pp. 40–57; Carroll Viera, ' "The Lifted Veil" and George Eliot's Early Aesthetic', *Studies in English Literature*, 24 (1984), pp. 749– 67.

2 George Eliot as the Angel of Destruction (*Scenes of Clerical Life*)*

SANDRA M. GILBERT AND SUSAN GUBAR

Sandra M. Gilbert and Susan Gubar are probably the major exponents of that form of feminist criticism which sees women's writing as having its own distinct tradition. They argue in their massive study, *The Madwoman in the Attic*, from which this reading of *Scenes from Clerical Life* (mainly written by Gubar) is drawn, that the works of major women writers of the nineteenth century are feminist texts, even if superficially they do not appear to be so. Thus beneath the calm surface of the stories that make up *Scenes of Clerical Life* there lurks an implicit feminine rage (see Introduction, pp. 19–20)

'But, my dear madam', the narrator of *Scenes of Clerical Life* (1857) occasionally cautions, 'you would gain unspeakably if you would learn with me to see some of the poetry and the pathos, the tragedy and the comedy, lying in the experience of a human soul that looks out through dull grey eyes, and that speaks in a voice of quite ordinary tones.'[1] His condescension is not unrelated to his determination to reform his audience's corrupt taste for melodrama. And certainly Eliot is centrally concerned in her earliest published fiction with sensitizing her readers to common human frailties. As in her later work, she wants to expand our faith in the redemptive possibilities of compassion. In addition, here, as elsewhere in her fiction, she portrays the impact of historical forces, such as Evangelicalism, on provincial life. But while the narrator calls our attention to the ordinary tones and everyday events he has substituted for the excitement and sentiment craved by readers steeped in too many silly novels by lady novelists, these *Scenes* only partly deal with three representative mild-mannered clergymen, since their drama actually depends upon quite extraordinary women. The stories told by Eliot are

* Reprinted from Sandra M. Gilbert and Susan Gubar, *The Madwoman in the Attic: The Woman Writer and the Nineteenth-Century Literary Imagination* (New Haven: Yale University Press, 1979, pp. 484–91; footnotes renumbered from the original.)

ignored by most critics in favor of the morals she expounds, in part because these plots are almost embarrassingly melodramatic. But such plots reveal a striking pattern of authorial vengeance in the service of female submission that informs Eliot's later fiction. If we focus exclusively on this pattern *Scenes*, to the exclusion of the philosophic, moralistic, and humorous bent of her narrator, it is partially to redress this imbalance and partially to understand what compels the emergence and the modulation of this voice as her fiction matures.

The first story, 'Amos Barton', introduces a churchman who is 'superlatively middling, the quintessential extract of mediocrity' (chapter 5), a man who gains our interest only because of his astonishingly virtuous wife, 'a large, fair, gentle Madonna, with . . . large, tender, short-sighted eyes' (chapter 2) not unlike those of Dorothea Brooke, the 'Blessed Virgin' of *Middlemarch*. The narrator exclaims over Milly Barton's virtues, "Soothing, unspeakable charm of gentle womanhood! which supersedes all acquisitions, all accomplishments. . . . You would even perhaps have been rather scandalized if she had descended from the serene dignity of *being* to the assiduous unrest of *doing*' (chapter 2). He even goes so far as to assert that she is suitably matched to a husband who reminds the narrator of 'mongrel ungainly dogs' because 'her sublime capacity of loving will have all the more scope' (chapter 2) with such a man. Plagued by a disreputable female houseguest and an insensitive husband, this angel in the house keeps her troubles to herself even when her 'delicate body was becoming daily less fit for all the many things that had to be done', and she continues to mend the clothes and arrange the dinners because 'A loving woman's world lies within the four walls of her own home' (chapter 7). Actually the trouble that Barton's mediocrity in his professional vocation makes for Milly suggests an implicit rejection of his canons of conduct. But it is Milly's death in childbirth which really represents her superiority to him; its message is the insignificance of the public world and the importance of private acts of love. Indeed, her family's helplessness at her deathbed only intensifies her authority as a spiritual guide for their lives after her death. Like funereal Aunt Pullet (in *The Mill on the Floss*) who always wears weeds, or lugubrious Liddy, whose predictions of imminent death serve as a chorus to Esther and Felix Holt, Milly Barton reveals Eliot's understanding that such female fascination with decline is a means of obtaining power, if only the power to predict catastrophe.

Since Milly's death is, after all, the logical extension of a life of being instead of doing, it also serves as a model for feminine submission, which is finally attained by the heroine of 'Mr Gilfil's Love-Story', but only after she has fully experienced the depth and futility of her own feelings. The Italian ward of Sir Christopher Cheverel is picked up like an *objet d'art* to furnish a plain brick English family house that Sir Christopher is transforming into a gothic mansion. She is one more foreign oddity among the clutter of 'Greek statues and busts of Roman emperors; low cabinets filled with curiosities, natural and antiquarian' (chapter 2). Indeed, Sir Christopher calls her his 'monkey' or 'songbird'. That his house is the same ancestral mansion we continually encounter is made clear by the inscription over the fireplace in the housekeeper's room: *Fear God and honour the King*. An orphan with no legitimate place here, Caterina is left to exercise her 'only talent [which] lay in loving' (chapter 4), by falling in love with Captain Wybrow, a man who 'always did the thing easiest and most agreeable to him from a sense of duty' (chapter 4), and whose lazy egotism therefore adumbrates that of all the later heirs in Eliot's novels: Arthur Donnithorne, Stephen Guest, Harold Transome, Tito Melema, Fred Vincy, and Mr Grandcourt.

When Captain Wybrow ignores his own implicit promises to Caterina and brings the haughty Beatrice Assher home to woo her as a bride before the petite dependant, the echoes of *Jane Eyre* are hard to ignore. Forced to watch the man she loves courting a wealthy, large-limbed, dark-haired beauty, Caterina is described as a 'poor bird . . . beginning to flutter and faintly dash its soft breast against the hard iron bars of the inevitable' (chapter 3). Like Jane or like Rochester's ward Adèle, Caterina experiences 'gleams of fierce resistance' to any harsh discipline. She even displays a 'certain ingenuity in vindictiveness' not unrelated to her financial and spiritual poverty. But it is her resemblance to Catherine of *Wuthering Heights* that helps explain the depth of Caterina's passion. Desiring her unobtainable relative, the captain, Caterina finds a dagger which 'she will plunge . . . into his heart' because she decides 'in the madness of her passion that she can kill the man whose very voice unnerves her' (chapter 13). But before she has an opportunity to use the knife (to which Eliot's publisher strongly objected), Caterina is inalterably separated from her childhood lover when she finds him dead of a heart attack in the garden. Like Catherine Earnshaw, Caterina Sarti finally marries her more civilized suitor, Mr Gilfil, and dies in childbirth. Only then is she fully possessed by her husband, who keeps a locked room full of miniature mementos: her little dressing table, her dainty looking glass, her small black kerchief, and so forth.

Although childbirth has so far brought nothing but death, the masculine narrator continues to announce in 'Janet's Repentance', as he had in the former stories, that motherhood 'stills all anxiety into calm content: it makes selfishness become self-denial, and gives even to hard vanity the glance of admiring love' (chapter 13). But while this encomium comes as an explanation of how Janet Dempster would be less sorrowful about her lot were she a mother, her lot is a life with 'a drunken tyrant of a midnight house' (chapter 7), a lawyer she was driven to marry because she 'had nothing to look to but being a governess' (chapter 3). 'Gypsy', as her husband calls her, is herself driven to secret drinking by his physical brutality:

> Every feverish morning, with its blank listlessness and despair, seemed more hateful than the last; every coming night more impossible to brave without arming herself in leaden stupor. The morning light brought no gladness to her: it seemed only to throw its glare on what had happened in the dim candle-light – on the cruel man seated immovable in drunken obstinacy by the dead fire and dying lights in the dining-room, rating her in harsh tones, reiterating old reproaches – or on a hideous blank of something unremembered, something that must have made that dark bruise on her shoulder, which ached as she dressed herself.
>
> (CHAPTER 13)

In her suffering she can only ask her mother why she was allowed to marry: 'Why didn't you tell me mother?' she asks; 'You knew what brutes men could be; and there's no help for me – no hope' (chapter 14). She is later echoed by Mrs Transome's heartfelt protest in *Felix Holt*: 'Men are selfish. They are selfish and cruel. What they care for is their own pleasure and their own pride' (chapter 5), and by Gwendolen Harleth's useless lament in *Daniel Deronda*: 'I don't care if I never marry any one. There is nothing worth caring for. I believe all men are bad, and I hate them' (chapter 14).

Unable to leave her husband because she is incapable of facing 'the blank that lay for her outside her married home', Janet is living with a man whom the servants believe capable of murdering her and shutting her up in a closet. But actually all Dempster need do to demonstrate his power over Janet is literally put her out on the street in her night-clothes one cold midnight. While we are told that Janet would be less sorrowful at this kind of treatment if she were a mother, it is really clear that 'Cruelty, like every other vice, requires no motive outside itself – it only requires opportunity' (chapter 13), because 'an unloving, tyrannous, brutal man needs no motive to prompt his cruelty; he needs only the perpetual presence of a woman he can call his own' (chapter 13), and marriage provides precisely this presence. In spite of the distaste of her publisher, John Blackwood, for the subject, Eliot insisted on writing about wife abuse and female alcoholism, but she does this very tactfully, from her description of Janet's 'wounded' consciousness of 'the riddle of her life' (chapter 13) to a factual explanation that her husband 'had all her little property in his hands, and that little was scarcely enough to keep her in comfort without his aid' (chapter 16). Like all the other marriages in *Scenes of Clerical Life*, this one is no happier than Bertha and Latimer's in 'The Lifted Veil'.

Eliot is concerned in 'Janet's Repentance', as she is in 'The Lifted Veil', to show us that 'Our daily familiar life is but a hiding of ourselves from each other behind a screen of trivial words and deeds, and those who sit with us at the same hearth are often the farthest off from the deep human soul within us, full of unspoken evil and unacted good' (chapter 16). Indeed, she seems to have written about clerical characters in her earliest fiction at least in part because these men are somehow 'feminine'. Inhabiting an emotional, moral, private sphere in which they are supposed to be exemplary, they are nevertheless profoundly aware of what goes on behind the veil, and they invite confessions from all who 'tremble to let in the daylight on a chamber of relics which we have never visited except in curtained silence' (chapter 18). Janet's repentance comes about, in fact, because of the 'fellowship in suffering' she attains with Mr Tryan, a model of submission himself (chapter 12). Confessing a sin similar to that committed by Captain Wybrow – inducing a girl below his station to an attachment that he fails to honor – he explains to Janet how only a sense of helpless guilt can prepare for salvation: 'There is nothing that becomes us but entire submission, perfect resignation' (chapter 18).

Reconciled with her mother, Janet even begins to believe that she must return to her husband since 'There were things in me that were wrong, and I should like to make up for them if I can' (chapter 20). And when, on his deathbed, her husband does need her, she gives unstintingly. Finally, her confidence in the human sympathy of Mr Tryan constitutes for her a faith in divine love that allows her to fight her temptation to drink. The fact that Janet Dempster is saved from drink and despair and is 'changed as the dusty, bruised, and sun-withered plant is changed when the soft rains of heaven have fallen on it' (chapter 26) testifies to the saintliness of Mr Tryan, as does his early death in the snug red-brick house Janet had furnished for him, and in her loving embrace. Indeed Janet's devoted nursing of the dying Mr Tryan reminds us that Eliot referred to the time when she nursed her father on his deathbed as the 'happiest days of life to me' (*Letters*, 1: 283–4).

The unintentional irony of this phrase is further illuminated by 'Janet's Repentance'. For this man who dies in Janet's arms, with her kiss on his lips, reminds us that another man has also died in her embrace with the belief that her kiss is deadly and her embrace will kill. On his deathbed, the brutal misogynist Dempster suffers from frightening visions of his wife's revenge. He thinks he sees

> 'her hair is all serpents . . . they're black serpents . . . they hiss . . . they hiss . . . let me go . . . she wants to drag me with her cold arms . . . her arms are serpents . . . they are great white serpents . . . they'll twine round me . . . she wants to drag me into the cold water . . . her bosom is cold . . . it is black . . . it is all serpents. . . .'
>
> (CHAPTER 23)

Nothing less than a female monster to her husband's sickened imagination, the repentant Janet has been transformed into an image which suggests that Dempster is simply mad with guilt over his mistreatment of her. At the same time, however, his death does seem fully connected with her agency, since she does wish him dead, and with ample reason, and since his death is so fortuitous a release for her from otherwise inescapable imprisonment. We are told, furthermore, about a female power that is definitively involved in causing Dempster's death: 'Nemesis is lame, but she is of colossal stature, like the gods; and sometimes, while her sword is not yet unsheathed, she stretches out her huge left arm and grasps her victim. The mighty hand is invisible, but the victim totters under the dire clutch' (chapter 13). The huge left arm of Nemesis, which recalls the great white serpent arms of Janet, rewards the repression of the suffering wife's murderous wish by enacting it.

Mr Tryan articulates the protest against resignation that we sense in all of Eliot's heroines when he admits, 'if my heart were less rebellious, and if I were less liable to temptation, I should not need that sort of self-denial' (chapter 11). Certainly Milly Barton, Caterina Sarti, and Janet Dempster all attain angelic submission only after considerable inward struggle against resentment and anger. Indeed, because they are too good for the kind of life they have to lead, all three are saved by death and thereby curiously linked to the forces of destruction. Having 'killed' themselves into ladylike docility and selflessness, all three heroines are instances of what Alexander Welsh calls the 'angel of death'.[2] Even their submission to death can be viewed, however, as a rejection of life. Not only ministering to the dying, these angels of destruction actually bring death, 'saving' their patient/victims by killing them off. Or, if they do not actually bring death to those they have every right to resent, the author does. Indeed, the angelic purity of the heroines seems to release the melodramatic response of their author. Thus Milly Barton's death allows her to live out her Madonna role and provides her with the only possible escape from a life of domestic drudgery, even as it punishes her husband for his neglect of her; the invisible left arm of Nemesis sends death to Captain Wybrow in the garden, thereby saving Caterina from killing him herself; and it frees Janet from a miserable marriage by dragging her husband 'into the cold water'. While each heroine represses her anger and submits to the necessity for renunciation, the author as the goddess Nemesis acts 'for' her in much the same way that Frankenstein's monster acted 'for' his creator or Bertha Mason Rochester acted 'for' Jane Eyre. Thus, interestingly enough, in *Scenes of Clerical Life*, it is the novelist – not as the male narrator, but as the female author behind the scenes – who plays the part of the madwoman.

The contradiction between Marian Evans as historical author and George Eliot as fictive narrator helps explain, then, how a title like *Scenes of Clerical Life* (which Eliot repeatedly insisted on with Blackwood) functions as a kind of camouflage or Austenian 'cover' to conceal the dramatic focus of the plot. Insisting on the primacy of male spheres of activity, Eliot aspires to the 'masculine' scientific detachment of an essayist reproducing and analyzing 'slices of life'. And in this respect, as in so many other, *Scenes of Clerical Life* forecasts the camouflages of her later fiction. *Adam Bede*, with its masculine title, relies on the story of fallen and female Hetty Sorrel for its suspense, just as *Felix Holt the Radical* maps the mental and moral development of Esther Lyon, while both *The Mill on the Floss* and *Middlemarch* announce themselves as sociological studies of provincial life, though they were originally conceived and still come across as portraits of female destiny. And at the end of her literary career Eliot wrote *Daniel Deronda*, a book that could as easily be entitled 'Gwendolen Harleth'.[3]

But *Scenes of Clerical Life* is also typical of Eliot's lifelong fascination with the angel of destruction, for the pattern we have seen in this early book – the contradiction between feminine renunciation countenanced by the narrator and female (even feminist) vengeance exacted by the author – remains an important one in Eliot's fiction, as Carol Christ has shown in her very useful essay on the function of providential death in Eliot's fiction.[4] But while Christ explains how Eliot's heroines are saved from performing acts of rage, she neither studies how all the heroines are nevertheless implicated in the author's violence, nor how the author is involved in punishing male characters who specifically symbolize patriarchal power.

Notes

1. George Eliot, *Scenes of Clerical Life* (Baltimore: Penguin, 1973), pp. 80–1. Subsequent citations appear parenthetically in the text. See Neil Roberts, *George Eliot: Her Belief and Her Art* (Pittsburgh: University of Pittsburgh Press, 1975), pp. 53–62, and Derek and Sybil Oldfield, '*Scenes of Clerical Life*: The Diagram and The Picture', *Critical Essays on George Eliot*, ed. Barbara Hardy (London: Routledge & Kegan Paul, 1970), pp. 1–18.
2. Alexander Welsh, *The City of Dickens* (Oxford: Clarendon Press, 1971), pp. 182–4.
3. The title that seems to be an exception to this rule, *Romola*, is also a kind of camouflage since it takes the emphasis off the demonic, fallen double (Baldassarre) and his plot of revenge, and emphasizes the angelically exemplary heroine.
4. Carol Christ, 'Aggression and Providential Death in George Eliot's Fiction', *Novel* (Winter 1976), pp. 130–40.

3 Reading Writing: Eliot (*Adam Bede*)*

J. HILLIS MILLER

J. Hillis Miller is one of the best known of American deconstructive critics. This chapter from his book *The Ethics of Reading* is the most recent of a series of essays he has written on George Eliot, all of which argue that her works consciously deconstruct the conventions of realism. Here he focuses on the notorious chapter 17 of *Adam Bede*, which appears to assert that the novel can and should reflect reality in a literal sense. Miller on the contrary argues that a close analysis of the chapter shows that George Eliot accepted that language could not avoid being figurative (see Introduction, pp. 9–11).

After the rigors of Paul de Man's intricate argumentation about the ethics of reading, the reader, it may be, turns with some expectation of relief to chapter 17 of George Eliot's *Adam Bede*, 'In Which the Story Pauses a Little', just as, within the chapter, Eliot's narrator turns with relief from paintings of 'cloud-borne angels, from prophets, sibyls, and heroic warriors' to those Dutch genre paintings 'which lofty-minded people despise'.[1] Surely, the reader thinks, Eliot believed in a straightforward realism in narration and surely that was associated with a confidence that readers could get straightforward moral lessons from her novels. For Eliot, a story is validated by its truth of correspondence to historical, social, and human reality, a human reality assumed to exist outside language. This goes along with a conviction that the function of such truth-telling is to teach us to be good, to love our neighbors, by offering examples of such goodness and of the disastrous consequences of its lack. Let us, however, look narrowly at the language of that famous chapter 17 and try to read what it says. It will be 'needful', to use one of her words and one of her metaphors, to question it closely, as if it were in the witness box narrating its experience upon oath.

---

* Reprinted from J. Hillis Miller, *The Ethics of Reading: Kant, de Man, Eliot, Trollope, James and Benjamin* (New York: Columbia University Press, 1987), pp. 61–80.

The theory of realism proposed in chapter 17 of *Adam Bede* depends on the notion that there can be a literal, nonfigurative, truth-telling language of narration. 'So I am content', says the narrator,

> to tell my simple story, without trying to make things seem better than they were; dreading nothing indeed, but falsity, which, in spite of one's best efforts, there is reason to dread. Falsehood is easy, truth so difficult. . . . Examine your words well, and you will find that even when you have no motive to be false, it is a very hard thing to say the exact truth, even about your own immediate feelings – much harder than to say something fine about them which is *not* the exact truth.

What, exactly, is this language, the words with which the novelist can say the exact truth about inner feeling or outer facts, without a fraction more or less, like a board cut by Adam Bede to perfect length and fit? The theory of the *function* of such language in the chapter is clear. It is a version of the definition of mimesis which goes back to Aristotle. This theory is one of the constants of occidental metaphysics. The theory is an economic one, in the broadest sense of that term. In Eliot's case it is an economic theory heavily tinged with the language of Protestant ethics. In Aristotle's *Poetics* the function of mimesis is knowledge. Imitation is natural to man, and it is natural for him to take pleasure in it. He takes pleasure in it because he learns from it. He learns from it the nature of the things or persons imitated, which without that detour through mimesis would not be visible and knowable.

In chapter 17 of *Adam Bede* the argument is not so much that I should know my neighbor as that I should love him or her:

> These fellow-mortals, every one, must be accepted as they are: you can neither straighten their noses, nor brighten their wit, nor rectify their dispositions; and it is these people – amongst whom your life is passed – that it is *needful* you should tolerate, pity and love: it is these more or less ugly, stupid, inconsistent people, whose movements of goodness you should be able to admire – [my italics].
>
> It is more *needful* that I should have a fibre of sympathy connecting me with that vulgar citizen who weighs out my sugar in a vilely-assorted cravat and waistcoat, than with the handsomest rascal in red scarf and green feather; – more *needful* that my heart should swell with loving admiration at some trait of gentle goodness in the faulty people who sit at the same hearth with me [my italics].

The argument here, like Aristotle's, depends on the notion that, paradoxically, things, in this case one's neighbors, cannot be seen as they are, therefore cannot be loved and admired, in themselves. It is necessary that they make a detour through the mirroring of art in order to become visible and hence lovable. A parallel argument is made by Fra Lippo Lippi in his defense of a 'realistic' art in Robert Browning's poem:

God's works – paint any one, and count it crime
To let a truth slip. Don't object, 'His works
Are here already; nature is complete:
Suppose you reproduce her – (which you can't)
There's no advantage! you must beat her, then.'
For don't you mark? we're made so that we love
First when we see them painted, things we have passed
Perhaps a hundred times nor cared to see;
And so they are better, painted – better to us,
Which is the same thing. Art was given for that;
God uses us to help each other so,
Lending our minds out . . .[2]

In Eliot's case the argument is that it is 'needful', we have an 'obligation', not only to reflect things accurately in the mirrors of our minds but to return that reflection with 'interest', so to speak, that is, in a represented form. The reflection must be turned into a genre painting or into a realistic novel. This must be done in such a way that what is reflected will be seen, understood, and loved. The obligation is economic, legal, and ethical, all at once. Eliot's narrator, at the end of the chapter, says: 'I herewith discharge my conscience.' This is the fulfillment of a categorical imperative, the one thing needful. At the same time it is the fulfillment of a contract, as when one has borrowed money from the bank and must pay it back with interest, 'discharge' the debt. At the same time, finally, it is the fulfillment of a legal obligation, as when one must tell the truth under oath in the witness box.

All three of these superimposed circuits of detour and return are guaranteed by their relation to a religious obligation. I must, in conscience, love God first and then love my neighbor as myself. The truthtelling of the witness is based on an oath sworn 'before God', or 'by God'. The painter or novelist, in his return with interest of what his mind has reflected, imitates God in that productivity whereby all the creation emanated from God only to be returned to him with a plus-value of that chorus of praise all nature raises in speaking back the name of God to God. This is stated in concentrated form in the simultaneously indicative, imperative, and performative* last line of Gerard Manley Hopkins' 'Pied

---

* [Ed.] **Performative**: A term used in the philosophy of language, introduced by J. L. Austin, to denote an utterance which is itself the performance of an act, such as 'I promise'. More generally a mode of language that brings reality into being through its rhetorical power to persuade or convince.

Beauty': 'He fathers forth whose beauty is past praise,/Praise him.' The syntax of this in the full grammar of the poem makes it mean at once: 'All created things do praise him'; 'Let all things praise him'; and 'I here, in the poem, perform the act of praising him.'

All three forms of the human circuit of detour and return, the economic, the ethical, and the legal, each grounded implicitly in the divine circuit of creation, and each functioning as a figure for the act of realistic representation, come together in Eliot's initial profession of obligation:

> But it happens, on the contrary, that my strongest effort is to avoid any such arbitrary picture, and to give a faithful account of men and things as they have mirrored themselves in my mind. The mirror is doubtless defective; the outlines will sometimes be disturbed, the reflection faint or confused; but I feel as much bound to tell you as precisely as I can what that reflection is, as if I were in the witness-box narrating my experience on oath.

The reflection here is double. This is true of the Victorian theory of realism generally, that system of intertwined figures and concepts about art or literature which governs in one way or another all Victorian discourse on that topic. Examples would include the abundant writings of Ruskin or, at the other end of a scale of complexity, the multitude of reviews of novels in Victorian periodicals. The diverse versions of this theory tend to be simultaneously subjective and objective in their notions about truth. They move uneasily back and forth between one and the other. The value of a novel, for Eliot, as for her contemporaries generally, lies in its truth of correspondence to things as they are, objectively. On the other hand, what is represented in the words of the novel is not the objective things as they are but those things as they have already been reflected in the mirroring mind of the novelist. That mirror, as Eliot here explicitly affirms and as her contemporaries agreed, always distorts. Subjectivity is like a mirror in a funhouse, concave, convex, or wavy, so that, as she says in a passage in *Middlemarch*, 'I am not sure that the greatest man of his age, if ever that solitary superlative existed, could escape these unfavorable reflections of himself in various small mirrors; and even Milton, looking for his portrait in a spoon, must submit to have the facial angle of a bumpkin.'[3] Even so, the novelist must represent as accurately as possible the reflection he finds in the defective mirror of his mind. The truth of correspondence in realism is not to objective things, or only indirectly to objective things. It is rather to things as they have already made a detour into necessarily distorted subjective reflections. Eliot's obligation is, as she says, 'to give a faithful account of men and things as they have mirrored themselves in my mind'.

From things to mental images to verbal account – the words on the page in a realistic novel are the product of a double translation. Their function is performative, not merely descriptive or cognitive. The obligation fulfilled in 'the faithful representing of commonplace things' is to generate the right feelings in the reader or beholder of such representations. These feelings bring the people who feel them to do the right thing, for 'it isn't notions set people doing the right thing – it's feelings.' The double mirroring of a realistic art makes something happen. It makes the right things happen by making people do the right thing. Commonplace things as they are must be returned back into those things as they are, after their double excursus, first into the mirroring mind, and then into the words which give a faithful account of that mind. They must be reintroduced into the culture which produced the art and which that art represents. They must be returned with the plus value of a power to generate good feelings and therefore good actions. Only then is the 'account' fully made and closed, the obligation fulfilled, the note discharged, the mortgage on the house of fiction paid off.

In the context of this economic–ethical–religious–affective–performative theory of realism George Eliot mounts his attack on idealizing art, the art of irrealism. (I say 'his' to remind the reader that the putative speaker in this chapter is not Mary Ann Evans, the author of *Adam Bede*, but a fictive personage, 'George Eliot', who narrates the story and who is given a male gender.) Eliot's attack on irrealism runs as a crossways woof through all the fabric of chapter 17, countering the positive argument. At first sight the attack on ideal beauty and goodness seems entirely reasonable. People are not like that, at least not those near home, and there can be no use, no obligation, nothing 'needful', in representing them as they are not. Much more is at stake here, however, than may at first appear.

What George Eliot explicitly rejects in the counterwoven argument of the chapter is that theological underpinning which is implicit in the economic theory of realism I have traced out. Though it is not a question here of direct influence, the best shorthand description of what Eliot rejects would give it the proper name Immanuel Kant. It was by no means necessary to know Kant's works in order to be a Kantian or an anti-Kantian in the nineteenth century, nor is it so in our own day. Kant in the *Critique of Judgment* codified a set of notions about art which is one of the constants of the Western tradition. The genius, according to Kant, imitates nature not by copying it, but by duplicating its manner of production. As God spoke nature into existence by means of the divine word and by means of his Son, the Word, so the genius, by virtue of a power given him by nature, speaks into existence a heterocosm which adds something hitherto unheard-of to nature. It adds the plus value of a new beauty which is beyond price. This new beauty is beyond measure by any slavish standards of mirroring correspondence to things as they are. The novel beauty the genius creates is grounded in the analogy between his *logos* and the divine *logos*. This analogy is based in nature or goes by way of nature, though only because nature is the word of God, a voice made into substantial things. Analogy, as the word suggests, is always a similarity in voices or in words.[4]

This Kantism George Eliot rejects. He rejects it by removing its ground in the analogy between God's way of producing nature and the way the genius produces his works. Without this analogy the works of 'genius' are simply unreal. They are a detour into the fictive from which there is no return to the real word of ugly, stupid, inconsistent neighbors. Therefore such works of art are of no use. They fulfill no obligation. They are the reverse of 'needful'.

George Eliot's way of expressing this is in several ways odd. It is odd for one thing in its effacement of the problem of language by a shift from language to another of the arts, painting. This sideways displacement occurs regularly throughout the chapter, for example in the famous appeal to Dutch genre painting as a model for truth-telling in literature. One effect of this is to make the reader forget the problem of the medium in literary realism. The implication is that the language of realism is a proper language functioning like a photograph or a scientific drawing. It goes by way of a one-to-one correspondence between the word and the thing.

The fact that language is the medium of realism and the fact that there are specific problems associated with the medium are intermittently confronted in the chapter. An example of one such problem which George Eliot at least implicitly recognizes is the temporality of narration. 'An account of men and things as they have mirrored themselves in my mind' is not a static spatial picture but a running narrative going from word to word, according to another meaning of 'account' alongside the economic and ethical ones. An 'account' is a telling over, an enumeration one by one of a series of items which are then added up to make a sum. In another place, in a passage cited above, George Eliot reminds the reader of the difficulty of finding the right word even for what is closest at hand and most intimate, one's own emotions; 'it is a very hard thing to say the exact truth even about your own immediate feelings.' The shift from language to painting or drawing invites the reader to forget all those problems which are specific to language. In invites him to think of narration in language as like making an exact atemporal drawing of something physically there before the artist's eyes, a lion or a jug:

> So I am content to tell my simple story, without trying to make things seem better than they were; dreading nothing, indeed, but falsity, which, in spite of one's best efforts, there is reason to dread. Falsehood

> is so easy, truth so difficult. The pencil is conscious of a delightful facility in drawing a griffin – the longer the claws, and the larger the wings, the better; but that marvellous facility which we mistook for genius is apt to forsake us when we want to draw a real unexaggerated lion.

'The pencil is conscious' – it is an odd phrase. It seems as though the phallic-shaped instrument of writing must have its own impulse toward falsehood. The impulse toward falsehood is given an implicit male gender, the gender of the narrator himself, whereas the faithful representing of commonplace things is perhaps therefore implicitly female. This may seem an implausibly large issue to pin on an innocent metonymy assigning consciousness to the means of writing rather than to the writer, but readers of *Middlemarch* or of Eliot's work as a whole will know that a contrast between male and female imaginations is a major feature of her work. Her work turns on a dismantling of the 'phallogocentric'* male system of metaphysics and its replacement by what, remembering one of the key metaphors of *Middlemarch*, one might call Ariadne's performative 'yes' to life. This speech act is dramatized in Dorothea's marriage to Will Ladislaw at the end of *Middlemarch*. I shall try elsewhere to demonstrate in detail how that works.

In chapter 17 of *Adam Bede*, to return to that, the facility of the conscious pencil which produces griffins is mistaken by the mind of the one holding the pencil for genius. It is taken in error as a God-given gift for generating works of art not copied from nature but nevertheless valid. In fact the conscious pencil produces nullities, empty fictions. This facility in falsehood is defined sardonically elsewhere in the chapter as 'the gift of that lofty order of mind who pant after the ideal'. The conscious pencil of the false genius produces by its lofty elevation those embodiments of religious, mythological, and heroic ideas which are so resolutely rejected throughout the chapter. They are rejected as 'falsehoods' or at best as validated only in a Feuerbachian way as projections of purely human values. All those paintings of the Madonna, for example, are for George Eliot, as for Ludwig Feuerbach, to be venerated not because Mary was the Mother of God but because a Madonna in art embodies the ideal of human motherhood. It is as if George Eliot were prepared to hurry with

---

* [Ed.] **Phallogocentric**: A term, coined by Jacques Derrida, that combines 'phallocentric' and 'logocentric'. 'Phallocentric' is a term used in feminist criticism to denote the cultural dominance of the masculine over the feminine. 'Logocentric' is a Derridean term used to indicate that the main tradition of Western thinking assumes that words reflect meanings which exist beyond the play of language. 'Phallogocentric', in substituting 'phallus' for 'logos', indicates that the phallus operates as a master-signifier in Western thinking, thus encoding masculinity as central and marginalizing the feminine.

averted face through all the rooms in the Louvre marked 'Renaissance Painting, Italy', in order to get to the room of Dutch genre paintings with all the relief of a man escaping the temptations of a false ideal in order to confront once more the real:

> I turn, without shrinking, from cloud-borne angels, from prophets, sibyls, and heroic warriors, to an old woman bending over her flowerpot. . . .
>
> Paint us an angel, if you can, with a floating violet robe, and a face paled by the celestial light; paint us yet oftener a Madonna, turning her mild face upward and opening her arms to welcome the divine glory; but do not impose on us any aesthetic rules which shall banish from the region of Art those old women scraping carrots with their work-worn hands, those heavy clowns taking holiday in a dingy pot-house, those rounded backs and stupid weather-beaten faces that have bent over the spade. . . .
>
> There are few prophets in the world; few sublimely beautiful women; few heroes. I can't afford to give all my love and reverence to such rarities: I want a great deal of those feelings for my everyday fellowmen, especially for the few in the foreground of the great multitude, whose faces I know, whose hands I touch, for whom I have to make way with kindly courtesy.

Rejecting an aesthetic of the sublime, the beautiful, the ideal, the rare, the distant, George Eliot affirms with great persuasive power a counter-aesthetic of the ugly, the stupid, the real, the frequent, the statistically likely, the near. It is the griffin replaced by the lion or, better, by the house cat. Once again the economic metaphor is essential. I have only so much love and reverence banked in my account of emotional savings, and I 'can't afford' to squander it on ideal rarities, if indeed they exist at all. All my emotion is needed for those who are near at hand, those 'more or less ugly, stupid, inconsistent people', my neighbors.

All this seems clear enough. It is consistent in its rejection not so much of the Kantian sublime as of a Kantism deprived of the analogy between the artist's voice and his power of production on the one hand, and the divine *logos*, with its performative power to make all by fiat, on the other.

Nevertheless, a question still remains. What exactly is the mode of language by which the novelist produces in literature something analogous to the adherence to the real of Dutch genre paintings? It would seem that the answer to this question would be easy to give. Surely the realistic novelist works primarily with referential, nonfigurative language, language validated by its truth of correspondence to things as they are. This is the sort of language that calls a spade a spade or an old woman scraping carrots an old woman scraping carrots.

As a matter of fact, the theory of language developed elsewhere in *Adam Bede* is considerably more problematic than this notion of referential literalism. This theory, dramatized in the way the characters live out, in the flesh, so to speak, problems of language, plays ironically against the notion of referential language affirmed in chapter 17 for the narrator's truth-telling. Though there is not space here for a demonstration of the way the action itself of *Adam Bede* dramatizes the age-old story of the disasters that follow taking figures of speech literally, it is needful for my reading of George Eliot's reading of himself to show that in fact the theory of language in chapter 17 is not so simple either. The question of the language of realism is the missing link in the chain of George Eliot's argument. This link can be reconstructed from the implications of the figures and negations he uses to tell the reader what that language is like and what it is not like. This process might be compared to the archeologist's reconstruction of the missing limb of an ancient statue or to the paleontologist's making of a complete skeleton from a few fossil bones. In this case too a rather unexpected animal emerges when the pieces are put together.

The question, the reader will remember, is what language will not only render a true account of things and men as they have mirrored themselves in the narrator's mind but also render that account in such a way as to add the interest of the one thing needful. The one thing needful is the creation of a fiber of sympathy tying the reader in love and reverence to his ugly, stupid, inconsistent neighbors. The narrator tells the reader that such language will be like genre paintings and unlike religious, mythological, or historical painting. Nothing is said about how one imitates in words the methods of those 'Dutch paintings, which lofty-minded people despise'. Exactly what linguistic procedures are involved?

The reader is told, at least implicitly, first by the narrator and then by Adam Bede himself in a long speech cited verbatim by the narrator from a conversation he had with Adam 'in his old age', that the proper language of storytelling will be like the sermons of Mr Irwine and unlike the sermons of Mr Ryde. This is an odd moment in the novel. The narrator elsewhere in the text has been anonymous, invisible, omniscient, and omnipresent, able to move freely and instantaneously in time and space, able to see without being seen, able to enter into the minds and hearts of the characters at will. In this chapter the narrator narrows down to a single 'real' person, dependent on individual reports for his information. This is especially apparent in his description of his encounter with the old Adam Bede. It is as if a cut-out photographed figure were inserted by collage into a Dutch painting. About this more must be said later. Now the question is the following: if the implicit comparison with two kinds of preaching gives a model for storytelling which is linguistic rather than graphic, what is the difference between Irwine's sermons and Ryde's? Again the reader is told little except negatively. Irwine, says Adam, 'was [not] much of a preacher'. '[H]e preached short moral sermons, and that was all.' Ryde, on the other hand, preached sermons full of 'notions' and 'doctrines', but these forms of language were ineffective in making his parishioners do the right thing and love their neighbors:

> 'But', said Adam, 'I've seen pretty clear ever since I was a young un, as religion's something else besides notions. It isn't notions sets people doing the right thing – it's feeling. . . . Mr Ryde was a deal thought on at a distance, I believe, and he wrote books; but as for math'matics and the natur o' things, he was as ignorant as a woman. [Note, by the way, the irony of the last phrase, when one thinks of it as written not by 'George Eliot' but by Mary Ann Evans, daughter of Robert Evans, the 'original' of Adam.] He was very knowing about doctrines, and used to call 'em the bulwarks of the Reformation; but I've always mistrusted that sort o' learning as leaves folks foolish and unreasonable about business.'

This seems to offer a clue to the proper language of storytelling in a double displacement, first to the question of the effective language of preaching and then from that to an apparent analogy between language causing 'feelings' or 'resolutions' and the language of mathematics, business, and 'the natur o' things'. This shift goes by way of a bifurcation between notions and doctrines, on the one hand, and some kind of language that will bring about 'resolutions', on the other. A measuring, hardheaded, literally naming, referential language, dramatized in the novel in Adam's profession of carpentry, seems to give the reader a model for the proper language of narration. But no, somewhat surprisingly, both the language of mathematics and the language of literal naming are dismissed as of no account, as ineffective, as unable to generate feelings and the good actions that follow from them:

> 'It's the same with the notions in religion as it is with math'matics, – a man may be able to work problems straight off in's head as he sits by the fire and smokes his pipe; but if he has to make a machine or a building, he must have a will and a resolution, and love something else better than his own ease.
>
> But I've seen pretty clear every since I was a young un as religion's something else besides doctrines and notions. I look at it as if the doctrines was like finding names for your feelings, so as you can talk of 'em when you've never known 'em, just as a man may talk o' tools

> when he knows their names, though he's never so much as seen 'em, still less handled 'em.'

If it is not the language of mathematics and if it is not the language of literal naming, then what is it? It must be some form of language which corresponds not to doctrines in religion, nor to the abstract calculations of mathematics, nor to the naming of tools but to doing something with those tools, to the performance of an action. Realistic fiction must make something happen in the pragmatic world of things and people. It must make the correct things happen. The search for the proper language of storytelling has eliminated one by one all the obvious candidates. The search has narrowed itself down into a corner where only one answer is possible. Realistic narration must depend, as this chapter of *Adam Bede* conspicuously does, on figurative language. Even more narrowly, it can be said to depend on a special form of figurative language: catachresis,* the use of terms borrowed from another realm to name what has no literal language of its own. Only such language can perform into existence feelings, a will, a resolution. The operation of such catachreses is itself necessarily described in figure in the chapter, as like this or as like that, since it cannot be literally described in itself.

Such a language will make a break in the remorseless chain of cause and effect which ordinarily operates, for Eliot, both in the physical or social worlds and in the internal world of the self. Only such a break, a fissure dividing before and after, can effect a redirection of the power of feeling in the self. This produces a consequent redirection of the power of doing in the outer world of the neighbors of that self. The renaming of things by the figure called catachresis is genuinely performative. It brings something altogether new into the world, something not explicable by its causes. Even though, like all performatives, it must use words already there in the language, it redirects those words to unheard-of meanings. It makes something happen in the 'real world' which would not otherwise have happened. This happening has no 'basis' other than the fictive, figurative, re-evaluation performed by the catachresis renaming one's ugly, stupid, inconsistent neighbors as lovable. George Eliot's language for this, or rather the language he borrows from Adam Bede, is borrowed from scripture, which borrows it from the natural world, in a multiple displacement, each realm of language supplementing a lack in the one of which it comes in aid. Just as the language of realism is catachresis, so it can only be spoken of as like this or as like that, as like religious

---

* [Ed.] **Catachresis:** In traditional rhetoric it refers to the misapplication of a word or to a strained metaphor, and therefore is regarded as essentially an abuse of language. Deconstructionist criticism in seeing catachresis as a central rather than a marginal figure, suggests that one cannot have an 'abuse' – free form of language.

experience, or as like violent changes in nature, which in turn are like religious experience. Realism is catachresis, and it can be named only in catachresis:

> 'I know, [says Adam] there's a deal in a man's inward life as you can't measure by the square, and say. "Do this and that'll follow", and, "Do that and this'll follow". There's things go on in the soul, and times when feelings come into you like a rushing mighty wind, as the Scripture says, and part your life in two a'most, so as you look back on yourself as if you was somebody else'.
>
> 'If we've got a resolution to do right, He gave it us, I reckon, first or last; but I see plain enough we shall never do it without a resolution, and that's enough for me.'

In the context of what Eliot says elsewhere in this chapter about the fictive status of religious ideals, angels, Madonnas, and so on, the word 'He' here, naming God as the base of sudden discontinuous changes in human feelings and actions, is another catachresis, perhaps the most extravagant of all. It gives the name of the personified deity to what are in fact, according to Eliot and according to her master-source, Ludwig Feuerbach, only human feelings. To Adam it seems that God gives feelings which give the proper resolutions. Eliot and the reader see plain enough that God is a name for human feelings. They see that it is such performative catachreses (for example, religious language naming God as the source of the rushing mighty wind in the soul) which function as that force of change parting a man's life in two almost.

Even though chapter 17 is strongly committed, in its overt affirmations, to realism as exact reproduction, the covert argument is for a use of figurative language. Such language does not say directly what it means. The language of realistic fiction is not based solidly on any extra-linguistic entities. It transforms such entities into something other than themselves, as your ugly, stupid, neighbor is made lovable when he or she has passed through the circuit of representation in a 'realistic' novel.

One example of figurative language stares the reader in the face in this chapter, so close at hand and so pervasive as to be almost invisible. In this it is like the big name written all across a map, and therefore undetectable, in Dupin's figure for the invisibility of the obvious in Poe's 'The Purloined Letter'. In chapter 17 of *Adam Bede*, as in the novel as a whole, the example of this is the voice of the fictitious narrator concocted by Mary Ann Evans. This narrator speaks as a male 'I'. He speaks as if all these things had really happened in history just as they are told. He bases his defense of realism on the purported conversation of another fictitious character, Adam Bede, and on Adam's analysis of religious experience.

This kind of experience is shown elsewhere in the novel to be a response to the 'ideal' in the sense of the unreal. Religious experience is a human projection, a fiction. The response of the reader who knows the 'source' of Adam in Mary Ann Evans' own life is an uneasy oscillation. This is Mary Ann Evans reporting accurately the speech and opinions of her father, thereby giving a faithful account of men and things as they have mirrored themselves in her mind. No, it is Mary Ann Evans pretending to be a male narrator reporting the speech of another invented character, 'based' perhaps on her father, but transposed into the realm of fiction where it can function as a performative force. The transposition of the author to the narrator, her father to Adam, corresponds, on the larger scale of the creation of character, to that smaller scale creation of figures of speech whereby a literal word is carried over not to substitute for another literal word but to name something that has no name other than a figurative one. Such nomination does not so much name something that already exists as make something happen, in the 'real' world, that would not otherwise have happened.

Like all performatives, this one is fundamentally ambiguous. Its 'undecidability' is to be defined by the fact that it is impossible to know whether anything really happens as a result of its force, or whether it only happens fictively, so does not happen at all. Can one hold in fact to the distinction between a real event and a fictive one? Does something really happen when a marriage is performed, a ship christened, or does it only happen in imagination? This is precisely the issue in Eliot's Feuerbachian treatment of religious experience and religious practices. Even if it can be decided that performatives do make something happen, it can never be decided exactly what that something is and whether that something is good or bad. All performatives are unpredictable and unmeasurable. A performative can never be controlled, defined, or have a decisive line put around its effects. The link between knowledge and power goes by way of language, and that link is both a barrier and a break, a gulf. Language used performatively makes something happen all right, but the link between knowing and doing can never be predicted exactly or understood perspicuously after the fact.

The peculiar final paragraph of chapter 17 of *Adam Bede* uneasily recognizes this. In the attempt to discriminate his own good performative evaluations from the other bad ones, George Eliot inadvertently reveals the structural kinship of all three. He is like a man who confesses to a criminal act by compulsively making a point of denying that he has committed it. In this final paragraph something odd about the initial ideal of a contractual debt almost comes to the surface as George Eliot, as he says, 'discharge[s] [his] conscience'. He pays this debt by confessing that he has had 'enthusiastic movements of admiration' for 'commonplace', 'vulgar' people, people 'who spoke the worst English'. At the beginning of the chapter he affirms, as I have shown, that the realistic novelist has an obligation to return what has been given to him in social experience by making an exact copy that will pay the debt with interest. This interest is an added power to generate enthusiastic movements of admiration for the ugly and the commonplace. The word 'enthusiastic' in its context rings with the irony of its etymology. It plays back and forth among the religious, aesthetic, and sentimental uses of the word. George Eliot's form of inflation, of being filled with a god, is not any of these. It is a sideways transposition of them all, as realism is a mirror image of something which is not, strictly speaking, there. To put this another way, realism is like the act of coinage. It is like that sort of performative which stamps an image on paper or metal and so makes it pass current, makes it worth so much as currency.

There is no way of using literal, conceptual, notional, or doctrinal languages for this mirroring with a difference. Only the performative catachresis of a figurative expression, that comes like a mighty rushing wind in upon the soul and breaks it in two almost, will work. The impact of such language is like religious experience, or like falling in love, or like a force of nature, according to the quadruple equation linking art, nature, love, and religion throughout *Adam Bede*. The ground or the 'like' in this analogical series running 'A is like B is like C is like D' is no solid ontological *logos*. The ground is analogy or figure itself. The base of these analogies is analogy. This means, in spite of the claim to a solid ground in 'reality', that realistic fiction brings groundless novelty into the social world. It brings, for example, my power to love my ugly neighbor. Realism inserts an infinite zero as multiplier or divisor into the circuit of the equation moving away from reality and back to it. This zero is something without ground or substance that nevertheless has power to make something happen. Its efficacy makes it dangerous, a force perhaps for good, perhaps for ill. In this it is analogous to the way the same unpredictable energy of human emotion and human dreaming, in the story proper, motivates a Hetty Sorrel as well as a Dinah Morris, the bad woman as well as the good.

The danger in performative figures almost surfaces in the attempt, in the final paragraph, to discriminate among three emotive attitudes: baseless idealism, cynical nihilism, and George Eliot's realism. The attempt to discriminate reveals, in spite of itself, a similarity. To try to erect barriers allowing a compartmentalization brings into the open an impossibility of deciding what difference there is among these three modes of valuing. There is a secret equivalence in measuring among them which might be defined by saying that any number multiplied by zero is zero, any number divided by zero is infinity.

The final paragraph of the chapter is of great 'interest', in the sense that it adds an increment to what has already been said, clarifying it and undermining it at once. The last paragraph seems at first a rather casual afterthought added to the main argument in defence of realism. In fact, it is of great importance as a revelation of the grounds, or rather the groundlessness, the zero base, of that argument. It asserts an equivalence in the low valuation given to the ugly real by 'that lofty order of minds who pant after the ideal', on the one hand, and by mean, narrow, selfish natures, on the other. Both idealists and cynics join in finding 'real' people of no account: 'For I have observed this remarkable coincidence, that the select natures who pant after the ideal, and find nothing in pantaloons or petticoats great enough to command their reverence and love, are curiously in unison with the narrowest and pettiest.' These two kinds of disvaluers are in turn opposed to George Eliot himself, who finds his neighbor of infinite account. Nevertheless, this comes to the same thing, as the paragraph covertly reveals. It makes the same sum, in the sense that both the low valuation and the high are figurative measures of what, as the chapter tells the reader over and over, are 'in fact' ugly, stupid, inconsistent people. To love such people is just as baseless as to call them, as Mr Gedge the pubkeeper did, 'a poor lot'. In fact Mr Gedge may be closer to an exact mirroring of people as Mary Ann Evans actually sees them, but Gedge's cynicism is also a baseless valuing as much as is George Eliot's loving reverence for commonplace people. The difference, all-important for Eliot, like a plus or minus sign before a zero, is that the positive evaluation is life enhancing. It creates and sustains the human community on the base of those baseless fictions which are absolutely 'needful' if there is to be a human community at all: 'It is more needful that I should have a fiber of sympathy connecting me with that vulgar citizen.'

All emotive evaluation is performative. It makes something happen which has no cause beyond the words which express it. Since my neighbor is 'really' ugly, stupid, inconsistent, to view a woman as not worth loving unless she dies before you possess her (French cynical idealism, the cynicism of those who reject the real and pant after the ideal); to measure everything by the norm of a mean and narrow mind, like Mr Gedge, and find it wanting ('A poor lot, sir, big and little, and them as comes for a go o' gin are no better than them as comes for a pint o' twopenny – a poor lot.'); to love one's ugly neighbor, knowing he or she is ugly, like George Eliot – all three come to the same thing. They are in unison. They make the same sum in the sense that they give measures which are analogies lacking a solid base in any *logos*. There is more than simple opposition in the relation between the closed circuit economy of realism, on the one hand, the ugly mirroring the ugly and returning the ugly to the ugly, and, on the other hand, the infinite economy of genius, the beautiful (angels and Madonnas, prophets, sibyls) mirroring nothing but the inventive soul of its creator, flying off into the inane ideal without possibility of return. Realism also adds a fictive plus value, and Madonnas or angels also make us admire human motherhood and self-denying aspiration.

George Eliot discharges his conscience, pays off his obligation, by covertly admitting his kinship with the positions he rejects. Extremes meet in their common baselessness. The cynicism which measures all people by a zero and finds them all equally poor comes to the same thing as the positive measure which gives my neighbor an infinite value, so generating a resolution to do good, to love him or her. It comes to the same thing yet comes to a very different thing in its effects, which makes all the difference between the maintenance and the dissolution of society. The cement of society is the fiction that my ugly, stupid neighbor is lovable. *Adam Bede* dramatizes in the story of its titular hero the dangers of too hardheaded and clear-seeing a power of judgment. Even the most charitable performative, however, has its dangers. The oscillation generated by the impossibility of distinguishing categorically between these two attitudes, the selfish and the unselfish, the cynical and the charitable, is the pervasive rhythm of thought and feeling in *Adam Bede* as a whole. It is dramatized in the secret identity and yet infinite difference between Hetty and Dinah. It is dramatized in the impossibility of deciding whether Adam's deluded love for Hetty is a good thing or a bad thing: 'He created the mind he believed in out of his own, which was large, unselfish, tender' (*Adam Bede*, chapter 33). It is mimed finally in the impossibility of deciding whether the 'I' who speaks in chapter 17 is Mary Ann Evans talking of the real, historical, autobiographical world of her father, her home county, and her childhood experience, or whether, as it must also be, it is those transposed into the fictive voice of an invented male narrator speaking of fictive events and valuing them in groundless figurative exchanges moving back and forth from love to nature to art to religion. It is both and so neither.

My reading of George Eliot's reading of his (or her) own writing has revealed an unsettling rift between the knowledge that writing gives in its resolute commitment to truth-telling, and the power to love one's neighbor the truth-telling story is supposed to give. This fissure is not too different, after all, from the gulf between the epistemology of metaphor and the necessary moment of 'ethicity', in Paul de Man's account of his 'paradigmatic' text, Rousseau's *Julie*.*

---

* [Ed.] This is discussed in chapter 3 of Miller's *The Ethics of Reading.*

Notes

1. All citations from *Adam Bede* will be from the Cabinet edition of George Eliot's works (Edinburgh and London: Blackwood, 1877–80), henceforth *AB*. This first citation is from vol. 1, pp. 267–8. Chapter 17 is vol. 1, pp. 265–78. Citations in the rest of this chapter, unless otherwise noted, are from this chapter.
2. 'Fra Lippo Lippi', ll. 295–306.
3. Chapter 10, Cabinet edition, 1:125.
4. See IMMANUEL KANT, *Kritik der Urteilskraft*, *Werkausgabe*, vol. 10 (Frankfurt am Main: Suhrkamp, 1979), especially paras 46–50, pp. 241–57. For an English translation see *Critique of Judgment*, tr. J. H. Bernard, (New York: Hafner, 1951), pp. 150–64. For a discussion of these patterns of thought in Kant, see Jacques Derrida, 'Economimesis', *Mimesis: Desarticulations* (Paris: Aubier-Flammarion, 1975), pp. 57–93.

4 Power and Knowledge in 'The Lifted Veil'*

TERRY EAGLETON

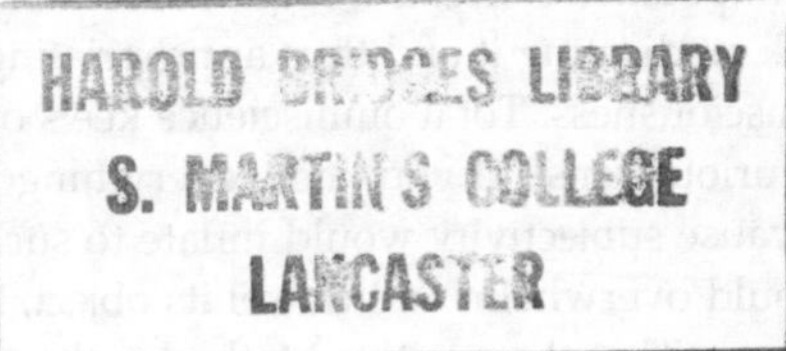

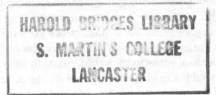

Terry Eagleton is one of the leading British literary theorists and one of the most influential of contemporary Marxist critics. His most recent work departs significantly from his earlier criticism in that it combines Marxist criticism with elements of post-structuralist theory. In this essay he argues that 'The Lifted Veil' is a particularly significant text since it not only reveals a relationship between the conventions of realism and the workings of capitalist society but it also exposes the contradictions underlying both (see Introduction, pp. 16–17).

It is always possible to undermine one kind of claim to 'disinterested' knowledge by asking why we should bother to find out anything in the first place. Since not much of our knowledge is directly relevant to physical survival – indeed 'culture' may be defined as all that is not – there must be some reasons, other than libidinal ones, for acquiring it. One plausible reason for science in the modern Western sense is that we need it, not so that we shall survive, but so that some shall survive better than others. Materialised in technology, science dominates Nature in such a way as to contribute to the reproduction of the social relations of exploitation in class-society. Power produces knowledge and knowledge produces power. Latimer's father in 'The Lifted Veil' considers a scientific education suitable for his son because he has recently acquired a connection with mining speculations.

In order for science to work efficiently, human subjects as well as Nature must be knowable and predictable; hence the birth of sociology. For a liberal bourgeoise like George Eliot, however, this produces a severe ideological contradiction. For the transparency of the human subject demanded by bourgeois scientific ideologies is at odds with that doctrine of the mysterious inscrutability of such subjects with which capitalism helps to mystify its social relations. All knowledge, as Romanticism knew,

* Reprinted from *Literature and History*, 9 (1983), pp. 52–61.

contains a secret irony or incipient contradiction: it must at once master the object and confront it as other, permit it an autonomy it simultaneously subverts. The bourgeois fantasy of technological omnipotence conceals a nightmare: in brutally appropriating Nature, you risk eradicating it and thus appropriating nothing but your own acts of consciousness. Total omniscience keels over inexorably into solipsism. In a curious sense, if you knew everything you would know nothing, because subjectivity would inflate to such immense proportions that it would overwhelm and cancel its object, leaving nothing outside itself to know. 'That the positive Method is the only method . . . on which truth can be found', wrote George Henry Lewes two years before the publication of 'The Lifted Veil', 'is easily proved; on it alone can *prevision* of phenomena depend. Prevision is the characteristic and test of knowledge.'[1] The essence of scientificity is predictability: once phenomena are predictable they are safely surrendered into the hands of the sociological priests. The problem with this, however, is that it threatens to abolish history. Science is what founds the great progressive narratives of bourgeois history, and what scuppers them too. Diachrony is unmasked as no more than the phenomenal movement of a secret synchrony. Bourgeois ideology, living history as enterprise and adventure, is in deadlock with the most privileged mode of bourgeois cognition. In order to safeguard the future you need to predict it; but in doing so you risk striking history dead, swallowing it into the solipsism of an eternal present. The future is secured precisely to the extent to which it is rendered uninteresting, known as 'future' only because it is secretly a present, and thus not known as future at all. The mechanism of the *Eros* of history is revealed as the *Thanatos* of science: the truth of life is the death of knowledge, as the life of knowledge is the death of history.

This contradiction never quite comes to fullness, but not for any particularly consoling reason. For the more social science manipulates its object, the more it uncovers its recalcitrance. The more it knows, the more it discovers it can't control – such as, for example, the tendency of the rate of profit to decline as a function of the proportionate increase of fixed over variable capital. Science is a lie because it does not yield the omnipotence it promises; the very social contradictions which allow it to flourish simultaneously defeat it. As with Hegel's great myth of master and slave, the master's secure possession of the slave is confounded by the latter's vestigial autonomy – by the ability to labour which makes him valuable to the master in the first place. If the slave is to be transparent to the master's desires, he must also be to some degree opaque to them. Just the same is true of the social relations between proletariat and bourgeoisie. The bourgeoisie must dominate the proletariat, shackle it materially and possess it as an object of reliable knowledge – but not to the point where it erases the proletariat's 'autonomy', that is to say, its labour-power. Its sociological omniscience is thus self-molesting: the most it can hope for is to measure its own ignorance with some precision. In one sense it does not *want* omniscience, for this could only signal the death of that very 'freedom' and irreducible randomness which is integral to its exploitation; but in another sense it wants it badly, for what could suit it better than a social formation rendered by knowledge entirely pliable to its desires? Omniscience is at once its dream and its terror.

Bourgeois knowledge is self-defeating because unpredictability is the very dynamic of bourgeois history. The capitalist's dream is to pre-calculate every competitor's move while remaining impervious to such science himself; but since everybody would want this knowledge it would cancel itself out. The capitalist accordingly finds himself in the precarious speculative situation in which his own calculations modify the terms on which others calculate, and so risk throwing his own plans out of gear. This is what is known as freedom, to be mourned from the standpoint of an impossible omniscience and celebrated by contrast with a history self-transparent to the point of deathly stasis. Desire – economic or sexual – requires knowledge, but that knowledge would in turn be the death of desire. Knowledge is power, but the more you have of it the more it threatens to rob you of your desire and render you impotent. If the future can be known it ceases properly to exist; and the present ceases to be present too, dwindles to a mere prolepsis which takes its meaning from elsewhere.

A solution to this dilemma might be sought in that alternative mode of cognition which is the aesthetic. Against the terrorism of positivist rationality may be pitted the responsiveness of imaginative sympathy, which seeks to enter its object without overwhelming it, holding appropriation and autonomy in tension. One of the gloomiest aspects of 'The Lifted Veil' is its recognition that this is no real way out either. For if science is an urge to omnipotence constantly thwarted by the recalcitrance it discloses, so in a different sense is sympathy, which in passively possessing its object is powerless to affect it. Sympathy doesn't get you anywhere. Like science, it tends to operate best on inanimate objects, at least according to Latimer's cynical view that we have a chance of meeting with some pity only when we are dead. Pressed to the caricaturing extremes of telepathy and prevision, sympathy merely writes large science's lethal drive to confiscate its object, sucking it into its own turbulent subjectivity while leaving it in reality outside and resistant. The epistemological imperialism of science and the self-diffusive motions of sympathy amount to much the same thing, opposites though they might appear: whether the object is introjected or the subject projected, the result is a fatal crippling of both. In science the object is at once cancelled and untouched, so that the subject, baffled either by its recalcitrance or evaporation or both, steadily disintegrates beneath its pose of transcendental unity. In sympathy the subject similarly risks collapse, whether this is seen as the sapping effect of projection into objects or the psychical disturbance of staggering around with them inside one's head. 'We must ponder the anomaly', writes Fredric Jameson, 'that it is only in the most completely humanized environment, the one the most fully and obviously the end product of human labor, production, and transformation, that life becomes meaningless, and that existential despair first appears as such in direct proportion to the elimination of nature, the non- or antihuman, to the increasing rollback of everything that threatens human life and the prospect of a well-nigh limitless control over the external universe.'[2] If this is true of science, it is true of sympathy too: as Nature is rolled back and history remorselessly 'humanised', all that seems left is the sickening tautology of a cultic intersubjectivity in which, suspended in a void, consciousness greedily or wearily absorbs consciousness.

It would be a mistake, then, to read 'The Lifted Veil' merely in *Künstler* versus *Bürger* terms, even though it interestingly invites such misrecognition. If this were so it would be difficult to account for the presence in the tale of Latimer's scientific friend Meunier, with whom he feels a special affinity, and whose 'large and susceptible mind' is an image of his own. When Latimer listens dreamily to Meunier's 'bold conceptions of future experiment and discovery', one has only to rewrite the phrase 'future-experiment' to describe Latimer's own career. The science/art opposition tacitly deconstructs itself: 'hungry for human deeds and human emotions' as a youth, Latimer is nevertheless forced to study science, 'plentifully crammed with the mechanical powers, the elementary bodies, and the phenomena of electricity and magnetism'. But what could be closer to his 'imaginative' apprehensions than electromagnetism? Latimer is more like his philistine father than he knows; art parodies the ideological dilemmas of science even as it seems to spurn them. The father may have the power and the son the knowledge, but power generates and is generated by knowledge, and Latimer's own knowledge is at times a form of power, a smug invulnerability. If they pulled together they could beat the world: imagine the outcome if Latimer trained his previsionary powers on his father's investments. But of course their mutual antagonism is essential, since in this society power and knowledge, while deeply implicating one another, are also, as we have seen, at odds. Knowledge castrates power by stifling desire, and power flourishes through a life-enhancing ignorance. The trick of the tale is partly to repress its own disruptiveness by highlighting the differences rather than complicities between father and son. In this way Latimer can come to seem just monstrous, the *poète maudit* or bohemian drop-out from a society which may be predatory but is at least sane. By presenting him as a psychical cripple, one of English fiction's epicene offspring of an uncouthly virile bourgeoisie, the story can at one ideological level quarantine him without too much trouble, offer him as a blood-sacrifice to bourgeois normality. But the symbolic implications of his prevision are not so easily sealed off: in so far as science hinges on precognition, normality is contaminated by its apparent antithesis. Latimer has the abnormality of the Lukácsian 'typical', which is never the average: he is a dreadful image of where, given a little extrapolation, the whole of bourgeois knowledge could land up. His monstrousness, far from being confined to armchair clairvoyance, reproduces itself daily in the laboratories.

Caught between the 'miseries of delusive expectation' and the 'miseries of true prevision', bourgeois society hesitates between desire and death, between the exhilarating terrors of speculative enterprise and the paralysing consolations of science. If it can sneak a glimpse of fatality behind the veil of contingency, it is because contingency, in a market society, is indeed what determines your fate. In case the connection between prevision and the stock exchange is thought to be symptomatic of Marxist paranoia, I should perhaps point out that the story makes the connection itself:

> So absolute is our soul's need of something hidden and uncertain for the maintenance of that doubt and hope and effort which are the breath of its life, that if the whole future were laid bare to us beyond today, the interest of all mankind would be bent on the hours that lie between; we should pant after the uncertainties of our one morning and our one afternoon; we should rush fiercely to the Exchange for our last possibility of speculation, of success of disappointment; we should have a glut of political prophets foretelling a crisis or a non-crisis within the only twenty-four hours left open to prophecy.

As a good bourgeois banker, Latimer's father prides himself on punctuality; and it is the unaccountable fact of his unpunctuality which precipitates his son's most shocking early experience of precognition:

> He was one of the most punctual of men and bankers, and I was always nervously anxious to be quite ready for him at the appointed time. But, to my surprise, at a quarter past twelve he had not appeared. I felt all the impatience of a convalescent who has just taken a tonic in the prospect of immediate exercise that would carry off the stimulus.
>
> Suddenly I was conscious that my father was in the room, but not alone: there were two persons with him . . .
>
> 'Well, Latimer, you thought me long', my father said . . .
>
> But while the last word was in my ears, the whole group vanished, and there was nothing between me and the Chinese painted folding-screen that stood before the door.

Disturbed by his father's lateness, Latimer manages to bring him there instead in imagination: prevision compensates for the father's fault, plugging the minatory gap he has created with an imaginary image. Latimer's own guilt about having failed his father betokens a concern for the old man which leads him to protect him from failing himself, arriving late in violation of his strict standards. It is, of course, Latimer the shiftless younger son who has 'arrived late', and the prevision is as much self-protection against the odd anxiety which the father's absence produces. Latimer is 'always nervously anxious to be quite ready for him', but he is in fact never 'quite ready' for him, and the 'absence' of this censorious patriarch is more than a quarter-of-an-hour affair. But if the scene underlines the son's subordination, it also secures his superiority: it is in the very gap created by the father's absence that Latimer's gift of prevision is fully born – that a faculty beyond his father's reach is realised. Knowledge is born of castrated desire, but it can make up for it too. Punctuality is a suitable virtue for those to whom time is linear, to be consumed in chopped-up fragments: you only need to worry about turning up on time if you can't foresee whether you will or won't. If Latimer senior is doomed to purely diachronic sequence, his son can transcend that to the point of synchronic vision. In this precognitive flash, then, he confesses his anxiety about his tyrannical father at the same time as he achieves in fantasy a compensatory sort of divinity; prevision is a 'supplement' in the double-sense of filling in for the father, repairing his absence, and yet exceeding him.

Art is born as the neurasthenic child of bourgeois power, crushed by its own pointless parasitism, but it has its revenge too: if it does not exactly strike the father dead (though Latimer, as we shall see, does the next best thing), it nevertheless attains a secret omniscience which can expose his inmost flaws, substituting esoteric knowledge for social dominance. Latimer, the incompletely oedipalised wretch whose 'natural' affections were thwarted by the premature withdrawal of an idealised mother's love, a withdrawal which abandoned him to the mercies of an oppressively masculine father, has lifted the forbidden skirt and received an enviable knowledge; but it is a terrible knowledge which strikes desire dead, as the knowledge of sexual difference and absence opens at a stroke the unconscious into which desire is repressed. For what he has glimpsed behind the veil is, precisely, nothing: the 'absence' of the future and so the 'absence' of the present which evaporates into it; the 'absence' of the father, marked by the sign of castration in his failure to come; the absence of the mother, that deliciously possessable imaginary object whose very brutal removal has generated these substitutive visions; and above all, consummating all of these absences in a single, stark metaphor, that absence which is his own future death, the non-being which is the ultimate ironic object of his knowledge. Foreseeing your own death is a striking figure of the tale's allegorical purposes, for there could be no sharper disjoining of knowledge and power. The more your knowledge veers into determinism, the more it will negate historical desire and thus yield you a purely Schopenhauerian form of mastery, reduce you like the later Latimer to the opposite of the hysteric, who has ceased even to desire desire. This will grant you the negative power of invulnerability, but it is not easy to distinguish that in practice from simple impotence. It is true that in a way knowledge *does* bring Latimer power: the evil eye of prevision topples the hated elder brother Alfred from his horse, an event which is at once a displaced fulfilment of Latimer's patricidal urge and a convenient way of scrambling into the empty space of his father's affections. But it is not a power which will bring you any good result: apart from Meunier, there is no knowledge in this fiction which is not either useless or malevolent. Knowledge is either predatory power over others or consciousness of one's impotence; prevision, that fantasmal caricature of art and science, induces an ontological lassitude which taints whatever goods it may deliver.

Latimer's empathy with other minds isn't easy to distinguish from a mere projection of his own arrogance, anxiety and aggressivity into them. Alfred has only to show a touch of hearty sympathy for him to sniff in it an odious condescension; other minds oppress this mean, maundering, indolent and egoistic spectator with their 'suppressed egoism, all the struggling chaos of puerilities, meanness, vague capricious memories, and indolent make-shift thoughts. . . . ' One would dearly love to hear Bertha's side of the story. Latimer, of course, knows well enough *what* she is from the moment he first sees her in prevision: a preying Water-Nixie, sharp, sarcastic and 'fatal-eyed'. Bertha (an ominous name in any case) is the phallic woman, triggering all of Latimer's repressed fantasies of the murderous female; she is unconsciously downgraded by contrast with the idealised mother, at the same time as the aggressive treatment of her may displace Latimer's resentment towards that mother, who died and left him. Bertha is 'keen, sarcastic, unimaginative, prematurely cynical', mainly because she doesn't instantly pander to his maudlin tastes in poetry. Coldly disillusioned about her, he nonetheless succeeds in remaining lamentably deluded, a contradiction which several alternative stabs at resolution can't quite dissolve. Typically, he manages to blame her for this fatal fascination while quietly complimenting himself: 'But there is no tyranny more complete than that which a self-centred negative nature exercises over a morbidly sensitive nature perpetually craving sympathy and support.' If only she weren't so exasperatingly aloof and he so naturally affectionate. Since Latimer has already told us elsewhere that his natural affections are somewhat thin on the ground (he feels compassion for his father only when he has triumphed over him through

Alfred's death), we might be more inclined to attribute his fascinations, as he does in part himself, to the fact that Bertha is the only person to evade his empathetic powers. She is a tantalising challenge to be conquered, not least because there is oedipal satisfaction to be gained in winning your brother's fiancée. 'Doubtless there was another sort of fascination at work', Latimer adds later on in a casual aside, briefly touching on physical attraction; but even so he manages to suggest that he marries Bertha in part to please the dear old father he despises. Bertha does indeed like Latimer at first, to the point of secretly wearing round her neck a ring he gives her: when she shows him the ring to placate his bleatings about being unfavoured, he tells us that the action 'completely fooled' him, as though it were she rather than he who was being emotionally manipulative. Perhaps he thought it was a hallucination. Once Alfred is dead, Bertha, with perfect decorum, behaves rather distantly to Latimer; but 'out of the subtlest web of scarcely perceptible signs' he discerns the truth or constructs the fantasy that she has always unconsciously loved him more than Alfred. She would have chosen him, 'but that, with the ignorant fluttered sensibility of a young girl, she had been imposed on by the charm that lay for her in the distinction of being admired and chosen by a man who made so brilliant a figure in the world as my brother'. This last acknowledgement is a remarkably complex affair for conveyance by 'scarcely perceptible signs': by the time we reach the end of the sentence we are half-convinced that this is something Bertha must have said rather than suggested.

After their marriage, Latimer grows sinisterly aware of an increasing coldness in Bertha, at first 'only perceptible in the dexterous avoidance of a tête-à-tête walk or dinner to which I had been looking forward'. Since the whining, self-piteous Latimer is hardly the kind of man one would choose as a companion for a world cruise, the appropriate criticism of Bertha is less of her supposed frigidity than of her lapse of taste in marrying him in the first place. A crisis of 'clairvoyance' ensues:

> . . . I saw myself in Bertha's thought as she lifted her cutting grey eyes, and looked at me: a miserable ghost-seer, surrounded by phantoms in the noon-day, trembling under a breeze when the leaves were still, without appetite for the common objects of human desire, but pining after the moonbeams. We were front to front with each other, and judged each other.

In a curious flash of esoteric knowledge, a preternatural power known only to the poetic few, Latimer sees that his wife rightly thinks him an idiot. The 'judging' is mutual only in so far as he naturally believes that anyone who defines him thus is a heartless ogre, even though he has just conceded the correctness of her judgement. It is difficult to square

Bertha's 'cutting' clear-sightedness with her supposed 'petty artifice', though Latimer contrives to object to both; if Bertha is indeed 'petty', it is only because discerning the truth of another is less of a *recherché* talent, at least where the palpably unpleasant Latimer is concerned, than he himself would have. The worst blow is that he lacks a monopoly on 'clairvoyance'.

Even so, you might think, all of this hardly justifies poisoning the poor wretch. Surely Latimer's suspicions of Bertha are finally proved not paranoid but just, in the dramatic accusations of the miraculously resuscitated Mrs Archer? 'Miraculous', in fact, is the word: the blood transfusion incident is a piece of tawdry melodrama, a grotesque and infelicitous flaw, a *fiction*. We can't believe it; and yet of course we must, for this is a 'realist' tale, and within those conventions what Latimer as observer says goes. It *must* have happened – Bertha must therefore be guilty – and yet, somehow, it didn't. Latimer has rigged his tale to frame his wife, impudently concocting an event as he may have previously, perhaps more permissibly, falsified perceptions. This, of course, is a wholly impermissible conclusion, unverifiable and unacceptable within realist hypotheses, and yet, knowing Latimer, who would put it past him? The *aporia** we stumble upon here forces us outside the frame of the realist fiction to ponder – as the story has surreptitiously done all along – the theoretical problem of realist fiction as such. For there is one compelling reason for Latimer's strange pre-marital fascination with Bertha which he cannot possibly disclose to us, namely that if this were not so then the narrative would come prematurely to a close. For the story to evolve at all, Latimer's prevision must mysteriously fail, or at least cease to matter, when it comes to his future wife. What is most striking is that it ceases to matter rather than fails: after Bertha's initial seductive opacity, Latimer is allowed a glimpse of his gloomy domestic future but helplessly perseveres in his courtship. His determination to plough on even though the upshot will be unpleasant is thus a little like Beckett's glum comment on the simultaneous absurdity and necessity of narrative: 'You must go on, I can't go on, I'll go on.' Carrying on regardless, narrating as though you don't know the end, assuming an ignorance where you acknowledge a truth, is clearly a dilemma at the very heart of realist writing. For narrative and desire to prosper, knowledge must be put in suspension; if knowledge castrates desire, desire is the blind spot of knowledge, the unrenunciable fantasy which keeps history moving against the grain of positivist fact. Of course, in so far as narrative suspends knowledge only to recuperate it, it can furnish a conciliatory model of these contradictions. Narrative is at once a desire not to know, in the name of the libidinal

* [Ed.] **Aporia**: A rhetorical term used in deconstructionist criticism to denote a self-generating, irresolvable impasse within a text.

gratifications of suspense, and a desire to know which will finally be satisfied in the triumphant restoration of whatever object or truth was temporarily removed for the narrative to generate itself in the first place. Ideally conceived, narrative represents as energising an interplay between freedom and determinism as does the 'free' market: there too, the temporary loss of both certainty and object which is speculative investment can be patiently borne because the object will return to you enriched and consolidated. Market society must work by fiction, speculative hypothesis, partial prevision, its insights as much the product of blindness as the visionary Latimer is the son of his benighted father. But in this society the reverse is also true: the muddle-headed Latimer is the child of his hard-headed father, blindness is born of knowledge, impotence of power. Knowledge is power but exposes what is intractable to it; desire gives birth to power but renders you its helpless prey; fiction is integral yet destructive, truth essential but unpalatable. Speculations in goods or other minds may go perversely awry, the cherished object may always not return. What generates Latimer's narrative is the removal by death of an object – his mother – which only his own death – which is to say, nothing at all – will restore.

Narrative, then, is not quite the ideal solution it looks; and neither, more generally, is writing itself. For it is certainly tempting to see in realist fiction a reconciliation of these difficulties – a form of omniscience which renounces domination, subtly responsive to the 'autonomy' of its own creations. But this, of course, is ideological delusion, a whole fiction in itself. If the bourgeoisie is enthralled by its own knowledge – exhilarated and enslaved by it – so is George Eliot, whose 'knowledge' as author of 'The Lifted Veil' consists, like Latimer's possibly paranoid intuitions, in searching out that which she has created in the first place. There is a pointless circularity about fiction which mimes the unhealthy solipsism of a Latimer. The parody of omniscience (as author you can 'know' what you like, since you're inventing it) fiction is thereby the parody of impotence, since what you 'know', like Latimer's confrontation with that black hole which opens and closes the narrative, is precisely nothing. Fiction only 'fictionally' knows. If Latimer projects his own malice and anxiety into others, perhaps Eliot does the same with him; if it is undecidable whether Latimer is seeing the truth or 'reading in', inscribing himself in others, textualising sweet nothings into sinister meanings, perhaps this is the guilty *aporia* of all fiction. What follows 'The Lifted Veil' is in this sense not *The Mill on the Floss* but *The Sacred Fount*. Nobody can gainsay Latimer just as nobody can gainsay Eliot, and this is the curse of omniscience, the epistemological circle of a bourgeois science which threatens to swallow the whole of Nature down its ravenous maw and so ends up knowing only its own innards. Fiction is a form of paranoia. Guilt-stricken by this insight, 'The Lifted Veil' at once concedes and refuses it, offers us the adventures of a narrative which contains its own negation, opens by aggressively denying us our libidinal pleasure in suspense only to reinstate that stimulation in its lurid, spooky storyline, and then obstinately refuses the gratifications of closure. Whether you are really seeing the future, or whether such apparent precognition is merely a textualising of the present, doesn't finally make much difference: in the first case you query the future's real existence, in the second case you deny the objectivity of the present, its status as anything but text. Writing historical novels is no way out either: either you make the past present as it 'really' was, in which case you are as powerless before it as Latimer is before the future; or you recognise the impossibility of such an enterprise only at the cost of relativising the past to a fiction of the present. 'Seeing' either past or future entails an insuperable contradiction: if you *do* see them then they aren't there, since their nature is to be elsewhere and invisible; if you don't see them they aren't there, either. But both projects are in any case tropes of a self-contradictory cognition which is rather more contemporary: 'knowing' an object – Nature, society, history – in conditions where all knowledge seems either active domination or passive empathy, 'masculine' or 'feminine', blinding its object with science or smothering it with subjectivity. In the same way the historical or previsionary novel, which conjures presence from absence, merely writes large the secret practice of 'contemporary' fiction, which does exactly the same.

What is certain about this society, at any rate, is that the truth is unpleasant. Whether the artist is someone who penetrates through to it, or whether as Bertha believes poetry is false consciousness, hold equally cheerless implications: at the extremes, the choice is one between death and delusion. Meanwhile, of course, we get along as best we can: we recognise the necessity of fiction, which is to say the historical indispensability of ideology. And this, for a rationalist, is certainly a depressing conclusion. We shall have to wait for the later Henry James to 'transcend' it, in those great moments in which an enormous knowledge, precisely by being divorced from domination, can veer on its axis into the most salvific, transformative (or ultimately dominative?) act of all. And as if this conclusion were not bleak enough, there is worse to come. For what if death were not the end after all? What if medicine were to perfect its transfusive techniques and raise future Mrs Archers permanently rather than temporarily from their death-beds? Is not this the true fantastic core of that bungled bit of melodrama? This particular narrative starts up again at the end, and why not, for there is nothing to stop it: Eliot has the empty freedom of prolonging it for another six volumes if she decides to. What if science were to reproduce that terrifying omnipotence, endlessly recycling its subjects, so that history, deprived of a closure, ceased to be narrative and became eternal recurrence? Then indeed would *Eros* be robbed of its last forlorn hope, *Thanatos*. In 'The Lifted Veil', the bourgeoisie dream their own death. Maybe we can help them out.

Notes

I am especially grateful to Charles Swann, of the University of Keele, whose essay 'Déjà Vu, Déjà Lu: "The Lifted Veil" as an Experiment in Art' (*Literature and History*, 5, No. 1, Spring 1979), first stimulated my interest in the story.

1. *The Biographical History of Philosophy* (London, 1857), pp. 659–60.
2. *The Political Unconscious: Narrative as a Socially Symbolic Act* (Ithaca and London, 1981), p. 251.

5 Rhetoric and Realism in Nineteenth-Century Fiction: Hyperbole in *The Mill on the Floss**

JONATHAN ARAC

Jonathan Arac is an American post-structuralist critic who, like J. Hillis Miller, attacks the widely-held view that the nineteenth-century novel is naïvely realistic. In particular he questions the view that the narrative structure of a novel like *The Mill on the Floss* is intended to be uniform and harmonious. He argues that there is a tension between those aspects of narrative and language which encourage a harmonious reading of the novel and the conscious use by George Eliot of rhetorical figures, such as hyperbole, which undermine that reading (see Introduction pp. 11–12).

My title does not signal a contrast between rhetoric, taken as empty and deceitful words, and realism, taken as the novelist's attempt to present life 'as it really was'. Rather, it suggests the cooperation of rhetorical self-consciousness in making the modern western tradition of prose fiction. Our age of French newer criticism seems no more willing than was that of American new criticism to recognize the energetic duplicities of language that activate nineteenth-century novels fully as much as they do more recent experimental writing. Despite Frank Kermode's attempts to demonstrate in 'pre-modern', 'readerly' works the textual plurality and heterogeneity that Roland Barthes has characterized as modern, as 'writerly,'[1] nineteenth-century fiction remains a straw man in some of the most outstanding recent work on the criticism of narrative. It is taken as willfully naïve and blind to the fictionality of literature, wishing instead to assert the reality of what it represents.[2] I find, however, that the naïve faith charged against the major nineteenth-century novelists quickly dissolves into theoretical and textual complexity.

In beginning to demonstrate this contention through reading an early novel of George Eliot, I have drawn from that work a rhetorical term as my tool for analysis in order to insist upon the self-consciousness in and

* Reprinted from *English Literary History*, 46 (1979), pp. 673–92.

about the language of the work. My figure of hyperbole bears the same name as a geometrical figure defining a shape generated from dual foci but from no center, suggesting the complexity and instability I wish to emphasize.[3] Furthermore, I find useful the arbitrary excess of such a geometrical metaphor for the 'form' of a literary work; as a term it is so alien, falls so far short of our usual critical metaphors, that its tentativity and purely exploratory value remains always in view. Such an analogy is much less likely to mislead us into false consequences than the organic, architectural, or textile metaphors that are more common. The barrenness may be fruitful as fresh provocation.

Such side-stepping of conventional linguistic models marks the realistic tradition in our fiction since its starting-point in Cervantes' *Don Quixote*.[4] Realistic novelists aim at the truth of life not by a direct and necessarily failed attempt at representing it, but through indirection, through exposure and criticism of alternative claims and strategies whose failures are exposed, leaving a residual sense of unstated truth. Cervantes does not tell us that the reality of Spain in his days was inns and windmills; instead he shows us the consequences of Quixote's trying to live in a world of castles and giants. We come to know the reality of Quixote's world as what exceeds and contradicts his model of romantic chivalry. So in the Quixotic tradition of the realistic novel, 'reality' is what escapes all rules and models.[5] The novel does not directly take on reality, and it carries along inside it the false models that must be overcome. If literature in general is a criticism of life, realism is that part of literature that begins through criticism of art, including its own.

The parodic presence of discarded models of action, expression, judgment, and feeling within a novel poses special problems for its critics, for 'viewed from a distance', a novel will look like a romance. This power of distance to romanticize motivates the constant new production of realistic works. The last word never lasts; an exposé of the follies of an age comes to seem itself one of the follies of that age. Thus the temporal distance that separated the romantics from Cervantes permitted their new interpretations that ennobled Quixote.[6] A similarly distanced reading may encourage us to find in *The Mill on the Floss* a perfect romantic spiral journey of circuitous return.[7] For the book moves from an initial unity of 'Boy and Girl' (title of Book First of the novel) through the alienation of 'Downfall' (Book Third) to the reunion of the 'Final Rescue' (Book Seventh), which raises the initial union to a higher plane through the dignity of the final biblical epigraph (identical to that on the title page). Not on such a broad pattern, but only in the intimacy of local interplay, can the realistic challenge to cultural models be read effectively. Only close reading preserves the critical dimension that Friedrich Schlegel demanded of modern literature and found typified in the novel.[8]

From a work like Erich Auerbach's *Mimesis* our age has all too easily taken only the emphasis on socio-historical particularity, the documentary aspect, and neglected the stylistic observations that define the recurrent problematic of the work.[9] Auerbach devotes his own major concern, however, to the break in linguistic principles of literary decorum. A social level appears that would once have demanded the 'low style' but now exists in language of 'tragic seriousness'. The 'mixture of styles' that permits the entrance of seriousness into 'everyday reality' is the real novelty in the realistic novel. A new freedom of language charges with the most moving significance a scene that previously 'would have been conceivable as literature only as part of a comic tale, an idyl, or a satire'.[10] The position of such a scene within the system and hierarchy of literature makes it truly revolutionary. Auerbach's sensitivity to 'levels' in the immediate texture of language allows him also to discriminate 'levels' in the narrative technique. The narrator has a power of linguistic formulation that exceeds the characters. This discrepancy between different ways of forming the world in words shapes novelistic form. Such splits between the book's norms and the norms of traditional literature, between the narrator's norms and those of the characters, between the chief character's norms and those of the world in which she lives, all create a heterogeneous texture in the book's prose and a complexity in the book's structure. It becomes difficult to grasp by what principle the work is to be integrated, unless we are willing to accept a definition of the clashes and demand nothing more definitive.

Himself aware of such splits, Henry James insisted on the artist's need for a 'geometry of his own' by which to 'draw . . . the circle' that shall 'happily *appear*' to contain the relations established within the work.[11] Yet James recognized as well that such appearances would not hold, that for the writer the 'inveterate displacement of his general centre' demands the production of 'specious and spurious centres . . . to make up for the failure of the true'.[12] As critics no less than as novelists we desire formal clarity, and we realize nonetheless that to impose such clarity in reading falsifies and omits much of what is most important. Let us begin with a harmonious reading of *The Mill on the Floss* in relation to a center and then attend to the waywardnesses that undo the pattern the geometrical eye has defined. Our path will lead out from a central fullness into increasing alienation and discrepancy, until finally a return to the center reveals the splits that had already from the start fractured it, making it 'specious and spurious'.

One of the most striking patterns woven into *The Mill on the Floss* presents a world of astonishing harmony and completeness, in which intuitions that we usually consider primitive are justified by the modern developments of science. The breadth of vision that encompasses all aspects of this world removes the terror of the disruptive. Not the extraordinary 'proverbial feather' and its terrifying ability to break a camel's back should concern us, but the 'previous weight of feathers' that has already placed the poor beast in imminent jeopardy.[13] The 'cumulative effect' of 'everyday things' (p. 69), the 'apparently trivial coincidences' and subtly nuanced 'incalculable states of mind' which are 'the favourite machinery of Fact,' rule the world, not the 'terrible dramatic scenes' (p. 295) which haunt our fearful imagination. If it is 'unaccountable' (p. 55) within the Dodson circle that Lucy should look so much as if she were a child of Mrs Tulliver's, while Maggie looks like no Dodson at all, the mystery is resolved when we remember that a child has two parents and that Maggie will grow up into the image of Mr Tulliver's mother (p. 233). The quest of science for 'a unity which shall bind the smallest things with the greatest' (p. 239) makes the world comprehensible as our home. Even in our little towns by our own hearths the principles and developments of nature and history are 'represented' (p. 239) as surely as within the Elizabethan microcosm. The reductive methods of scientific analysis (the 'Mill' of Enlightenment as seen by Carlyle and Novalis) combine with the flow and flux of nature (the 'Floss') in a familiar order.

Continuous development from a 'traceable origin' (p. 63) marks this world, whether in the historical and political sphere of the British Constitution or the astronomical, of the solar system and fixed stars. Whatever certain idealists may claim about the mind's capacity to transcend its environment, one finds that 'the Basset mind was in strict keeping with its circumstances' (p. 70). The word-play that joins in the name 'Basset' a technical geological term and a familiar hunting dog suggests the complete interrelation of levels, just as do the book's innumerable comparisons between human actions and characteristics and those of animal nature. If it is 'humiliating' (p. 36) that Tom and Maggie Tulliver as they take together their sacrament of cake resemble 'two friendly ponies', it is also a bringing back to earth that renews their vitality.[14] Social developments may sometimes make people 'out of keeping with the earth on which they live' (p. 238), but this disproportion can be cured by a return to the privileged 'spot' where our childhood sight of nature in its 'sweet monotony' of the 'same' fixed forever for us the 'mother tongue' of our 'imagination' (pp. 37–8). Through fidelity to such a past, and only through it, can Maggie be sure in life of a ground 'firm beneath [her] feet' (p. 420).

The description of the Mill at the book's opening adumbrates this pattern of unity in the processes of man and nature as it evokes the 'dwelling-house . . . old as the elms' and the coincidence of perspective that unites the 'masts' of 'distant ships . . . close among the branches of the spreading ash' (p. 7). Language itself appears to testify to this relation in the sentences describing the Ripple. It first is 'lively' in its current and 'lovely' to see, and then at once it seems 'living' and its sound like the voice of a 'loving' person.

In the description of St Ogg's this pattern emerges most compactly as a mass. St Ogg's is 'one of those old, old towns which impress one as a continuation and outgrowth of nature, as much as the nests of the bower-birds or the winding galleries of the white ants: a town which carries the traces of its long growth and history like a millennial tree, and has sprung up and developed in the same spot between the river and the low hill' (p. 104) since Roman times. Echoing a phrase from Wordsworth's *Excursion* that describes the Wanderer's growth among the presences of Nature, Eliot summarizes the town as 'familiar with forgotten years'.[15] This family intimacy, based on the bonds of the physical, yet affecting as well every other aspect of human life, links that life to nature, and to its own past as the source of sustenance and value.

This pattern emphasizes the fundamental importance of childhood experience in the development of our mature selves and thus protects the book against the charge of excessive attention to nursery trivialities with which some contemporary reviewers greeted it.[16] It provides as well, however, the basis for expectations of stability and continuity and of an emphasis upon the small and subtle, and many readers have seen the latter portion of the book as a deviation from this basis into excess of emotion and action alike. This discrepancy is attributed to extra-textual causes, whether a psychological over-identification with Maggie that destroys control, or the author's necessity of finishing within the canonical three-volume size after having already lavished upon the earlier portions an 'epic breadth' that could not be maintained.[17]

Within *The Mill on the Floss*, however, even within the first two-thirds of it, another pattern can be found that has no priority over the pattern that I have just defined, but is different from it and incommensurable with it. One can see in this second pattern 'romantic' excess contrasted to the 'realistic' fine-grain of the first, or one may see the first as a compensatory, romantic myth of order, built up by the mind's attempt to defend itself against the real violence of the second. I call this second pattern the hyperbolic. It breaks up the smooth continuity of linkages we have been examining. It is hard to regulate a force that breaks order, but I shall try to specify the hyperbolic in three stages. First, I explore the most literal, 'grammatical' cases of hyperbole, the inappropriately excessive word that disrupts the continuity of perception and expression. This involves primarily the language of the characters – both in their speech and thought – and the narrator's relation to that language. Next, I analyze the place of the hyperbolic in the narrator's deeper investigation of human psychology and of our attitudes toward character. This involves primarily the narrator's language and its relation to the language of the audience. Finally, I emphasize the philosophical implications of the hyperbolic as a force disfiguring the harmonious notions of origin, cause and truth.

The narrator introduces the notion of 'hyperbole' early in the book during Bob Jakin's quarrel with Tom Tulliver: 'To throw one's pocket-knife after an implacable friend is clearly in every sense a hyperbole, or throwing beyond the mark' (p. 48). This comment is itself an instance of rhetorical hyperbole, for it overstates the case. As Maggie insists, 'Almost every word . . . may mean several things' (p. 129). 'Throwing beyond the mark' is not a hyperbole in 'every sense' for there are in the *OED* three other senses of 'Hyperbole': the rhetorical, 'a figure of speech consisting in exaggerated or extravagant statement, used to express strong feeling or to produce a strong impression, and not intended to be understood literally'; a rare general sense, 'excess, extravagance'; and an obsolete geometrical sense, 'hyperbola'. Indeed, so far is Eliot's usage from being 'clearly' the sense, that it is not even recorded in the *OED*. It is evidently a nonce-usage, derived etymologically from the Greek *hyperbolé*, for 'throwing beyond', 'overshooting' is the primary sense given in Liddell and Scott, which then gives further meanings that parallel the usual English senses. There is one more Greek sense that is especially noteworthy, for it suggests a strange split within the word; it is one of those words that seem to mean almost opposite things, for it also means 'deferring, delay', an undershooting as well as an overshooting, inhibition as well as excess. It is finally worth remarking that the verb *hyperbállo*, from which the noun derives, has a specialized sense with regard to water, 'to run over, overflow'. The Floss and its floods make an important part in the hyperbolic pattern of the book.

This narrative foregrounding of the term, naming, defining and exemplifying it all in one sentence, in itself calls our attention to the term's significance. This setting of learned word-play in close proximity to the movement of Bob Jakin's unlearned mind exemplifies one of the book's major techniques, the exploitation of a discrepancy between narrator and characters, presenting characters' minds in words that they would never themselves use, offering an interpretation of their world unlike any that they could make. The narrator regularly hyperbolizes in going beyond the bounds of the characters' intellectual limitations. This gap established between the world and powers of the narrator and those of the characters contradicts our harmonious reading of Dorlcote Mill in the narrator's dream, in which there had seemed to be a smooth continuity between that past world, so available to memory, and the present standpoint of retrospection. There is then a danger of violence, of forcing, in the narrator's relation to the represented world of the book.

The etymological play of superiority in this 'hyperbole' passage clearly relates it to the discussion of metaphor that occurs in the course of Tom's schooling. In trying to teach Tom etymology, Stelling is guided himself by an etymological pun, taken seriously as a paradigm for action. He considers the cultivation of Tom's mind like the 'culture' of fields, and thus the resistant mind, like impervious earth, must be 'ploughed and harrowed' all the more by the means it resists. The violence here is evident, all the more so as the narrator compares the situation to making Tom eat cheese 'in order to remedy a gastric weakness which prevented him from digesting it'. Reflecting on this new analogy, the narrator observes, 'It is astonishing what a different result one gets by changing the metaphor!' This change in the model for thought totally reverses the obvious course of remedy. The narrator concludes by lamenting 'that we can so seldom declare what a thing is, except by saying it is something else' (p. 124).[18] When we aim our words at a thing, we're always off the mark. All language contains a hyperbolic potential.

The geometric figure of the hyperbola condenses into an emblem many of the most important aspects of the hyperbolic pattern of the book and its difference from the first pattern of centered wholeness that I described. The hyperbola is a discontinuous function; it is not a closed figure but open, and split into two parts; it is a set of points related not to a single origin but to two given points (the foci), and the defining relation is a constant difference.

Linguistic hyperbole demands attention at many points in the book beyond the place where it is named. Bob Jakin admires Tom's control of his speech, 'His tongue doesn't overshoot him as mine does' (p. 340). This comment establishes the same contrast between Bob and Tom that marked the earlier scene of their quarrel, but more frequently Maggie is contrasted with Tom in this respect. In 'The Family Council' at the time of the Tulliver 'Downfall', Tom behaves with earnest restraint, 'like a man'. In contrast, Maggie suddenly 'burst[s] out' like a 'young lioness' and in a 'mad outbreak' (p. 190) denounces her relatives. In these instances the hyperbolic marks its user as belonging to the wrong class or sex, as falling outside the charmed circle of respectability and masculinity, though Tom is himself caught up at other moments in the hyperbolic pattern. Just as the first pattern follows the emphasis of Maggie's wishes for the firm ground of the sacred spot and its memories, so in the hyperbolic pattern Maggie's wish for '*more*' (p. 250) predominates.

Maggie's unfamiliarity with the heights of provincial society makes her 'throw' 'excessive feeling' into 'trivial incidents' (p. 329). Maggie's imagination leads her also into perceptual hyperbole, an atmospheric heightening that melodramatically colors a scene of no outer significance. As she is led back from the gypsies to home, she is 'more terrified' than Bürger's Leonore, and for her, 'The red light of the setting sun seemed to have a portentous meaning, with which the alarming bray of the second donkey with the log on its foot must surely have some connection'

(p. 102). This deluded, obsessively precise and symbolic view of the world here is deflated by the pattern of stability and everyday causality; elsewhere in the book, however, it is not always canceled but may also prevail.

Bob and Maggie are not the only hyperbolists. The whole speech-community of St Ogg's agrees in calling 'the "Hill"' what the narrator tells us is only 'an insignificant rise of ground', a 'mere bank' (p. 260) walling off the Red Deeps, where Philip had Maggie have their clandestine meetings. Just as Aunt Pullet had earlier 'unconsciously us[ed] an impressive figure of rhetoric' (p. 52) in substituting 'gone' for 'dead', so her unconscious hyperbole, in what the narrator calls a 'wide statement' (p. 297), triggers the revelation to Tom of Maggie's meetings with Philip. The narrator describes Tom's consequent state of mind in terms that relate it to Maggie's as she returned from the gypsies. He was 'in that watchful state of mind which turns the most ordinary course of things into pregnant coincidences' (p. 298). The tone of irony in this statement works only against any reader trustful enough in the stability of things to believe that the 'ordinary course' will prevail. For a comment of Bob's about Philip sends Tom off to intercept Maggie and to accompany her to the Red Deeps, there to denounce Philip.

In that terrible scene of humiliation, Maggie's imagination, 'always rushing extravagantly beyond an immediate impression' (pp. 301–2), superadds a phantasm of 'her tall strong brother grasping the feeble Philip bodily, crushing him and trampling on him'. This further heightening of the original 'terrible dramatic . . . scene' of confrontation that had 'most completely symbolised' (pp. 295) her fear still does not prepare Maggie for the repetition soon thereafter, in which father Tulliver flogs father Wakem until Maggie, as if in compensation for the helplessness that she suffered in the earlier scene, rescues both men. In such moments life again knows 'those wild, uncontrollable passions which create the dark shadows of misery and crime' (p. 238), those 'giant forces' that used to 'shake the souls of men' as they 'used to shake the earth' (p. 106). Uniformitarianism has not wholly removed the possibility of catastrophe.

This possibility exists within the force of language as it exists within the forces of nature. In considering Mr Stelling's violent metaphor of 'culture', humor held the dangers in control, but our superior amusement at Mr Tulliver's entanglement in language dwindles as we realize that words are the immobilizing net that binds him for the kill. The narrator notes the dangers to life inherent within the necessary excesses of language as he summarizes the situation after Philip and Maggie have begun to declare their love in the Red Deeps: 'It was one of those dangerous moments when speech is at once sincere and deceptive – when feeling, rising high above its average depth, leaves flood-marks which are never reached again' (p. 294). The duplicity of speech emerges clearly, and the resemblance of this duplicity to the vagaries and discontinuities of the river. This example might suggest a polarization of place in the novel, the Red Deeps being the 'place of excess', set against the central scene. But the language here resonates with Maggie's being 'Borne along by the Tide' (p. 401) with Stephen and swept along the flood with Tom at the end. There is no special place of excess in the book. Like a field of force, a force of displacement, the hyperbolic traverses the whole world of the book, wherever the 'fluctuations' of a 'moral conflict' reveal a 'doubleness', wherever 'inward strife' wishes to 'flow' (p. 380) into release. The 'demon forces for ever in collision with beauty, virtue, and the gentle uses of life' are not restricted to the bygone days of the 'robber-barons' (p. 237) on the Rhine.

Is it possible for a 'secret longing' of which we are not 'distinctly conscious' and 'running counter' to all our conscious intentions to 'impel' our actions? The narrator urges us, 'Watch your own speech, and notice how it is guided by your less conscious purposes, and you will understand that contradiction' (pp. 402–3). We must double ourselves into an actor and observer in order to achieve the full, if transient, self-consciousness necessary to allow us to judge the splits within others. Even being 'thoroughly sincere' does not protect Maggie from duplicity in her conversation with Lucy; for by revealing her love-history with Philip, Maggie unwittingly tempts Lucy to see nothing of significance in the strange vibrations between Maggie and Stephen: 'Confidences are sometimes blinding, even when they are sincere' (p. 338). In a book that has invoked Oedipus (p. 117) and that broods on the Oedipal contrast between the 'earth-born' and those out of harmony 'with the earth on which they live' (pp. 237–8), such an observation suggests a relationship between the force of words here and the literally blinding consequence for Oedipus of the words that reveal his ancestry.[19]

In a similar way, Semele is invoked humorously early in the book (p. 153), with Tom in her place and Poulter like Jove withholding his immediate glory by not showing his sword. But Maggie's 'perpetual yearning' with 'its root deeper than all change' to have 'no cloud between herself and Tom' (p. 398) proves like Semele's to find full immediacy only in the permanent embrace of death. Conflict is the stuff of human life, for 'all yielding is attended with a less vivid consciousness than resistance' (p. 410). Only in the state of strife, of duality, of hyperbolically saying more than we mean, though not all that we mean, do we remain human. What are the other possibilities? The silence and unconsciousness of death, the total yielding to the flow of unconsciousness in madness, or the purity of sainthood. In the book's only perfect act of communication, Ogg names the force and source of the Virgin's wish, 'It is enough that thy heart needs it', and she accepts as complete his definition of her 'heart's need' (pp. 104–05).[20]

Yet what place has a saint's legend in this story of provincial mediocrity? The narrator recognizes that any suggested elevation, whether beatific or tragic, jars with the chosen level of milieu and action (in ways like those that Auerbach investigates). The narrator must therefore try to come to terms with this discrepancy between the world evoked and the world represented, this hyperbolic tendency of comparison. The narrator must find ways of mediating between the characters' psychologies and the audience's psychological expectations and levels of sympathy. One strategy uses the principle of the everyday, stable, and continuous. It reduces the hyperbole by devaluing the excessive term. Thus at one point the narrator compares the 'unwept, hidden . . . tragedy' of Mr Tulliver and 'other insignificant people' to the 'conspicuous, far-echoing tragedy' (pp. 173–4) of the royal. The fundamental base of comparison, however, is not greatness but weakness: 'Mr Tulliver . . . though nothing more than a superior miller and maltster, was as proud and obstinate as if he had been a very lofty personage.' The vices of pride and obstinacy join low and high in moral equality that negates distinctions of status. Eliot adds a further element to the comparison. The tragedy of high life 'sweeps the stage in regal robes', while we pass obscure tragedy 'unnoticingly on the road every day'. High tragedy is obvious, showy, in fact is only art, while to appreciate everyday tragedy shows our discernment of reality. Thus the hyperbole is erased; everyday suffering is realer and deeper than that of the exceptional monster; we are back within the domestic circle of continuity and security, even within suffering.

Quite different is another moment in which the narrator begins with hyperbole and then transforms it by estranging us from the familiar term. Rhetorical hyperbole, in which an excessive term is contrasted with one of common measure, yields to a vision of a hyperbolic world, in which everything exceeds common measure. After Maggie has cut off her hair, the narrator hyperbolically compares her sitting 'helpless and despairing among her black locks' to 'Ajax among the slaughtered sheep' (p. 59). Recognizing that Maggie's 'anguish' may seem 'very trivial' to adults,[21] the narrator suggests that it may be 'even more bitter . . . than what we are fond of calling antithetically the real troubles of mature life'. Rather than simply exploiting the antithesis of imagination and real life, the narrator calls it into question, even suggests that there may be no reality except that arbitrarily created by drawing a bar of antithesis. Without the axial coordinates we could not say that one branch of a hyperbola is positive and one negative. Furthermore, the narrator goes on, the discontinuity which establishes reality in the world of value may correspond to a necessary developmental discontinuity within the growth of the individual to maturity:

> We have all of us sobbed so piteously, standing with tiny bare legs above our little socks, when we lost sight of our mother or nurse in some strange place; but we can no longer recall the poignancy of that moment and weep over it. . . . Every one of those keen moments has left its trace, and lives in us still, but such traces have blent themselves irrecoverably with the firmer texture of our youth and manhood; and so it comes that we can look on at the troubles of our children with a smiling disbelief in the reality of their pain. Is there any one who can recover the experience of his childhood, not merely with a memory of what he did and what happened to him . . . but with an intimate penetration, a revived consciousness of what he felt then? . . . Surely if we could recall . . . the strangely perspectiveless conception of life that gave the bitterness its intensity, we should not pooh-pooh the griefs of our children.
>
> (pp. 59–60)

The significance of this passage in relation to Wordsworth, Freud, and Proust is beyond the scope of my present discussion. I want only to emphasize that the project of recovering the past is set under the sign of impossibility. We usually read that impossibility as a modest irony, disclaiming the narrator's actual achievement of this goal. Even so, we must recognize that just as a psychoanalytic cure requires 'transference', so here too there is a necessary displacement. Only through George Eliot can Marian Evans recover her past, and only through Maggie Tulliver can we recover ours.

In contrast to the analysis of Mr Tulliver's tragic status, the discrimination of two states here is made not through contrasting life and art, but rather through comparing two kinds of art, our adult art of perspective and the 'perspectiveless' primitive art of children. The flatness of this original art hides from us the 'intensity' within it. Thus a radical challenge is posed to both our sense of reality and our canons of representation. In perspectiveless art no single point organizes the whole into a continuum, and the process of maturation forces us to lose consciousness of the continuity of our present feelings with our past. Nonetheless, Eliot's art is not itself perspectiveless; perhaps most clearly in such moments of circumspection and direct appeal, her art keeps its distance. To speak of childhood's sense of the 'measureless' space from summer to summer, one must be capable of measurement.

From the grammatical to the psychological to the more largely philosophical the force of hyperbole pervades the book, leaving intact none of the certainties with which we were familiar in the first pattern. Thus, the hyperbolical description of Maggie moves beyond the bounds of rhetorical hyperbole to show the hyperbolic principle at work in the realm of cause, effect, and intention. In the sequence in which she pushed Lucy into the mud, Maggie is twice compared to a 'Medusa' (pp. 88, 91), a disproportion all the more exaggerated because Maggie's hair is cut, depriving her of the primary Medusan attribute. The narrator justifies the comparison: 'There were passions at war in Maggie at that moment to have made a tragedy, if tragedies were made by passion only; but the essential *τι μεγεθος* which was present in the passion was wanting to the action' (p. 90). The book's first pattern showed a regular harmony between cause and effect, circumstance and mind, but the hyperbolic pattern constantly signals discrepancy. Any possible explanations to flatten out these discrepancies are unknown or incomprehensible, and this 'mystery of the human lot' drives men to the consolations of 'superstition' (p. 238).

Maggie's tremendous childhood passion can express itself only in trivial actions, and the same gap between spirit and world prevails elsewhere. Some of the results that she most laments arise from no conscious intention. She 'never *meant*' (p. 33) Tom's rabbits to die from neglect, any more than she 'really . . . mean[t] it' (p. 78) when she toppled Tom's 'wonderful pagoda' of cards.[22] This disproportion holds in the adult world as well. We 'spoil the lives of our neighbours' unintentionally, and the 'sagacity' that seeks to reduce these results to causes in 'distinct motives' and 'consciously proposed end[s]' is in fact hyperbolic, 'widely misleading', for such proportions hold only in the 'world of the dramatist' (p. 23). The same tactic of setting life against art that reduced the hyperbolic relation between royal and domestic tragedy here insists upon the excess of suffering over aim. The stable, continuous world is a fiction.

In the same way, 'small, unimpassioned revenges' have an 'enormous effect in life, running through all degrees of pleasant infliction, blocking the fit men out of places, and blackening characters'. Since there is no appreciable source of agency, we surmise that 'Providence, or some other prince of this world . . . has undertaken the task of retribution for us' (p. 223). If we wish to avoid such superstitious metaphors, then we may think of 'apparently trivial coincidences and incalculable states of mind' as the 'machinery of Fact' (p. 295) rather than of fate, but the metaphor of machinery only gives us the illusion of comprehensibility. We still have no way of calculating the results.

The narrator tries to demystify the 'hypothesis of a very active diabolical agency' that Mr Tulliver requires to explain his 'entanglements' by changing the metaphor and proposing that Wakem was 'not more guilty' towards Tulliver 'than an ingenious machine, which performs its work with much regularity, is guilty towards the rash man who, venturing too near it, is caught up by some fly-wheel or other, and suddenly converted into unexpected mincemeat' (pp. 218–19). We laugh at this analogy, and thus laugh at Mr Tulliver, but the comedy depends precisely upon the disproportion, the sudden excess of the result, postponed until the end, which we could never have expected. How are we to know when is 'too near', and does the reference to 'some fly-wheel or other' indicate any more real knowledge of the process than Mr Tulliver has? Indeed, the very phrase 'ingenious machine' carries paradoxically animistic overtones. At the end of the book 'some wooden machinery' appears as the agency of Tom and Maggie's drowning, but the narrator cannot resist transforming it into an active agent, 'huge fragments, clinging together in fatal fellowship' that overwhelm the boat and then are seen 'hurrying on in hideous triumph' (p. 456). The hyperbolic pattern escapes our analogies, which are rooted in the will for a natural continuity that this pattern denies, and which demonstrate the pattern in failing to master it.

Even our most cherished cultural institutions work hyperbolically: 'Allocaturs, filing of bills in Chancery, decrees of sale, are legal chain-shot or bomb-shells that can never hit a solitary mark, but must fall with widespread shattering' (p. 215). Thus it is no real amelioration of human life that the 'floods' of old have yielded to 'fluctuations of trade' (p. 106) as the cause of uncertainty. For 'so inevitably diffusive is human suffering, that even justice makes its victims, and we can conceive no retribution that does not spread beyond its mark in pulsations of unmerited pain' (p. 215). Justice itself is unjust, as indifferent as the river is to the excess in what it sweeps away. Our machinery does not serve our purposes. The very idea 'which we call truth', the finest tool of our cultural creation, crumbles into a 'complex, fragmentary, doubt-provoking knowledge'. Truth can no longer be the satisfying goal of our inquiry but will only further provoke us, and it is not even at one with itself, any more than is our memory of our past. Only 'prejudice' is the 'natural food' of our 'tendencies' (p. 400) toward wholeness and uniformity. If earlier we saw Enlightenment and nature reconciled, here we recall the hyperboles of Burke's polemic intransigence.

Now we may return to the familiar, family world of living and loving together at the Mill on the Floss, which formed the basis for our sketch of the book's pattern of harmony. But those figures of harmony are now disfigured, while in a new reversal the force of hyperbole proves productive as well as disruptive. The split between truth and prejudice that we have just noted echoes that between Tom and Maggie, the once-united 'Boy and Girl'. Tom is the man of prejudice, while to Philip, Maggie 'was truth itself' (p. 409), although he is unaware of the terrible revelation that awaits him of what truth is really like. Tom is 'a character at unity with itself' (p. 271), while Maggie must fear, yet constantly find herself in, 'doubleness' (p. 265). While Tom is 'concentrating' (p. 242) himself on recovering his father's position in life and matching his father's 'concentration' (p. 243) on the same purpose, the two of them are falling into a 'perpetually repeated round' (p. 245) of mechanical recurrence. Maggie in contrast feels 'the strong tide of pitying love almost as an inspiration' (p. 243). Thus the harmony of the Mill and the Floss that marks the first pattern of the book is contradicted by a contrast of the 'mill-like monotony' (p. 166) of deadening singleness with the dangerously double eddies of passionate fluxes and refluxes. The 'habitual . . . deepening . . . central fold' (p. 299) in Tom's brow is the disfiguring mark of his commitment, his attachment to his place. Maggie's dream on her way back after floating away with Stephen shows the profound wish for a wholeness to unite the Mill and the Floss, for in it she capsizes her boat in reaching out after Tom, but as she begins to sink, she becomes 'a child again in the parlour at evening twilight, and Tom was not really angry' (p. 413). But the book's ending grants such wholeness only in death.

The 'parlour' itself, if it were as available to the full, 'intimate penetration' of Maggie's memory as it is to the reader's, has been from the beginning a scene of conflict and discontinuity. There Mr Tulliver conceives the book's initially disruptive act of overreaching, his hyperbolic 'plan' for Tom which Mrs Glegg defines as 'bringin' him up above his fortin'' (p. 64). Mr Tulliver explains his intention in terms of that fundamental paternal ambivalence that to modern readers is the most striking link between him and Oedipus: 'I don't *mean* Tom to be a miller. . . . [H]e'd be expectin' to take to the mill an' the land, an' a-hinting at me as it was time for me to lay by an' think o' my latter end. . . . I shall give Tom an eddication an' put him to a business, as he may make a nest for himself, and not want to push me out o' mine' (p. 15). Thus the principle of generational continuity is split at its center; the 'nest' has no place for two and therefore demands displacement.

Tom himself manifests similar ambivalence toward his father. Even while working to redeem his father's credit, he keeps his efforts secret from a 'strange mixture of opposite feelings . . . that family repulsion which spoils the most sacred relations' (p. 283). Maggie also suffers from this split within Tom, for he feels a 'repulsion' towards her that 'derived its very intensity from their early childish love' (p. 437). She finds that he always 'checked her . . . by some thwarting difference' (p. 252). This split within family feelings echoes the opening description of the 'loving tide', which with its 'impetuous embrace' does not welcome the Floss but rather 'checks' (p. 7) it. There is a split in the very source of love, for the loved one's difference from us makes a 'fear spring . . . in us' (p. 422).

Maggie, then, is terrified at the 'anger and hatred' against her family that 'would flow out . . . like a lava stream' (p. 252) within her. From such contradictions proceeds 'that partial, divided action of our nature which makes half the tragedy of the human lot' (p. 439). But the book makes clear also that the other half of the tragedy comes from the concentrated singleness that seems the only alternative.

If both wholeness and division make life tragic, each also makes life livable. The pattern of orderly growth and causation is not the only source of positive value. Dr Kenn may seem to speak with the authority of the whole book when he laments the present tendency 'towards the relaxation of ties – towards the substitution of wayward choice for the adherence to obligation, which has its roots in the past' (p. 433). But his own relation to Maggie has begun through a chance encounter at the charity-bazaar, 'one of those moments of implicit revelation which will sometimes happen even between people who meet quite transiently. . . . There is always this possibility of a word or look from a stranger to keep alive the sense of human brotherhood' (pp. 381–2). This brief confluence between him and Maggie echoes the kindness shown her in her need by Mrs Stelling, who was not generally a loving woman and 'whom she had never liked'. In kissing Mrs Stelling, Maggie first feels a 'new sense' of 'that susceptibility to the bare offices of humanity which raises them into a bond of loving fellowship' (p. 170). An extravagant comparison marks the point: 'To haggard men among the icebergs the mere presence of an ordinary comrade stirs the deep fountains of affection.' Thus the wayward and the transient have the same potential for enriching and sustaining life as do long-established ties and deep roots. 'Brotherhood' is a matter of contiguity as well as of genealogical continuity, something people may find, or make, for themselves as well as receive from nature. Such a hyperbolic pattern is not, however, easy to grasp. Tom finds Maggie's life a 'planless riddle' (p. 343), and in despair he can only expect that in her life one 'perverse resolve' will 'metamorphose itself . . . into something equally perverse but entirely different' (p. 400). From that metamorphic point of discontinuity, the hyperbolic springs as a constant source of difference, of change, in contrast to the orderly growth of the same from a fixed and presently revisitable center.

This wayward, hyperbolic energy ensures that all the literary types that help to structure the book are different in their return, whether Oedipus or Semele or St Ogg, or Saul and Jonathan, the father and son whose memorial lament serves as epitaph for brother and sister. If one pattern of the book depends on the recurrence of the 'same flowers . . . the same hips and haws . . . the same red-breasts' and is best fixed in a landscape description of a town 'familiar with forgotten years', another landscape best carries the hyperbolic pattern: 'Nature repairs her ravages – but not all. The uptorn trees are not rooted again; the parted hills are left scarred:

if there is a new growth, the trees are not the same as the old, and the hills underneath their green vesture bear the marks of past rending. To the eyes that have dwelt on the past, there is no thorough repair' (p. 457). I have used the tag quotation from Wordsworth ('familiar with forgotten years') to recall the first pattern of the book, which in many ways corresponds to what we call the Wordsworthian in George Eliot and in nineteenth-century culture generally, but within Wordsworth's text itself the same kinds of conflict and contradiction occur. In its context the quoted phrase also evokes hills 'scarred' from 'past rending' In describing the youth of the Wanderer, as he turned his eyes from the books he was reading to the book of nature, Wordsworth says he saw:

some peak
Familiar with forgotten years, that shows
Inscribed upon its visionary sides,
The history of many a winter storm,
Or obscure records of the path of fire.[23]

Such violence sets in action the conflict between contrasting linguistic registers (and associated forms of experience and action) that makes *The Mill on the Floss* realistic in its attempt to unsettle cultural complacencies yet allows it as well to avoid the merely prosaic and routine. Eliot's awareness of this conflict makes her book an active clash between the hope of a fitting language and the recognition that language is never at one with reality, any more than the world is at one with itself. Rather than trying to heal such splits through formulas of artistic integration that weld the book into a specious wholeness, or trying to naturalize such splits by inserting them into a biographical interpretation of George Eliot, I find it most fruitful to grasp the complexities of *The Mill on the Floss* within the larger history of the realistic novel, which takes its beginning and elaborates its practice from just such splits.

Notes

1. Frank Kermode, *The Classic* (New York: Viking, 1975), pp. 130ff., and Roland Barthes, *S/Z* (Paris: Seuil, 1970). See also Fredric Jameson, 'The Ideology of the Text', *Salmagundi*, 31–32 (Fall 1975–Winter 1976), pp. 232–3.
2. See for example Northrop Frye, *The Secular Scripture* (Cambridge: Harvard University Press, 1976), p. 46 (Nineteenth-century realism is based on the 'naive confidence that words have an unlimited ability to represent things outside themselves.'); Jonathan Culler, *Flaubert* (Ithaca: Cornell University Press, 1974), p. 80 ('The basic enabling convention of the novel as a genre' is 'confidence in the transparent and representative power of language.'); Paul de Man, 'The

Rhetoric of Temporality', in *Interpretation*, ed. Charles Singleton (Baltimore: Johns Hopkins University Press, 1969), p. 204 (The nineteenth-century 'regression in critical insight' finds 'its historical equivalent in the regression from the eighteenth-century ironic novel . . . to realism.').

3. See comments on 'dual-focus form' by Peter K. Garrett, 'Double Plot and Dialogical Form in Victorian Fiction', *Nineteenth-Century Fiction* (*NCF*), 32 (1977), pp. 1–17; and the 'double-reading' of *Daniel Deronda* by Cynthia Chase, 'The Decomposition of the Elephants', *Publications of the Modern Language Association* (*PMLA*), 93 (1978), pp. 215–27. Both examine works, however, in which double plots make textual duality more naturalistically manageable.

4. See Harry Levin, 'The Example of Cervantes', in *Contexts of Criticism* (Cambridge: Harvard University Press, 1957), pp. 79–96; and José Ortega y Gasset, *Meditations on Quixote* (1914), trans. Evelyn Rugg and Diego Marín (New York: Norton, 1961).

5. On the absence of 'reality' from direct representation, see Margaret Homans, 'Repression and Sublimation of Nature in *Wuthering Heights*', *PMLA*, 93 (1978), pp. 9–19. Cf. also J. Hillis Miller, 'Nature and the Linguistic Moment', in *Nature and the Victorian Imagination*, ed. U. C. Knoepflmacher and G. B. Tennyson (Berkeley: University of California Press, 1977), especially pp. 440, 444–5.

6. See Anthony Close, *The Romantic Approach to 'Don Quixote'* (Cambridge: Cambridge University Press, 1978), especially pp. 26–67.

7. On this pattern see M. H. Abrams, *Natural Supernaturalism* (New York: Norton, 1971), *passim*. Abrams I think overestimates romantic confidence in this pattern, just as many readers do Eliot's.

8. See the famous fragment on 'romantische Poesie' (that is, both 'modern' and 'novelistic' literature), *Charakteristiken und Kritiken*, I (1796–1801), ed. Hans Eichner (Munich: Schöningh, 1967), pp. 182–3.

9. See for example David Carroll, '*Mimesis* reconsidered', *Diacritics*, 5 (Summer 1975), pp. 5–12.

10. Erich Auerbach, *Mimesis* (1946), trans. Willard Trask (1953; reprinted New York: Doubleday, 1957), p. 430.

11. Henry James, *The Art of the Novel* (New York: Scribner, 1934), p. 5.

12. *The Art of the Novel*, pp. 302, 86. See also J. Hillis Miller, *The Form of Victorian Fiction* (Notre Dame: University of Notre Dame Press, 1968), pp. 29–30.

13. George Eliot, *The Mill on the Floss*, ed. Gordon S. Haight (1860; Boston: Houghton, 1961), p. 140. All subsequent references to this edition are given parenthetically.

14. 'Humiliate' is derived from Latin *humus*, 'earth'. *Humus* and 'human' are etymologically related, which may reinforce our sense that what is 'humiliating' by one standard is humanizing by another. On the social and stylistic transgressions committed by Christian *sermo humilis* in bringing the highest meanings into everyday life and language, see Erich Auerbach, *Literary Language and its Public in Late Latin Antiquity and in the Middle Ages* (1958), trans. Ralph Manheim (New York: Random, 1965), pp. 25–66.

15. Eliot uses this same phrase to characterize the qualities of a 'resonant language' that will 'express life' and give a 'fitful shimmer of many-hued significance' because it is historically rooted rather than scientifically transparent and 'de-odorized'. See 'The Natural History of German Life' (1856), in *Essays of George Eliot*, ed. Thomas Pinney (New York: Columbia University Press, 1963), pp. 287–8.

16. See for example the *Dublin University Magazine* review (1861), in *George Eliot: The Critical Heritage*, ed. David Carroll (New York: Barnes, 1971), p. 147.

17. On psychology, see F. R. LEAVIS, *The Great Tradition* (1948; reprinted New York: Doubleday, 1954), p.58; on 'epic breadth', *The George Eliot Letters*, ed. Gordon S. Haight, (New Haven: Yale University Press, 1954–55), III, 317 (9 July, 1860).

18. J. HILLIS MILLER relates this passage to speaking 'parabolically'. See 'Optic and Semiotic in *Middlemarch*', in *The Worlds of Victorian Fiction*, ed. Jerome H. Buckley (Cambridge Mass.: Harvard University Press, 1975), p. 144.

19. On Oedipus and autochthony (a form of 'humiliation') see Claude Lévi-Strauss, 'The Structural Study of Myth', in *Myth: A Symposium*, ed. Thomas A. Sebeok (1955; reprinted Bloomington and London: Indiana University Press, 1965), pp. 91–2. On Eliot's pervasive references to Greek tragedy see Vernon Rendall, 'George Eliot and the Classics' (1947–48), in *A Century of George Eliot Criticism*, ed. Gordon S. Haight (1965; reprinted London: Methuen, 1966), pp. 215–21.

20. ELIOT saw tragedy arising from the 'dramatic collision' the *'conflict'* between 'valid claims' that will continually renew itself until the 'outer life of man' achieves 'harmony with his inward needs'. ('The Antigone and its Moral', 156, in *Essays of George Eliot*, pp. 263–4.) Eliot's own tangled language and troubled plots belong to a world that lacks this perfect correspondence of 'heart's need' to language and action. For more on Eliot's theory of tragedy see U. C. Knoepflmacher, *George Eliot's Early Novels* (Berkeley and Los Angeles: University of California Press, 1968), pp. 171–4.

21. In ELIOT's frequent loaded use of 'trivial' may we recall the intersection of three roads where Oedipus met Laius?

22. On this pattern of spoiling see Lynne Tidaback Roberts, 'Perfect Pyramids: *The Mill on the Floss*', *Texas Studies in Language and Literature* (*TSLL*), 13 (1971), pp. 111–24.

23. *The Excursion*, Book I, II. 275–9, in *The Poetical Works of William Wordsworth*, eds. Ernest de Selincourt and Helen Darbishire (Oxford: Clarendon, 1940–49), V, 17.

6 Men of Maxims and *The Mill on the Floss**

Mary Jacobus

Mary Jacobus's work combines a feminist perspective with post-structuralism. Like post-structuralist critics she is much concerned with the question of language, but for her language cannot be considered separately from gender. She argues that *The Mill on the Floss* exposes how men's domination of women operates through their control over language. But she sees the ending of the novel as regressive since it implies that difference and division can be transcended (see Introduction, pp. 20–1).

> The first question to ask is therefore the following: how can women analyze their own exploitation, inscribe their own demands, within an order prescribed by the masculine? *Is a women's politics possible within that order?*
>
> (Luce Irigaray)[1]

To rephrase the question: Can there be (a politics of) women's writing? What does it mean to say that women can analyze their exploitation only 'within an order prescribed by the masculine'? And what theory of sexual difference can we turn to when we speak, as feminist critics are wont to do, of a specifically 'feminine' practice in writing? Questions like these mark a current impasse in contemporary feminist criticism. Utopian attempts to define the specificity of women's writing – desired or hypothetical, but rarely empirically observed – either founder on the rock of essentialism (the text as body), gesture toward an avant-garde practice which turns out not to be specific to women, or, like Hélène Cixous in 'The Laugh of the Medusa' do both.[2] If anatomy is not destiny, still less can it be language.

A politics of women's writing, then, if it is not to fall back on a

* Reprinted from Mary Jacobus, *Reading Woman: Essays in Feminist Criticism* (London: Methuen, 1986), pp. 62–79.

biologically based theory of sexual difference, must address itself, as Luce Irigaray has done in 'The Power of Discourse and the Subordination of the Feminine', to the position of mastery held not only by scientific discourse (Freudian theory, for instance), not only by philosophy, 'the discourse of discourses', but by the logic of discourse itself. Rather than attempting to identify a specific practice, in other words, such a feminist politics would attempt to relocate sexual difference at the level of the text by undoing the repression of the 'feminine' in all the systems of representation for which the Other (woman) must be reduced to the economy of the Same (man). In Irigaray's terms, 'masculine' systems of representation are those whose self-reflexiveness and specularity disappropriate women of their relation to themselves and to other women; as in Freud's theory of sexual difference (woman equals man-minus), difference is swiftly converted into hierarchy. Femininity comes to signify a role, an image, a value imposed on women by the narcissistic and fundamentally misogynistic logic of such masculine systems. The question then becomes for Irigaray not 'What is woman?' (still less Freud's desperate 'What does a woman want?') but 'How is the feminine determined by discourse itself?' – determined, that is, as lack or error or as an inverted reproduction of the masculine subject.[3]

Invisible or repressed, the hidden place of the feminine in language is the hypothesis which sustains the model of the textual universe, like ether. We know it must be there because we know ourselves struggling for self-definition in other terms, elsewhere, elsehow. We need it, so we invent it. When such an article of faith doesn't manifest itself as a mere rehearsal of sexual stereotypes, it haunts contemporary feminist criticism in its quest for specificity – whether of language, or literary tradition, or women's culture. After all, why study women's writing at all unless it is 'women's writing' in the first place? The answer, I believe, must be a political one, and one whose impulse also fuels that gesture toward an elusive '*écriture féminine*' or specificity. To postulate, as Irigaray does, a 'work of language' which undoes the repression of the feminine constitutes in itself an attack on the dominant ideology, the very means by which we know what we know and think what we think. So too the emphasis on women's writing politicizes in a flagrant and polemical fashion the 'difference' which has traditionally been elided by criticism and by the canon formations of literary history. To label a text as that of a woman, and to write about it for that reason, makes vividly legible what the critical institution has either ignored or acknowledged only under the sign of inferiority. We need the term 'women's writing' if only to remind us of the social conditions under which women wrote and still write – to remind us that the conditions of their (re)production are the economic and educational disadvantages, the sexual and material organizations of society, which rather than biology, form the crucial determinants of women's writing.

Feminist criticism, it seems to me, ultimately has to invoke as its starting point this underlying political assumption. To base its theory on a specificity of language or literary tradition or culture is already to have moved one step on in the argument, if not already to have begged the question, since by then one is confronted by what Nancy Miller, in a recent essay on women's fiction, has called 'the irreducibly complicated relationship women have historically had to the language of the dominant culture'.[4] Perhaps that is why, baffled in their attempts to specify the feminine, feminist critics have so often turned to an analysis of this relationship as it is manifested and thematized in writing by and about women. The project is, and can't escape being, an ideological one; concerned, that is, with the functioning and reproduction of sexual ideology in particular – whether in the overtly theoretical terms of Luce Irigaray or in the fictional terms of, for instance, George Eliot. To quote Miller again, the aim would be to show that 'the maxims that pass for the truth of human experience, and the encoding of that experience in literature, are organizations, when they are not fantasies, of the dominant culture'.[5]

But Irigaray's 'women's politics', her feminist argument, goes beyond ideology critique in its effort to recover 'the place of the feminine' in discourse. The 'work of language' which she envisages would undo representation altogether, even to the extent of refusing the linearity of reading. '*Après-coup*', the retroactive effect of a word ending, opens up the structure of language to reveal the repression on which meaning depends; and repression is the place of the feminine. By contrast, the 'style' of women – *écriture féminine* – would privilege not the look but the tactile, the simultaneous, the fluid. Yet at the same time, we discover, such a style can't be sustained as a thesis or made the object of a position; if not exactly 'nothing', it is nonetheless a kind of discursive practice that can't be thought, still less written. Like her style, woman herself is alleged by Irigaray to be an unimaginable concept within the existing order. Elaborating a theory of which woman is either the subject or the object merely reinstalls the feminine within a logic that represses, censors, or misrecognizes it. Within that logic, woman can only signify an excess or a deranging power. Woman for Irigaray is always the 'something else' that points to the possibility of another language, asserts that the masculine is not all, does not have a monopoly on value, or still less, 'the abusive privilege of appropriation'. She tries to strike through the theoretical machinery itself, suspending its pretension to the production of a single truth, a univocal meaning. Woman would thus find herself on the side of everything in language that is multiple, duplicitous, unreliable and resistant to the binary oppositions on which theories of sexual difference such as Freud's depend.[6]

Irigaray's argument is seductive precisely because it puts all systems in question, leaving process and fluidity instead of fixity and form. At the same time, it necessarily concedes that women have access to language only by recourse to systems of representation that are masculine. Given the coherence of the systems at work in discourse, whether Freudian or critical, how is the work of language of which she speaks to be undertaken at all? Her answer is 'mimetism', the role historically assigned to women – that of reproduction, but deliberately assumed; an acting out or role playing within the text which allows the woman writer to know better and hence to expose what it is she mimics. Irigaray, in fact, seems to be saying that there is no 'outside' of discourse, no alternative practice available to the woman writer apart from the process of undoing itself:

> To play with mimesis is thus, for a woman, to try to recover the place of her exploitation by discourse, without allowing herself to be simply reduced to it. It means to resubmit herself – inasmuch as she is on the side of the 'perceptible', of 'matter' – to 'ideas', in particular to ideas about herself, that are elaborated in/by a masculine logic, but so as to make 'visible', by an effect of playful repetition, what was supposed to remain invisible: the cover-up of a possible operation of the feminine in language. It also means 'to unveil' the fact that, if women are such good mimics, it is because they are not simply resorbed in this function. *They also remain elsewhere.*[7]

Within the systems of discourse and representation which repress the feminine, woman can only resubmit herself to them; but by refusing to be reduced by them, she points to the place and manner of her exploitation. 'A possible operation of the feminine in language' becomes, then, the revelation of its repression, through an effect of playful rehearsal, rather than a demonstrably feminine linguistic practice.

Irigaray's main usefulness to the feminist critic lies in this half-glimpsed possibility of undoing the ideas about women elaborated in and by masculine logic, a project at once analytic and ideological. Her attack on centrism in general, and phallocentrism in particular, allows the feminist critic to ally herself 'otherwise', with the 'elsewhere' to which Irigaray gestures, in a stance of dissociation and resistance which typically characterizes that of feminist criticism in its relation to the dominant culture or 'order prescribed by the masculine'. But like Irigaray herself in 'The Power of Discourse', feminist criticism remains imbricated within the forms of intelligibility – reading and writing, the logic of discourse – against which it pushes. What makes the 'difference', then? Surely, the direction from which that criticism comes – the elsewhere that it invokes, the putting in question of our social organization of gender; its wishfulness, even, in imagining alternatives. It follows that what pleases the feminist critic most (this one, at any rate) is to light on a text that seems to do her arguing, or some of it, for her – especially a text whose story is the same as hers; hence, perhaps, the drift toward narrative in recent works of feminist criticism such as Sandra Gilbert and Susan Gubar's influential *The Madwoman in the Attic*.[8] What's usually going on in such criticism – perhaps in all feminist criticism – is a specificity of relationship that amounts to a distinctive practice. Criticism takes literature as its object, yes; but here literature in a different sense is likely to become the subject, the feminist critic, the woman writer, woman herself.

This charged and doubled relationship, an almost inescapable aspect of feminist criticism, is at once transgressive and liberating, since what it brings to light is the hidden or unspoken ideological premise of criticism itself. *Engagée* perforce, feminist criticism calls neutrality into question, like other avowedly political analyses of literature. I want now to undertake a 'symptomatic' reading of a thematically relevant chapter from Eliot's *The Mill on the Floss* (1860) in the hope that this quintessentially critical activity will bring to light if not 'a possible operation of the feminine in language' at least one mode of its recovery – language itself. I will return later to the final chapter of Irigaray's *This Sex Which Is Not One* in which an escape from masculine systems of representation is glimpsed through the metaphors of female desire itself.

Nancy Miller's 'maxims that pass for the truth of human experience' allude to Eliot's remark near the end of *The Mill on the Floss* that 'the man of maxims is the popular representative of the minds that are guided in their moral judgement solely by general rules'.[9] Miller's concern is the accusation of implausibility leveled at the plots of women's novels: Eliot's concern is the 'special case' of Maggie Tulliver – 'to lace ourselves up in formulas' is to ignore 'the special circumstances that mark the individual lot'. An argument for the individual makes itself felt as an argument against generalities. For Eliot herself, as for Dr Kenn (the repository of her knowledge at this point in the novel), 'the mysterious complexity of our life is not to be embraced by maxims' (p. 628). Though the context is the making of moral, not critical, judgments, I think that Eliot, as so often at such moments, is concerned also with both the making and the reading of fiction; with the making of another kind of special case. Though Maggie may be an 'exceptional' woman, the ugly duckling of St Ogg's, her story contravenes the norm, and in that respect it could be said to be all women's story. We recall an earlier moment, that of Tom Tulliver's harsh judgment of his sister ('You have no resolution to resist a thing that you know to be wrong'), and Maggie's rebellious murmuring that her life is 'a planless riddle to him' only because he's incapable of feeling the mental needs which impel her, in his eyes, to wrongdoing or absurdity (pp. 504, 505). To Tom, the novel's chief upholder of general rules and patriarchal law (he makes his sister swear obedience to his prohibitions on the family Bible), the planless riddle of Maggie's life is only made sense of by a 'Final Rescue' which involves her death: 'In their death they were not divided' (p. 657). But the reunion of brother and sister in the floodwaters of the Ripple enacts both reconciliation and revenge, consummation and cataclysm; powerful authorial desires are at work.[10] To simplify this irreducible swirl of contradictory desire in the deluge that 'rescues' Maggie as well as her brother would be to salvage a maxim as 'jejune' as '*Mors omnibus est communis*' (one of the tags Maggie finds when she dips into her brother's Latin grammar) stripped of its saving Latin.[11] We might go further and say that to substitute a generality for the riddle of Maggie's life and death, or to translate Latin maxims into English commonplaces, would constitute a misreading of the novel as inept as Tom's misconstruction of his sister, or his Latin. Maggie's incomprehensible foreignness, her drift into error or impropriety on the river with Stephen Guest, is a 'lapse' understood by the latitudinarian Dr Kenn. For us, it also involves an understanding that planlessness, riddles and impropriety – the enigmas, accidents and incorrectness of language itself – are at odds with the closures of plot (here, the plot of incestuous reunion) and with interpretation itself, as well as with the finality of the maxims denounced by Eliot.

For all its healing of division, *The Mill on the Floss* uncovers the divide between the language or maxims of the dominant culture and the language itself which undoes them. In life, at any rate, they remain divided – indeed, death may be the price of unity – and feminist criticism might be said to install itself in the gap. A frequent move on the part of feminist criticism is to challenge the norms and aesthetic criteria of the dominant culture (as Miller does in defending Eliot), claiming, in effect, that 'incorrectness' makes visible what is specific to women's writing. The culturally imposed or assumed 'lapses' of women's writing are turned against the system that brings them into being – a system women writers necessarily inhabit. What surfaces in this gesture is the all-important question of women's access to knowledge and culture and to the power that goes with them. In writing by women, the question is often explicitly thematized in terms of education. Eliot's account of Tom's schooling in 'School-Time', the opening chapter of Book 2, provides just such a thematic treatment – a lesson in antifeminist pedagogy which goes beyond its immediate implications for women's education to raise more far-reaching questions about the functioning of both sexual ideology and language. Take Maggie's puzzlement at one of the many maxims found in the *Eton Grammar*, a required text for the unfortunate Tom. As often, rules and examples prove hard to tell apart:

> The astronomer who hated women generally caused [Maggie] so much puzzling speculation that she one day asked Mr. Stelling if all astronomers hated women, or whether it was only this particular astronomer. But, forestalling his answer, she said,
>
> 'I suppose it's all astronomers: because you know, they live up in high towers, and if the women came there, they might talk and hinder them from looking at the stars.'
>
> Mr. Stelling liked her prattle immensely.
>
> (p. 220)

What we see here is a textbook example of the way in which individual misogyny becomes generalized – 'maximized', as it were – in the form of a patriarchal put-down. Maggie may have trouble construing *'ad unam mulieres'*, or 'all to a woman', but in essence she has got it right.[12] Just to prove her point, Mr Stelling (who himself prefers the talk of women to star gazing) likes her 'prattle', a term used only of the talk of women and children. Reduced to his idea of her, Maggie can only mimic man's talk.

Inappropriate as he is in other respects for Tom's future career, Mr Stelling thus proves an excellent schoolmaster to his latent misogyny. His classroom is also an important scene of instruction for Maggie, who learns not only that all astronomers to a man hate women in general but that girls can't learn Latin; that they are quick and shallow, mere imitators ('this small apparatus of shallow quickness', Eliot playfully repeats); and that everybody hates clever women, even if they are amused by the prattle of clever little girls (pp. 214, 211, 216). It's hard not to read with one eye on her creator. Maggie, it emerges, rather fancies herself as a linguist, and Eliot too seems wishfully to imply that she has what one might call a 'gift' for languages – a gift, perhaps, for ambiguity too. Women, we learn, don't just talk, they double-talk, like language itself; that's just the trouble for boys like Tom:

> 'I know what Latin is very well', said Maggie, confidently. 'Latin's a language. The are Latin words in the Dictionary. There's bonus, a gift.'
>
> 'Now, you're just wrong there, Miss Maggie!' said Tom, secretly astonished. 'You think you're very wise! But "bonus" means "good", as it happens – bonus, bona, bonum.'
>
> 'Well, that's no reason why it shouldn't mean "gift",' said Maggie stoutly. 'It may mean several things. Almost every word does.'
>
> (p. 214)

And if words may mean several things, general rules or maxims may prove less universal than they claim to be and lose their authority. Perhaps only 'this particular astronomer' was a woman-hater or hated only one woman in particular. Special cases or particular contexts – 'the special circumstances that mark the individual lot' (p. 628) – determine or render indeterminate not only judgment but meaning too. The rules of language itself make Tom's rote learning troublesome to him. How can he hope to construe his sister when her relation to language proves so treacherous – her difference so shifting a play of possibility, like the difference within language itself, destabilizing terms such as 'wrong' and 'good'?

Maggie, a little parody of her author's procedures in *The Mill on the Floss,* decides 'to skip the rule in the syntax – the examples became so absorbing':

> These mysterious sentences snatched from an unknown context, – like strange horns of beasts and leaves of unknown plants, brought from some far-off region, gave boundless scope to her imagination, and were all the more fascinating because they were in a peculiar tongue of their own, which she could learn to interpret. It was really very interesting – the Latin Grammar that Tom had said no girls could learn: and she was proud because she found it interesting. The most fragmentary examples were her favourites. *Mors omnibus est communis* would have been jejune, only she likes to know the Latin; but the fortunate gentleman whom every one congratulated because he had a son 'endowed with *such* a disposition' afforded her a great deal of pleasant conjecture, and she was quite lost in the 'thick grove penetrable by no star', when Tom called out,
>
> 'Now, then, Maggie, give us the Grammar!'
>
> (pp. 217–18)

Whereas maxims lace her up in formulas, 'these mysterious sentences' give boundless scope to Maggie's imagination; for her, as for her author (who makes them foretell her story), they are whole fictional worlds, alternative realities, transformations of the familiar into the exotic and strange. In their foreignness she finds herself, until roused by Tom's peremptory call, as she is later to be recalled by his voice from the Red Deeps. Here, however, it is Maggie who teaches Tom his most important lesson, that the 'dead' languages had once been living: 'that there had once been people upon the earth who were so fortunate as to know Latin without learning it through the medium of the Eton Grammar' (p. 221). The idea – or, rather, fantasy – of a language that is innate rather than acquired, native rather than incomprehensibly foreign, is a consoling one for the unbookish miller's son; but it holds out hope for Maggie too, and presumably also for her creator. Though Latin stands in for cultural imperialism and for the outlines of a peculiarly masculine and elitist classical education from which women have traditionally been excluded, Maggie can learn to interpret it. The 'peculiar tongue' had once been spoken by women, after all – and they had not needed to learn it from Mr Stelling or the institutions he perpetuates. Who knows, she might even become an astronomer herself, or, like Eliot, a writer who by her pen name had refused the institutionalization of sexual difference as cultural exclusion. Tom and Mr Stelling tell Maggie that 'Girls never learn such things'; 'They've a great deal of superficial cleverness but they couldn't go far into anything' (pp. 214, 221). But going far into things – and going far – is the author's prerogative in *The Mill on the Floss*. Though Maggie's quest for knowledge ends in death, as Virginia Woolf thought Eliot's own had ended,[13] killing off this small apparatus of shallow quickness may have been the necessary sacrifice in order for Eliot herself to become an interpreter of the exotic possibilities contained in mysterious sentences. Maggie – unassimilable, incomprehensible, 'fallen' – is her text, a 'dead' language which thereby gives all the greater scope to authorial imaginings, making it possible for the writer to come into being.

We recognize in 'School-Time' Eliot's investment – humorous, affectionate, and rather innocently self-lovingly – in Maggie's gifts and haphazard acquisition of knowledge. In particular, we recognize a defense of the 'irregular' education which until recently had been the lot of most women, if educated at all. Earlier in the same chapter, in the context of Mr Stelling's teaching methods (that is, his unquestioning reliance on Euclid and the *Eton Grammar*), Eliot refers whimsically to 'Mr Broderip's amiable beaver' which 'busied himself as earnestly in constructing a dam, in a room up three pairs of stairs in London, as if he had been laying his foundation in a stream or lake in Upper Canada. It was 'Binny's function to build' (p. 206). Binny the beaver, a pet from the pages of W. J. Broderip's *Leaves from the Note Book of a Naturalist* (1852), constructed his dam with sweeping brushes and warming pans, 'hand-brushes, rush-baskets, books, boots, sticks, clothes, dried turf or anything portable'.[14] A domesticated *bricoleur*, Binny makes do with what he can find. A few lines later, we hear of Mr Stelling's 'educated' condescension toward 'the display of various or special knowledge made by irregularly educated people' (p. 207). Mr Broderip's beaver, it turns out, does double duty as an illustration of Mr Stelling's 'regular' (not to say 'rote') mode of instruction – he can do no otherwise, conditioned as he is – and as a defense of Eliot's own display of irregularly acquired 'various or special knowledge'. Like Maggie's, this is knowledge drawn directly from books, without the aid of a patriarchal pedagogue. Mr Stelling and the institutions he subscribes to (Aristotle, deaneries, prebends, Great Britain and Protestantism – the Establishment, in fact) are lined up against the author-as-eager-beaver. Eliot's mischievous impugning of authority and authorities – specifically, cultural authority – becomes increasingly explicit until, a page or so later, culture itself comes under attack. Finding Tom's brain 'peculiarly impervious to etymology and demonstration', Mr Stelling concludes that it 'was peculiarly in need of being ploughed and harrowed by these patent implements: it was his favourite metaphor, that the classics and geometry constituted that culture of the mind which prepared it for the reception of any subsequent crop.' As Eliot rather wittily observes, the regimen proves 'as uncomfortable for Tom Tulliver as if he had been plied with cheese in order to remedy a gastric weakness which prevented him from digesting it' (p. 208). Nor is Eliot only, or simply, being funny. The bonus or gift of language is at work here, translating dead metaphor into organic tract.

Like Maggie herself, the metaphor here is improper, disrespectful of authorities, and, as Tom later complains of his sister, not to be relied on. Developing the implications of changing her metaphor from agriculture to digestion, Eliot drastically undermines the realist illusion of her fictional world, revealing it to be no more than a blank page inscribed with a succession of arbitrary metaphoric substitutions:

> It is astonishing what a different result one gets by changing the metaphor! Once call the brain an intellectual stomach, and one's ingenious conception of the classics and geometry as ploughs and harrows seems to settle nothing. But then, it is open to some one else to follow great authorities and call the mind a sheet of white paper or a mirror, in which case one's knowledge of the digestive process becomes quite irrelevant. It was doubtless an ingenious idea to call the camel the ship of the desert, but it would hardly lead one far in training that useful beast. O Aristotle! if you had had the advantage of being 'the freshest modern' instead of the greatest ancient, would you not have mingled your praise of metaphorical speech as a sign of high intelligence, with a lamentation that intelligence so rarely shows itself in speech without metaphor – that we can so seldom declare what a thing is, except by saying it is something else?
>
> (pp. 208–9)

In the *Poetics* Aristotle says: 'It is a great thing to make use of . . . double words and rare words . . . but by far the greatest thing is the use of metaphor. That alone cannot be learned; it is the token of genius. *For the right use of metaphor means an eye for resemblances.*'[15] Of course there's authorial self-congratulation lurking in this passage, as there is in Eliot's affectionate parade of Maggie's gifts. But an eye for resemblances (between Binny and Mr Stelling, for instance, or brain and stomach) is also here a satiric eye. Culture as (in)digestion makes Euclid and the *Eton Grammar* hard to swallow; Aristotle loses his authority to the author herself. On one level, this is science calling culture into question, making empiricism the order of the day. But there's something unsettling to the mind, or, rather, stomach, in this dizzy progression from culture, digestive tract, and *tabula rasa* to ship of the desert (which sounds like a textbook example of metaphor). The blank page may take what imprint the author chooses to give it. But the price one pays for such freedom is the recognition that language, thus viewed, is endlessly duplicatous rather than single-minded (as Tom would have it be); that metaphor is a kind of impropriety or oxymoronic otherness; and that 'we can so seldom declare what a thing is, except by saying it is something else'.

Error, then, must creep in where there's a story to tell, especially a woman's story. Maggie's 'wrong-doing and absurdity', as the fall of women often does, not only puts her on the side of error in Tom's scheme of things but gives her a history; 'the happiest women', Eliot reminds us, 'like the happiest nations, have no history' (p. 494). Impropriety and metaphor belong together on the same side as a fall from absolute truth or unitary schemes of knowledge (maxims). Knowledge in *The Mill on the Floss* is guarded by a traditional patriarchal prohibition which, by a curious slippage, makes the fruit itself as indigestible as the ban and its thick rind. The adolescent Maggie, 'with her soul's hunger and her illusions of self-flattery', begins 'to nibble at this thick-rinded fruit of the tree of knowledge, filling her vacant hours with Latin, geometry, and the forms of the syllogism' (p. 380). But the Latin, Euclid and Logic, which Maggie imagines 'would surely be a considerable step in masculine wisdom', leave her dissatisfied, like a thirsty traveler in a trackless desert. What does Eliot substitute for this mental diet? After Maggie's chance discovery of Thomas à Kempis, we're told that 'the old books, Virgil, Euclid and Aldrich – that wrinkled fruit of the tree of knowledge – had been all laid by' for a doctrine that announces: 'And if he should attain to all knowledge, he is yet far off' (pp. 387, 383). Though the fruits of patriarchal knowledge no longer seem worth the eating, can we view Thomas à Kempis as anything more than an opiate for the hunger pains of oppression? Surely not. The morality of submission and renunciation is only a sublimated version of Tom's plain-spoken patriarchal prohibition, as the satanic mocker, Philip Wakem, doesn't fail to point out. Yet in the last resort, Eliot makes her heroine live and die by this inherited morality of female suffering – as if, in the economy of the text, it was necessary for Maggie to die renouncing in order for her author to release the flood of desire that is language itself.[16] Why?

The Mill on the Floss gestures toward a largely unacted error, the elopement with Stephen Guest which would have placed Maggie finally outside the laws of St Ogg's. Instead of this unrealized fall, we are offered

a moment of attempted transcendence in the timeless death embrace which abolishes the history of division between brother and sister – 'living through again in one supreme moment, the days when they had clasped their little hands in love' (p. 655). What is striking about the novel's ending is its banishing not simply of division but of sexual difference as the origin of that division. The fantasy is of a world where brother and sister might roam together, 'indifferently', as it were, without either conflict or hierarchy. We know that their childhood was not like that at all, and we can scarcely avoid concluding that death is a high price to pay for such imaginary union. In another sense, too, the abolition of difference marks the death of desire for Maggie; 'The Last Conflict' (the title of the book's closing chapter) is resolved by her final renunciation of Guest, resolved, morever, with the help of 'the little old book that she had long ago learned by heart' (p. 648). Through Thomas à Kempis, Eliot achieves a simultaneous management of both knowledge and desire, evoking an 'invisible' or 'supreme teacher' within the soul, whose voice promises 'entrance into that satisfaction which [Maggie] had so long been craving in vain' (p. 384). Repressing the problematic issue of book learning, this 'invisible teacher' is an aspect of the self which one might call the voice of conscience or, alternatively, sublimated maxims.
In 'the little old book', Maggie finds the authorized version of her own and Eliot's story, 'written down by a hand that waited for the heart's prompting . . . the chronicle of a solitary, hidden anguish . . . a lasting record of human needs and human consolations, the voice of a brother who, ages ago, felt and suffered and renounced' (pp. 384–5).

Where might we look for an alternative version or, for that matter, for another model of difference, one that did not merely substitute unity for division and did not pay the price of death or transcendence? Back to the schoolroom, where we find Tom painfully committing to memory the *Eton Grammar*'s 'Rules for the Genders of Nouns', the names of trees being feminine, while some birds, animals, and fish '*dicta epicoena* . . . are said to be epicene'.[17] In epicene language, as distinct from language imagined as either neutral or androgynous, gender is variable at will, a mere metaphor. The rules for the genders of nouns, like prescriptions about 'masculine' or 'feminine' species of knowledge, are seen to be entirely arbitrary. Thus the lament of David for Saul and Jonathan can be appropriated as the epitaph of brother and sister ('In their death they were not divided'), and 'the voice of a brother who, ages ago, felt and suffered and renounced' can double as the voice of a sister-author, the passionately epicene George Eliot. One answer, then, to my earlier question (why does Eliot sacrifice her heroine to the morality of renunciation?) is that Eliot saw in Thomas à Kempis a language of desire but desire managed as knowledge is also managed – sublimated, that is, not as renunciation but as writing. In such epicene writing, the woman writer finds herself in metaphor.

For Irigaray, the price paid by the woman writer for attempting to inscribe the claims of women 'within an order prescribed by the masculine' may ultimately be death; the problem as she sees it is this: '[How can we] disengage ourselves, *alive*, from their concepts?'[18] The final, lyrical chapter of *This Sex Which Is Not One*, 'When Our Lips Speak Together', is, or tries to be, the alternative she proposes. It begins boldly: 'If we keep on speaking the same language together, we're going to reproduce the same history' (p. 205). This would be a history of disappropriation, the record of the women writer's self loss as, attempting to swallow or incorporate an alien language, she is swallowed up by it in turn:

> Outside, you try to conform to an alien order. Exiled from yourself, you fuse with everything you meet. You imitate whatever comes close. You become whatever touches you. In your eagerness to find yourself again, you move indefinitely far from yourself. From me. Taking one model after another, passing from master to master, changing face, form, and language with each new power that dominates you. You/we are sundered; as you allow yourself to be abused, you become an impassive travesty.
>
> (p. 210)

This, perhaps, is what Miller means by 'a posture of imposture', the uncomfortable posture of all woman writers in our culture, within and without the text'.[19] Miming has become absorption into an alien order. One thinks of Maggie, a consumer who is in turn consumed by what she reads, an imitative 'apparatus' who, like the alienated women imagined by Irigaray, can only speak their desire as 'spoken machines, speaking machines'. Speaking the same language, spoken in the language of the Same ('If we keep on speaking sameness, if we speak to each other as men have been doing for centuries, as we have been taught to speak, we'll miss each other, fail ourselves'), she can only be reproduced as the history of a fall or a failure (p. 205). Eliot herself, of course, never so much as gestures toward Irigaray's jubilant utopian love language between two women – a language of desire whose object ('my indifferent one') is that internal (in)difference which, in another context, Barbara Johnson calls 'not a difference between . . . but a difference within. Far from constituting the text's unique identity, it is that which subverts the very idea of identity.' What is destroyed, conceptually, is the 'unequivocal domination of one mode of signifying over another'.[20] Irigaray's experiment in 'When Our

Lips Speak Together' is of this kind, an attempt to release the subtext of female desire, thereby undoing repression and depriving metalanguage of its claim to truth. 'The exhausting labor of copying, miming' is no longer enough (p. 207).

But for all Irigaray's experimentalism, the 'difference' is not to be located at the level of the sentence, as Miller reminds us.[21] Rather, what we find in 'When Our Lips Speak Together' is writing designed to indicate the cultural determinants that bound the woman writer and, for Irigaray, deprive her of her most fundamental relationship: her relationship to herself. In fact, what seems most specifically 'feminine' about Irigaray's practice is not its experimentalism as such but its dialogue of one/two, its fantasy of the two-in-one: 'In *life* they are not divided', to rephrase David's lament. The lips that speak together (the lips of female lovers) are here imagined as initiating a dialogue not of conflict or reunion, like Maggie and Tom's, but of mutuality, lack of boundaries, continuity. If both Irigaray and Eliot kill off the woman engulfed by masculine logic and language, both end also – and need to end – by releasing a swirl of (im)possibility:

> These rivers flow into no single, definitive sea. These streams are without fixed banks, this body without fixed boundaries. This unceasing mobility. This life – which will perhaps be called our restlessness, whims, pretenses, or lies. All this remains very strange to anyone claiming to stand on solid ground.
>
> (p. 215)

Is that, finally, why Maggie must be drowned, sacrificed as a mimetic 'apparatus' (much as the solidity of St Ogg's is swept away) to the flood whose murmuring waters swell the 'low murmur' of Maggie's lips as they repeat the words of Thomas à Kempis? When the praying Maggie feels the flow of water at her knees, the literal seems to have merged with a figural flow; as Eliot writes, 'the whole thing had been so rapid – so dream-like – that the threads of ordinary association were broken' (p. 651). It is surely at this moment in the novel that we move most clearly into the unbounded realm of desire, if not of wish fulfillment. It is at this moment of inundation, in fact, that the thematics of female desire surface most clearly.[22]

We will look in vain for a specifically feminine linguistic practice in *The Mill on the Floss*; 'a possible operation of the feminine in language' is always elsewhere, not yet, not here, unless it simply reinscribes the exclusions, confines and irregularities of Maggie's education. But what we may find in both Eliot and Irigaray is a critique which gestures beyond cultural boundaries, indicating the perimeters within which their writing is produced. For the astronomer who hates women in general, the feminist critic may wish to substitute an author who vindicates one woman in particular or, like Irigaray, inscribes the claims of all women. In part a critic of ideology, she will also want to uncover the ways in which maxims or *idées reçues* function in the service of institutionalizing and 'maximizing' misogyny, or simply deny difference. But in the last resort, her practice and her theory come together in Eliot's lament about metaphor – 'that we can so seldom declare what a thing is, except by saying it is something else'. The necessary utopianism of feminist criticism may be the attempt to declare what is by saying something else – that 'something else' which presses both Irigaray and Eliot to conclude their very different works with an imaginative reaching beyond analytic and realistic modes to the metaphors of unbounded female desire in which each finds herself as a woman writing.

Notes

1. Luce Irigaray, 'The Power of Discourse and the Subordination of the Feminine', *This Sex Which Is Not One*, Catherine Porter, trans. (Ithaca: Cornell University Press, 1985), p. 81.
2. See Hélène Cixous, 'The Laugh of the Medusa', Elaine Marks and Isabelle de Courtivron (eds), *New French Feminisms*, pp. 245–64 (Amherst: University of Massachusetts Press, 1980). The implications of such definitions of *'écriture féminine'* are discussed briefly in 'The Difference of View', section II. 1, and by Nancy K. Miller, 'Emphasis Added: Plots and Plausibilities in Women's Fiction', Publications of the Modern Language Association (*PMLA*) (January 1981), 96(1), p. 37; my own essay is indebted to Miller's account of *The Mill on the Floss* in the context of 'women's fiction'.
3. See Irigaray, *This Sex Which Is Not One*, pp. 68–85 *passim*, and her *Speculum of The Other Woman*, (Ithaca: Cornell University Press, 1985), pp. 133–46. See also Carolyn Burke, 'Introduction to Luce Irigaray's "When Our Lips Speak Together",' *Signs* (Autumn 1980), 6(1), p. 71.
4. Miller, Emphasis Added', p. 38.
5. Ibid., p. 46.
6. See Irigaray, *This Sex Which Is Not One*, pp. 74–80 *passim*.
7. Irigaray, *This Sex Which Is Not One*, p. 76.
8. See, for instance, Gilbert and Gubar, 'Toward a Feminist Poetics,' Part I of *The Madwoman in the Attic* (New Haven: Yale University Press, 1979), pp. 3–104; Gilbert and Gubar's is above all a work of literary (her)story.
9. George Eliot, *The Mill on the Floss*, ed A. S. Byatt (Harmondsworth: Penguin, 1979), p. 628; subsequent page references in the text are to this edition. I am escpecially indebted to Byatt's helpful annotations.
10. See Gilbert and Gubar, *The Madwoman in the Attic,* who succinctly state that

Maggie seems 'at her most monstrous when she tries to turn herself into an angel of renunciation' (p. 491), and Gillian Beer, 'Beyond Determinism: George Eliot and Virginia Woolf', in Mary Jacobus, (ed.), *Women Writing and Writing About Women* (London: Croom Helm, 1979), p. 88, on an ending that 'lacks bleakness, is even lubricious' in its realization of 'confused and passionate needs'.

11. '*Mors omnibus est communis* would have been jejune, only [Maggie] liked to know the Latin'; Eliot, *The Mill on the Floss*, pp. 217–18; see below.
12. '*Astronomer: ut* – "as", *astronomus* – "an astronomer", *exosus* – "hating", *mulieres* – "women", *ad unum* [mulierem] – "to one" [that is, in general]. (*Eton Grammar*, 1831 edition, p. 279)'; Eliot, *The Mill on the Floss*, p. 676, note 55.
13. See Virginia Woolf, 'George Eliot', *Collected Essays of Virginia Woolf*, 4 vols, Leonard Woolf (ed), London: Hogarth Press, 1966–67), 1; p. 204: 'With every obstacle against her – sex and health and convention – she sought more knowledge and more freedom till the body, weighted with its double burden, sank worn out.'
14. See Eliot, *The Mill on the Floss*, pp. 675–6, note 44.
15. Aristotle, *Poetics*, 22:16 (my italics); see Eliot, *The Mill on the Floss*, p. 676, *n.* 46. J. Hillis Miller notes apropos of this passage that it 'is followed almost immediately by an ostentatious and forceful metaphor [that of a shrewmouse imprisoned in a split tree (p. 209)], as if Eliot were compelled . . . to demonstrate that we cannot say what a thing is except by saying it is something else'; 'The Worlds of Victorian Fiction', *Harvard English Studies* (1975), 6, p. 145*n*.
16. See Carol Christ, 'Aggression and Providential Death in George Eliot's Fiction', *Novel* (Winter 1976), 9 (2), pp. 130–40, for a somewhat different interpretation.
17. See Eliot, *The Mill on the Floss*, p. 676, note 53.
18. Luce Irigaray, 'When Our Lips Speak Together,' *This Sex Which Is Not One*, p. 212.
19. Miller, 'Emphasis Added', p. 46.
20. Barbara Johnson, *The Critical Difference* (Baltimore: Johns Hopkins University Press, 1981), pp. 4, 5.
21. See Miller, 'Emphasis Added', p. 38.
22. Cf. Gillian Beer, 'Beyond Determinism', in Jacobus, (ed.), *Women Writing and Writing About Women*, p. 88: 'Eliot is fascinated by the unassuageable longings of her heroine. She allows them fulfillment in a form of plot which simply glides out of the channelled sequence of social growth and makes literal the expansion of desire. The river loses its form in the flood.'

7 Life's Empty Pack: Notes toward a Literary Daughteronomy (*Silas Marner*)*

SANDRA M. GILBERT

Sandra M. Gilbert's essay on *Silas Marner* is an ambitious attempt to bring together literary criticism with a wider cultural critique, a significant tendency in much contemporary criticism. Drawing upon Freudian and Lacanian psychoanalytic theory, structuralist anthropology, and contemporary feminist theory, she explores the father–daughter relationship in the novel and argues that it is a culturally crucial text since it reveals the connection between father–daughter incest and patriarchy (see Introduction, pp. 21–2).

No mother gave me birth. Therefore the father's claim
And male supremacy in all things . . .
. . . wins my whole heart's loyalty.

(Athene, in Aeschylus, *The Eumenides*)

If underneath the water
  You comb your golden hair
With a golden comb, my daughter,
  Oh would that I were there!

(Christina Rossetti, 'Father and Lover')

Sad and weary I go back to you, my cold father, my cold mad father, my cold mad feary father . . . I rush, my only, into your arms.

(Anna Livia Plurabelle, in James Joyce, *Finnegans Wake*)

O father, all by yourself
You are pity and historical as the Roman Forum.

(Sylvia Plath, 'The Colossus')

For the first time all of us, men and women alike, can look back on nearly

---

* Reprinted from *Critical Inquiry*, 11 (1985), pp. 355–84.

two centuries of powerful literary ancestresses. Aside from the specifically literary–historical implications of such a phenomenon – an issue that Susan Gubar and I have addressed elsewhere[1] – what effects has this unprecedented situation had? In particular, what paradigms of female sexuality have strong female precursors passed on to other women writers? These are questions I want to begin to address here – specifically, by exploring an aspect of female psychosexual development. A dark, indeed problematic, pattern emerges when we juxtapose the accounts of female maturation and obligation that are offered by theorists like Sigmund Freud and Claude Lévi-Strauss with the meaning that George Eliot's frequently studied *Silas Marner* may have had for the women who are in a sense that powerful literary mother's aesthetic daughters.

I choose Eliot as my paradigm of the female precursor because, as Virginia Woolf put it, she was 'the first woman of the age', a thinker who became, in one historian's words, a 'Man of Ideas', her official importance sanctioned by the biography Woolf's own father dutifully produced for the English Men of Letters Series.[2] At the same time, however, I see Eliot as paradigmatic because her very power – the success that made her into what we call a 'precursor' – evidently disquieted so many of her female contemporaries and descendants. As Elaine Showalter reminds us, 'most nineteenth-century women novelists seem to have found [Eliot] a troubling and demoralizing competitor, one who had created an image of the woman artist they could never equal'. 'George Eliot *looks* awful. Her picture frightens me!' exclaims a character in Elizabeth Robins' novel *George Mandeville's Husband*.[3] Even Eliot's most fervent female admirers, moreover, express ambivalence toward her in the rhetoric through which they try to come to terms with her. Two of these notable Eliotian heiresses are Emily Dickinson and Edith Wharton. Both offer commentaries curiously haunted by ambiguities, and though these commentaries are ostensibly about the writer's life story, they provide a dramatic set of metaphors that can help us interpret the messages these literary daughters extracted from such an apparently 'legendary' story as *Silas Marner*.[4]

In 1883, after having waited with great anxiety to receive a copy of the Eliot biography written by John Walter Cross, the novelist's husband in the last year of her life, Dickinson wrote a thank-you note to the Boston publisher Thomas Niles, in which she succinctly mythologizes the career of her English precursor. 'The Life of Marian Evans had much I never knew', she begins. 'A Doom of Fruit without the Bloom, like the Niger Fig', and a poem follows this strange introduction.

Her Losses make our Gains ashamed—
She bore Life's empty Pack
As gallantly as if the East

Were swinging at her Back.
Life's empty Pack is heaviest,
As every Porter knows—
In vain to punish Honey—
It only sweeter grows.[5]

'A Doom of Fruit without the Bloom.' 'Life's empty Pack.' 'In vain to punish Honey.' These are striking but mysterious phrases. Where do they come from, and what do they mean?

Several remarks by Wharton, though almost equally paradoxical, begin to provide some clarification. Reviewing Leslie Stephen's English Men of Letters Series volume on Eliot, Wharton writes that 'unconsciously, perhaps, [the Victorian novelist] began to use her books as a vehicle of rehabilitation, a means, not of defending her own course, but of proclaiming, with increasing urgency and emphasis, her allegiance to the law she appeared to have violated'. Earlier in her essay, Wharton offers a metaphorical, almost Dickinsonian statement of what she means by 'the law': 'The stern daughter of the voice of God', she writes, 'stands ever at the side of Romola and Dorothea, of Lydgate and Maggie, and lifts even Mr Farebrother and poor Gwendolyn to heights of momentary heroism.'[6]

Putting statements like these together with Woolf's sense of Eliot's success and centrality, we can begin to see why the author of *Silas Marner* was both a paradigmatic and a problematic female precursor. Metaphorically speaking, such a conflation of reactions suggests that Eliot represents the conundrum of the empty pack which until recently has confronted every woman writer. Specifically, this conundrum is the riddle of daughterhood, a figurative empty pack with which – as it has seemed to many women artists – not just every powerful literary mother but every literal mother presents her daughter. For such artists, the terror of the female precursor is not that she is an emblem of power but, rather, that when she achieves her greatest strength, her power becomes self-subverting: in the moment of psychic transformation that is the moment of creativity, the literary mother, even more than the literal one, becomes the 'stern daughter of the voice of God' who paradoxically proclaims her 'allegiance to the law' she herself appears to have violated.

As such a preceptor, the literary mother necessarily speaks both of and for the father, reminding her female child that she is not and cannot be his inheritor: like her mother and like Eliot's Dorothea, the daughter must inexorably become a 'foundress of nothing'.[7] For human culture, says the literary mother, is bound by rules which make it possible for a woman to speak but which oblige her to speak of her own powerlessness, since such rules might seem to constitute what Jacques Lacan calls the 'Law of the Father', the law that means culture is by definition both patriarchal and phallocentric and must therefore transmit the empty pack of disinheritance to every daughter.[8] Not surprisingly, then, even while the literary daughter, like the literal one, desires the matrilineal legitimation incarnated in her precursor/mother, she fears her literary mother: the more fully the mother represents culture, the more inexorably she tells the daughter that she cannot have a mother because she has been signed with and assigned to the Law of the Father.[9] Like Eliot, who aspired to be a 'really cultured woman', this 'culture-mother' uses her knowledge, as Eliot advised in her scornful essay 'Silly Novels by Lady Novelists', 'to form a right estimate of herself' – that is, to put herself (and, by implication, her daughters) in the 'right' place.[10]

This speculation rests of course on syntheses of Freud and Lévi-Strauss that psychoanalytic thinkers like Lacan and Juliet Mitchell have lately produced. Concentrating on the Oedipus complex, such writers have argued that every child enters the language-defined system of kinship exchange that we call 'culture' by learning that he or she cannot remain permanently in the state of nature signified by the embrace of the mother; instead, the child must be assigned a social place denoted by the name (and the Law) of the Father, the potent symbol of human order who disrupts the blissful mother–child dyad. What this means for the boy – a temporary frustration of desire coupled with the promise of an ultimate accession to power – has been elaborately and famously explored by both Freud and Lacan (and also, in a different way, by Lévi-Strauss). What it means for the girl is much less clearly understood; hence, in meditating on the empty pack of daughterhood, I am necessarily improvising both literary and psychoanalytic theory. But my task will, I hope, be made possible by Eliot's status as paradigmatic female precursor, or symbolic culture-mother, and made plausible by the juxtaposition of one of Eliot's texts, *Silas Marner*, with what we might call a revisionary daughter-text, Wharton's *Summer*.

A definition of Eliot as renunciatory culture-mother may seem an odd preface to a discussion of *Silas Marner* since, of all her novels, this richly constructed work is the one in which the empty pack of daughterhood appears fullest, the honey of femininity most unpunished. I want to argue, however, that this 'legendary tale', whose status as a schoolroom classic makes it almost as much a textbook as a novel, examines the relationship between woman's fate and the structure of society in order to explicate the meaning of the empty pack of daughterhood. More specifically, this story of an adoptive father, an orphan daughter, and a dead mother broods on events that are actually or symbolically situated on the margins or boundaries of society, where culture must enter into a dialectical struggle with nature, in order to show how the young female human animal is converted into the human daughter, wife and mother. Finally, then, this fictionalized 'daughteronomy' becomes a female myth of origin narrated by a severe literary mother who uses the vehicle of a half-allegorical family romance to urge acquiescence in the Law of the Father.

If *Silas Marner* is not obviously a story about the empty pack of daughterhood, it is plainly, of course, a 'legendary tale' about a wanderer with a heavy yet empty pack. In fact, it is through the image of the packman that the story, in Eliot's own words, 'came *across* my other plans by a sudden inspiration' – and, clearly, her vision of this burdened outsider is a re-vision of the Romantic wanderer who haunts the borders of society, seeking a local habitation and a name.[11] I would argue further, though, that Eliot's depiction of Silas Marner's alienation begins to explain Ruby Redinger's sense that the author of this 'fluid and metamorphic' story 'is' both Eppie, the redemptive daughter, and Silas, the redeemed father. For in examining the outcast weaver's marginality, this novelist of the 'hidden life' examines also her own female disinheritance and marginality.[12]

Almost everything that we learn about Silas and the tribe of pack-bearing wanderers he represents tends to reinforce our sense that he belongs in what anthropologists call a 'liminal zone'.[13] Pallid, undersized, alien-looking, he is one of the figures ordinary country folk see at the edges of time and place – 'on the upland, dark against the early winter sunset', 'far away among the lanes, or deep in the bosom of the hills'. As a weaver, moreover, he is associated with those transformations that take place on the borders of culture – activities that seem to partake 'of the nature of conjuring'.[14] Again, he is liminal because, both shortsighted and cataleptic, he cannot participate meaningfully in the social world. That he dwells on the edge of Raveloe, near the disused Stone-pits, and never strolls 'into the village to drink a pint at [the local pub called] the Rainbow' further emphasizes his alienation, as does the story of his Job-like punishment when the casting of lots in Lantern Yard 'convicted' him of a theft he had not committed (*SM*, 1. 1). Finally, his obsessive hoarding, in which gold is drained of all economic signification, reduces the currency of society to absurdity, further emphasizing his alienation.

Considering all these deprivations and denials of social meaning, it is no wonder that this wanderer's pack seems to be heavy with emptiness. Psychologically, moreover, it is no wonder that Eliot in some sense 'is' the Silas whom we first encounter at the Stone-pits, if only because through him she examines the liminality that Marian Evans experienced in fact and Maggie Tulliver in fiction. Her own metaphors frequently remind us, furthermore, that just as he weaves textiles, she 'weaves' texts – and at the time his story 'thrust itself' into the loom of her art, her texts were turning to gold as surely (and as problematically) as his textiles did.[15] In addition, as the man without a place, Silas carries with him the dispossession that she herself had experienced as part of the empty pack of daughterhood.

Perhaps, indeed, it is because he shares to some extent in what Sherry Ortner has seen as woman's liminal estate that Silas is often associated not only with the particulars of Marian Evans' femaleness but also with a number of socially defined female characteristics, including a domestic expertise which causes him, in the words of one Raveloer, to be 'partly as handy as a woman' (*SM*, 1. 14).[16]

Paradoxically, however, it is his handily maternal rearing of Eppie that redeems Silas as a *man* even while his transformation from outcast to parent reflects a similar but more troubled metamorphosis that Marian Evans was herself undergoing at the time she wrote the novel. Significantly, at the moment the plot of *Silas Marner* began to 'unfold' in her mind, George Eliot was becoming a 'mother' to George Henry Lewes' children. But where her ambiguous status as 'mother' of 'a great boy of eighteen . . . as well as two other boys, almost as tall' isolated her further from the society that had cast her out, Silas' status as father of a golden-haired daughter definitively integrates him into a community that had previously thought him diabolic.[17] His transformations of role and rank, therefore, suggest at least one kind of redemption a fallen literary woman might want to imagine for herself: becoming a father.

Silas' redemptive fatherhood, which originates at Christmastime, is prepared for by Eliot's long meditation on the weaver's relationship to his gold, perhaps the most compelling passage of psychological analysis in the novel and the one that most brilliantly propounds the terms of the submerged metaphor that is to govern the book's dramatic action. For the miser, as I noted earlier, what would ordinarily be a kind of language that links members of society is empty of signification and therefore not only meaningless but dead-ended. Halted, static, even regressive, the currency does not flow: nothing goes out into the world, and therefore nothing returns.[18] Silas' history is thus a history without a story because it is without characters – without, that is, both persons and signifiers. Yet its terror consists not merely in the absence of meaning but in the presence of empty matter: the shining purposeless heaps of coins which 'had become too large for the iron pot to hold them' (*SM*, 1. 2). It is this mass of lifeless matter that must be imprinted with vital signification if the outcast weaver is to be resurrected and redeemed. And ultimately, indeed, Silas' transformation from fall to fatherhood is symbolized, in a kind of upside-down myth of Midas, by the metamorphosis of his meaningless gold into a living and meaningful child, a child whose Christmas coming marks her as symbolically divine but whose function as divine daughter rather than sacred son is to signify, rather than to replace, the power of her newly created father.

To make way for Eppie, who is his gold made meaningful, Silas must first, of course, be separated from his meaningless gold. What is surely most important about this loss, however, is that the absence of the gold forces the miser to confront the absence that his gold represented. In addition, if we think of this blank, this empty pack, in relation to the Christmas myth for which Eliot is preparing us, we can see that Silas' dark night of the soul is the long dark night of the winter solstice, when dead matter must be kindled and dead flesh made Word if culture is to survive. That 'the invisible wand of catalepsy' momentarily freezes the weaver in his open doorway on the crucial New Year's Eve that is to lead to his resurrection merely emphasizes this point. His posture is that of the helpless virgin who awaits annunciation 'like a graven image . . . powerless to resist either the good or evil that might enter there' (*SM*, 1. 12).

Because it depends on drastic role reversals, however, Eliot's deliberate parody by the Christmas story suggests that she is half-consciously using the basic outlines of a central culture myth to meditate not on the traditionally sanctified relationship of Holy Mother and Divine Son but on another, equally crucial, bond – that of Holy Father and Divine Daughter. In doing so, she clarifies for herself and for her readers the key differences between sonship and daughterhood. For when the divine child is a son he is, as the Christian story tells us, an active spiritual agent for his mother. To put the matter in a Freudian or Lacanian way, he is the 'Phallus' for her, an image of sociocultural as well as sexual power.[19] But when the divine child is a daughter, or so the story of Silas Marner tells us, she is a treasure, a gift the father is given so that he can give it to others, thereby weaving himself into the texture of society. To put the matter in a Lévi-Straussian way, she is the currency whose exchange constitutes society, a point Eliot stunningly anticipated in her submerged metaphor of the girl who is not only as good as but better than gold because her very existence is a pot of gold not at the end but at the beginning of the Rainbow covenant between man and man.

This last allusion is, of course, a reference to the central notion of *The Elementary Structures of Kinship*, in which Lévi-Strauss argues that both the social order, which distinguishes culture from nature, and the incest taboo, which universally manifests the social order, are based upon the exchange of women.[20] In this anthropological view, a daughter is a treasure whose potential passage from man to man insures psychological and social well-being: if the very structure of a patrilineage guarantees that ultimately, inexorably, a man's son will *take* his place and his name, it also promises that a daughter will never be such a usurper since she is an instrument – rather than an agent – of culture. In fact, because she is the father's wealth, his treasure, she is what he *has*, for better or worse.

That Silas christens his Christmas child 'Hephzibah' dramatizes this point even while it begins to weave him deeply into the common life of 'Bible names' and knit him back into his own past (*SM*, 1. 14). 'Hephzibah', or 'Eppie,' was the name of both Silas' mother and his sister:

in gaining a new Hephzibah, he has regained the treasure of all his female kin. Even more significantly, the name itself, drawn from Isaiah, refers to the title Zion will be given after the coming of the Messiah. Literally translated as 'my delight is in her', 'Hephzibah' magically signifies both a promised land and a redeemed land (see Isaiah 62:4 and 5). Diffusely female, this delightful land incarnates the treasure that is possessed and exchanged by male citizens, and therefore it represents the culture that is created by the covenant between man and man as well as between God and man. A philological fact upon which Eliot herself once meditated enriches further such an association. According to an etymology given by the *Oxford English Dictionary* and based upon Grimm's law, the Anglo-Saxon word 'daughter' can be traced back to the Indo-European root *dhugh*, meaning 'to milk'. Hence, this daughter named Hephzibah is not only milkmaid but milk-giver, she who nurtures as well as she who is nurtured – for, as defined by the Law and reinforced by the lexicon of the Father, a daughter *is* the promised land of milk and honey, the gift of wealth that God the Father gives to every human father.[21]

Most of these points are made quite explicit in the concern with weddings that permeates *Silas Marner*, a concern which surfaces in the famous conversation that happens to be taking place at the Rainbow Tavern just when Silas is discovering the loss of his gold. Old Mr Macey, the parish clerk, is recounting the story of the Lammeter marriage, a ceremony in which the minister got his phrases oddly turned around. The tale asks the question, 'Is't the meanin' or the words as makes folks fast i' wedlock?' and answers that 'it's neither the meaning nor the words – it's the regester does it – that's the glue' (*SM*, 1. 6). But of course, as we learn by the end of *Silas Marner*, it is the very idea of the wedding itself, the having and giving of the daughter, that is the glue.[22] For as Silas and Eppie, Aaron and Dollie parade through Raveloe on their way back to Silas' enlarged cottage after Eppie's marriage to Aaron, the harmony of the bridal party contrasts strikingly with our memory of Silas' former isolation. In marrying Aaron, Silas' daughter has married Silas – married him both to the world and to herself.[23] What had been the 'shrunken rivulet' of his love has flowed into a larger current and a dearer currency, a treasure he has given so that it can return to him. And it has returned: 'O father', says Eppie, just as if she had married *him*, 'What a pretty home ours is' (*SM*, 'Conclusion'). Unlike that other Romantic wanderer, the Ancient Mariner, Silas Marner is a member of the wedding. But then, the Ancient Mariner never got the Christian Christmas gift of a daughter.

How does the gift feel about herself, however? What does it mean to Eppie to mean all this for Silas? Certainly Eliot had long been concerned with the social significance and cultural possibilities of daughterhood. Both *The Mill on the Floss* – the novel that precedes *Silas Marner* – and *Romola* – the one that follows it – are elaborate examinations of the structural inadequacies of a daughter's estate. As for Marian Evans, moreover, her real life had persistently confronted her with the problematic nature of daughterhood and its corollary condition, sisterhood. As biographers have shown, her feelings for her own father were ambivalent not only during his lifetime but throughout hers; yet his superegoistic legacy pervaded other relationships she formed. When she was in her early twenties, for instance, she became a dutiful disciple to the Casaubon-like Dr Brabant, who 'punningly baptized her *Deutera* because she was to be a second daughter to him'.[24] And even when she was a middle-aged woman, she remembered her older brother Isaac as a kind of miniature father, 'a Like unlike, a Self that self restrains', observing wistfully that 'were another childhood-world my share, / I would be born a little sister there'.[25] Since 'Eppie' was the name of Silas' little sister, it seems likely that, in being 'born' again to the mild weaver, Marian Evans did in fiction if not in fact re-create herself as both daughter and little sister.

Certainly Eppie's protestations of daughterly devotion suggest that she is in some sense a born-again daughter. 'I should have no delight i' life any more if I was forced to go away from my father,' she tells Nancy and Godfrey Cass (*SM*, 2. 19). Like the Marian Evans who became 'Deutera', Eppie is not so much a second daughter as twice a daughter – a doubly daughterly daughter. As such a 'Deutera', she is the golden girl whose being reiterates those cultural commandments Moses set forth for the second time in Deuteronomy. Thus, although scrupulous Nancy Lammeter Cass has often been seen as articulating Eliot's moral position on the key events of this novel, it is really the more impulsive Eppie who is the conscience of the book.

This becomes clearest when Nancy argues that 'there's a duty you owe to your lawful father'. Eppie's instant reply, with its counterclaim that 'I can't feel as I've got any father but one', expresses a more accurate understanding of the idea of fatherhood (*SM*, 2. 19). For in repudiating *God-free* Cass, who is only by chance (*casus*) her natural father, and affirming Silas Marner, who is by choice her cultural father, Eppie rejects the lawless father in favor of the lawful one, indicating her clear awareness that fatherhood itself is both *a* social construct (or, in Stephen Dedalus' words, 'a legal fiction') and *the* social construct that constructs society.[26] Having achieved and acted on this analysis, she is rewarded with a domestic happiness which seems to prove Dickinson's contention that it is 'vain to punish Honey, / It only sweeter grows'. At the same time, in speaking such a law, this creature of milk and honey initiates the re-education and redemption of Godfrey Cass: the cultural code of Deuteronomy speaks through her, suggesting that, even if she is a Christmas child, she is as much a daughter of the Old Testament as of the New, of the first telling of the law as of its second telling.[27]

Happy and dutiful as she is, however, Eppie is not perfectly contented, for she has a small fund of anxiety that is pledged to her other parent – her lost mother. This intermittent sadness, which manifests itself as a preoccupation with her mother's wedding ring, directs our attention to a strange disruption at the center of *Silas Marner*: the history of Eppie's dead mother. On the surface, of course, the ring that Silas has saved for his adopted daughter is an aptly ironic symbol of that repressed plot, since there never was any bond beyond an artificial one between Molly Farren and Godfrey Cass, the lawless father 'of whom [the ring] was the symbol'. But Eppie's frequent ruminations on the questions of 'how her mother looked, whom she was like, and how [Silas] had found her against the furze bush' suggest that there is something more problematic than a traditional bad marriage at issue here (*SM*, 2. 16). As so often in this 'legendary tale', what seems like a moral point also offers an eerily accurate account of what Freud sees as the inexorable psychosexual growth and entry of the daughter into a culture shaped by the codes of the father. 'Our insight into [the pre-Oedipus] phase in the little girl's development comes to us as a surprise, comparable . . . with . . . the discovery of the Minoan–Mycenaean civilization behind that of Greece', remarks Freud, explaining that 'everything connected with this first mother-attachment has . . . seemed to me . . . lost in a past so dim and shadowy . . . that it seemed as if it had undergone some specially inexorable repression'.[28]

Indeed, Molly Farren *has* undergone a 'specially inexorable repression' in this novel. Three or four pages of a single chapter are devoted to her, though her damned and doomed wanderings in the snow strikingly recapitulate the lengthier wanderings of fallen women like Hetty Sorrel and Maggie Tulliver. I suggest that Eliot attempts this drastic condensation precisely because *Silas Marner*, in allowing her to speak symbolically about the meaning of daughterhood, also allowed her to speak in even more resonant symbols about the significance of motherhood. What she said was what she saw: that it is better to be a daughter than a mother and better still to be a father than a daughter. For when the Deuteronomy of culture formulates the incest laws that lie at the center of human society, that severe code tells the son: 'You may not have your mother; you may not kill your father.' But when it is translated into a 'Daughteronomy' preached for the growing girl, it says: 'You must bury your mother; you must give yourself to your father.'[29] Since the daughter has inherited an empty pack and cannot *be* a father, she has no choice but to be *for* the father – to be his treasure, his land, his voice.

Yet, as Eliot shows, the growing girl is haunted by her own difficult passage from mother to father, haunted by the primal scene in the snow when she was forced to turn away from the body of the mother, the emblem of nature which can give only so much and no more, and seek the hearth of the father, the emblem of culture that must compensate for nature's inadequacies.[30] This moment is frozen into the center of *Silas Marner* like the dead figure of Molly Farren Cass, whose final posture of self-abandonment brings about Eppie's 'effort to regain the pillowing arm and bosom; but mammy's ear was deaf, and the pillow seemed to be slipping away backward' (*SM*, 1. 12). Indeed, for women the myth that governs personality may be based on such a moment, a confrontation of the dead mother that is as enduring and horrifying to daughters as Freud (in *Totem and Taboo*) claimed the nightmare of the dead father was to sons. Finally, the garden that Eppie and Silas plant at the end of the novel memorializes this moment. '"Father",' says the girl 'in a tone of gentle gravity . . . , "we shall take the furze bush into the garden"' – for it was against the bush that Molly died (*SM*, 2. 16). Now, fenced in by the garden of the law, the once 'straggling' bush will become a symbol of nature made meaningful, controlled and confined by culture (*SM*, 1. 12).

In the end, then, it is Silas Marner, the meek weaver of Raveloe, who inherits the milk and honey of the earth, for he has affirmed the Law of the Father that weaves kin and kindness together. Not coincidentally, when Silas' adopted daughter's engagement to Aaron knits him definitively into the world, Dunstan Cass' skeleton is uncovered and the gold is restored: since Silas has been willing to give his treasure to another, his treasure is given back to him. The intricate web of nemesis and apotheosis that Eliot has woven around Silas reminds us, moreover, that the very name 'Raveloe' preserves two conflicting meanings along with an allegorical pun on the word 'law'. According to *Webster's*, to 'ravel' means both to 'entangle' or 'make intricate' and to '*un*ravel' or 'disentangle'. And indeed, in this 'legendary' domain the nots and knots of the law are unraveled – untangled and clarified – in an exemplary manner, even while the *Ravel* or entanglement of the *Law* weaves people together with Rainbow threads of custom and ceremony.

Finally, too, all is for the best in this domain because this tale of ravelings and unravelings has been told both by and about a daughter of wisdom. Indeed, though Silas as Job is, of course, no Jove and the daughter of his single parenthood is no Minerva, the structure of the relationship between innocently wise Eppie and her lawful father repeats the structure of the relationship between the goddess of wisdom and her law-giving father, just as the frozen burial of Molly Farren Cass affirms the fateful judgment of *The Oresteia* that the mother 'is not the true parent of the child / Which is called hers'.[31] In Hélène Cixous's wry words, there is 'no need for mother – provided that there is something of the maternal: and it is the father then who acts as – is – the mother'.[32] With no Eumenides in sight, the redeemed land of Raveloe belongs to fathers and daughters. It is no wonder that Wharton begins her revisionary *Summer* with Charity Royall, an angry transformation of Eppie, trapped in a library ruled by a plaster bust of Minerva.

Writing to Wharton in 1912 about *The Reef*, perhaps the most Jamesian of her novels, Henry James thought of Eliot and suggested that his friend's revisionary clarification of Eliot's message was so radical that the American writer had made herself, metaphorically speaking, into her English culture-mother's primordial precursor. 'There used to be little notes in you that were like fine benevolent finger-marks of the good George Eliot – the echo of much reading of that excellent woman', he told Wharton. 'But now you are like a lost and recovered "ancient" whom *she* might have got a reading of (especially were he a Greek) and of whom in *her* texture some weaker reflection were to show.'[33] In fact, James' remarks were more prophetic than analytic, for if the not altogether successful *Reef* was quasi-Jamesian rather than proto-Eliotian, the brilliantly coherent *Summer* does surface the *Ur*-myth, and specifically the dark 'Daughteronomy', on which *Silas Marner* is based.

It may seem odd to argue that *Summer*, a sexy story of an illicit love affair, has anything in common with Eliot's pedagogically respectable *Silas Marner*. Yet, like *Silas Marner*, *Summer* is a family romance which also incorporates a female *Bildungsroman*, the account of a daughter's growth to maturity. As in *Silas Marner*, too, both the covert symbolic romance and the overt educational *roman* are resolved through the relationship between an adopted daughter and a man who seems to act as both her father and her mother. Again, like *Silas Marner*, *Summer* broods on the winter of civilization's discontent and the summer of reproduction; in doing so, moreover, Wharton's romance, like Eliot's fable, explores events that are situated on the margins of society, where culture must enter into a dialectical struggle with nature in order to transform 'raw' female reality into 'cooked' feminine sex roles.[34] In addition, as a corollary of this exploration, *Summer*, like *Silas Marner*, traces the redemption that the father achieves through his possession of the daughter. Finally, therefore, the two novels illuminate each other with striking reciprocity: in the conciliatory coziness with which it evades desire, *Silas Marner* is the story Wharton might have liked to tell, while in the relentless rigor with which it renounces desire, *Summer* is the tale Eliot may have feared to confront.

As James' remark about her 'ancient' quality implied, Wharton had begun to become a fierce mythologist by the time she wrote this short novel; in particular, she had started to read Joseph Conrad, whose grasp of archaic symbolism she much admired and imported into *Summer*, strengthening her implicit reading of *Silas Marner* with a quest plot that mimics the psychic journey at the heart of his *Heart of Darkness*. Thus, as my epigraph from Sylvia Plath's poem 'The Colossus' is meant to suggest, 'a blue sky out of the Oresteia' does arch over *Summer*, infusing and illuminating every detail of a mythic narrative that revolves around three figures: a father who 'all by [himself is] pithy and historical as the Roman Forum', a daughter who marries the 'winter of [his] year' as helplessly as Aeschylus' Electra or Plath's 'Electra on Azalea Path' marry the shadow of Agamemnon, and a dead mother who must be as definitively consigned to barren ground as Clytemnestra or the Eumenides.[35] Appropriately enough, therefore, *Summer* begins as its heroine, teenage Charity Royall, walks down the main street of the New England village of North Dormer to her part-time job in a library presided over by a plaster cast of 'sheep-nosed' Minerva,[36] the divine daddy's girl who resolved *The Oresteia* by ruling in favor of 'the father's claim / And male supremacy in all things'. A representative of nature bewildered by culture, Charity is a sort of foundling who, we learn, was 'brought down' from a nearby mountain (always mysteriously called 'the Mountain', with an ominous capital *M*) when she was very little, an origin which places her among the 'humblest of the humble even in North Dormer, where to come from the Mountain was the worst disgrace'. At the same time, however, both her job as librarian and the odd fact that she keeps the lace she is making 'wound about the buckram back of a disintegrated copy of "The Lamp-lighter"' significantly qualify her humbleness (*S*, pp. 22, 14). For, like Eliot's Eppie and like Gerty, the heroine of Maria Cummins' 1854 best-seller, Wharton's Charity is the ward of a solitary older man who dotes on and delights in her youth, her dependence.[37]

Where both Eliot's Silas Marner and Cummins' Trueman Flint are sympathetic men almost from the first, however, Charity's guardian is an equivocal figure, and his difference begins to reveal the secret dynamics such apparently divergent works as Cummins' and Eliot's novels share with Wharton's. For Lawyer Royall, says the narrator of *Summer*, 'ruled in North Dormer; and Charity ruled in lawyer Royall's house. . . . But she knew her power, knew what it was made of, and hated it.' *Lawyer* Royall: so far as we know, this 'magnificent monument of a man' has no other name (*S*, pp. 23, 27). Indeed, as Charity's father/guardian/suitor and (eventually) husband, he is, ultimately, no more than the role his professional title and allegorical surname together denote: a regal law-giver, a mythologized superego whose occupation links him with the library and with culture, that is, with the complex realm of patriarchal history that both puzzles and imprisons the wild child he is trying to make into a desirable daughter/bride.

Even while he is a 'towering' public man, however, Lawyer Royall is a notably pathetic private man. From the first, Wharton deconstructs the colossus of the father to make explicit the ways in which this paradigmatic patriarch is as dependent on his Charity as Silas Marner was on his Eppie or, indeed, as Agamemnon was on Iphigenia or Electra,

Oedipus on Antigone and Ismene, or the biblical Jephthah on his (nameless) daughter. To begin with, we learn that Charity had long ago perceived Lawyer Royall as 'too lonesome' for her to go away to school (*S*, p. 26); later, more dramatically, we discover that his 'lonesomeness' manifested itself in an abortive attempt to rape her. Finally, we are told that it was this episode which drove the girl to try to establish her independence by taking her deathly job in the library. But, of course, this attempt at escape, as in some Sophoclean case history, simply impels her even more inexorably toward her fate.

For it is in 'Minerva's' library that Charity meets her lover-to-be, a handsome architect named Lucius Harney – a far more glamorously equivocal representative of culture than the aging Lawyer Royall. Town-bred, easy with books, this dashing young man is culture's heir; at the same time, he is a golden boy whose 'lusciousness', as Andrea Hammer has observed, links him to nature, even seems to make him nature's emissary – and that is why *he* is an equivocal figure. Young, sensual, magnetic, he is frequently associated with the grass, the sky, the 'flaming breath' of summer; indeed, he and Charity conduct their affair while he is 'camping' halfway up the Mountain in a little abandoned house surrounded by a fallen fence, 'crowding grasses', and rosebushes that have 'run wild' (*S*, p. 166).[38] That he is often connected in Charity's mind with her mysterious Mountain relative Liff Hyatt, whose initials echo his, seems at first to suggest, moreover, that, like Liff, Lucius is a brother figure – and his earliest advances *are* described as 'more fraternal than lover-like' (*S*, p. 95).[39] Yet, just as Eppie Marner's marriage to the brother figure Aaron also marries her definitively to her father, Silas, so Charity's apparently illegitimate romance with Lucius Harney moves her inexorably into the arms of Lawyer Royall, and this not just because it is Lawyer Royall who marries her to 'rescue' her from unwed motherhood but because it eventually becomes plain that even Lucius Harney's desire for her is entangled in feelings of rivalrous identification with the patriarchally 'majestic' lawyer (see *S*, p. 191).

For Charity, in every sense of that word, must be given to the father. And, as *Summer's* denouement finally makes clear, even while Lucius Harney has seemed to act against the patriarchal Royall, he has also acted *for* the lawyer, appearing as if by magic in the library to deflower Charity and impregnate her so that she is at last ready for the marriage to her guardian that she had earlier persistently refused. Indeed, it is arguable that throughout the affair in which he seems to have functioned as nature's emissary by drawing the girl into the wilderness of her own sexuality, Harney has really perfomed as culture's messenger and, specifically, as a vivid and vital 'Phallus' whose glamour seduces the daughter into the social architecture from which she would otherwise have tried to flee. For in patriarchal marriage, says Wharton's plot, the brother/equal inevitably turns into the father/ruler. Not surprisingly, therefore, when Charity and Lawyer Royall start on their journey toward the allegorically named town of *Nettle*ton, where the girl's sexual initiation began and where she is finally going to be married to her legal guardian, Charity briefly imagines that she is 'sitting beside her lover with the leafy arch of summer bending over them'. But 'this illusion [is] faint and transitory' because it implies a deceptive liberty of desire (*S*, p. 273). As Wharton reluctantly observed, the daughter's summer of erotic content blooms only to prepare her for what Dickinson called 'a Doom of Fruit without the Bloom' – an autumn and winter of civilized discontent in which, like her precursor, the first Mrs Royall, she will be 'sad and timid and weak' (*S*, p. 24). As in Wharton's pornographic 'Beatrice Palmato' fragment – a more melodramatic tale of father–daughter incest which makes overt some of the psychodynamics that even in *Summer* are only covert – the symbolic father will 'reap [the] fruit' borne from the son/lover's deflowering of the daughter.[40]

Charity does, however, make one last frantic effort to flee the wintry prison house of culture that is closing around her, and that is in her wild pilgrimage up the Mountain in search of her mother. As the girl's affair with Lucius Harney has progressed, she has become increasingly concerned about her origins and begun to try, the way Eppie did in *Silas Marner*, to explain to herself what it means both to have and to be a mother. Finally, when she realizes she is pregnant, she also understands that there is 'something in her blood that [makes] the Mountain the only answer to her questioning', and in an astonishing episode, which includes some of the most fiercely imagined scenes in American fiction, she journeys toward the originary heart of darkness where she will find and lose her mother (*S*, p. 236).

Appropriately enough, Charity's mother's name is *Mary* Hyatt. Equally appropriately, Charity arrives in the outlaw community on the Mountain only to discover that the woman has just died. It is as if the very idea of the daughter's quest must necessarily kill her female progenitor, not only to emphasize the unavailability of female power but also to underscore the Oresteian dictum that 'The mother is not the true parent of the child / Which is called hers. She is [merely] a nurse who tends the growth / Of young seed planted by its true parent, the male.'[41] Worse still, this anti-Virgin Mary is not only dead, she is horrifyingly dead, dead 'like a dead dog in a ditch', 'lips parted in a frozen gasp above . . . broken teeth', one leg drawn up under a torn skirt and the other 'swollen glistening leg' flung out, 'bare to the knee', in a death paroxysm that parodies the paroxysm of birth and suggests the nausea of nakedness in which the flesh of the mother expels and repels the flesh of the child (*S*, pp. 250, 248). As Mr Miles, the clergyman who ascends the Mountain only for funerals, prepares to bury the woman's uncoffined body in frozen ground, nameless and indistinguishable squatters, Charity's undefinable relatives, squabble over the pitiful furnishings in the shanty where Mary Hyatt died on a mattress on the floor. Nothing, they say, was hers: 'She never had no bed'; 'And the stove warn't hers.' Nor does the reading of the Bible, the Book of patriarchal Law, offer any hope of redemption for the dead woman. When Mr Miles intones 'yet in my flesh shall I see God', Charity thinks of 'the gaping mouth and stony eyes [and] glistening leg', and when he proposes that Jesus Christ shall change this 'vile body that it may be like unto His glorious body', a last spadeful of earth falls heavily 'on the vile body of Mary Hyatt' (*S*, pp. 251, 255).

Where women poets from Elizabeth Barrett Browning and Emily Dickinson transformed mothers into 'multitudinous mountains sitting in / [A] magic circle, with [a] mutual touch / Electric', and 'Sweet Mountains' into 'Strong Madonnas', Wharton, like her culture-mother George Eliot, saw the mother as blind, deaf, and stony and the maternal Mountain as a place of mourning.[42] As if Eliot anticipated the French feminist psychoanalyst Christiane Olivier's contention that the mirror which man holds toward woman 'contains only the image of a dead woman' and, more specifically, a dead Jocasta, the morbid moment of Molly Farren Cass' death in the snow and her daughter Eppie's discovery that 'mammy's ear was deaf' is – as we saw – frozen into the center of *Silas Marner*.[43] Similarly, frozen into the center of *Summer* is the moment of Mary Hyatt's burial in the snow and her daughter Charity's mortifying discovery that there is no salvation from or for her mother's 'vile body'.

Neither is there salvation or even significant charity for Charity from other women in the novel. To be sure, one of the girl's unnamed relatives – Liff Hyatt's mother – lets her spend the night on a mattress on the floor 'as her dead mother's body had lain', but as that simile suggests, such an act of kindness only promises to induct Charity into the 'passive promiscuity' lived by the matriarchal horde on the Mountain, a life entirely outside the comforts and controls of culture, a life in which the mother – possessionless and unpossessed – is 'glad to have the child go' (*S*, pp. 258, 260). As for the other women, the semi-senile figure of Verena Marsh, the Royalls' housekeeper, 'with her old deaf-looking eyes' foreshadows the blind deaf stony figure of Charity's mother; the 'fallen' Julia Hawes and her impoverished sister Ally, together with the 'indestructible' Annabel Balch, reemphasize women's dependence on male legal and financial protection; and the pseudo-motherly abortionist, Dr Merkel, suggests that a daughter who wants to live apart from the father must kill her baby or else, like Mary Hyatt, be 'cut down' and killed by the 'savage misery' of a life apart from culture (*S*. pp. 155, 254, 259).

Taken together, therefore, the decisions and destinies of all these women italicize Charity's own perception that 'in the established order of things as she [knows] them, [there is] no place for her individual adventure.' In fact, the pregnancy that signals her transformation from girl to woman, from daughter to mother, has so severely depersonalized her that she feels herself 'a mere speck in the lonely circle of the sky'. Like dead Mary Hyatt, she has nothing and is nothing but a vessel for her child; thus the impersonal biological imperative of the coming life is, as Wharton brilliantly puts it, 'like a load that [holds] her down, and yet like a hand that pull[s] her to her feet' (*S*, pp. 235, 264, 265). The annunciation of summer, Charity discovers, inexorably entails the renunciation that is winter, a divestment of desire that definitively prepares her for her final turn toward the rescuing father. Fated to move from father to library to lover to father, she goes to Nettleton and marries her guardian. And by now even the Romantic nature she had experienced with her lover has been transmuted into culture – that is, into a set of cultural artifacts: an engraving of a couple in a boat that decorates her bridal chamber, and a pin set with a lake blue gem which implies that in the bloomless winter of her maturity the lake itself must turn to stone.

But if a stone is all Charity has, Charity is what Lawyer Royall has, an emblem of redemption that he needs as much as Silas Marner needs 'his' Eppie. For if, as Freud argues, the girl arrives at 'the ultimate normal feminine attitude in which she takes her father as love-object' only after 'a lengthy process of [symbolically castrating] development' ('FS,' p. 199) which, in Helene Deutsch's words, 'drive[s]' her 'into her constitutionally predetermined passive role', then the daughter's desire for the father must be understood to be, like Charity's need for Lawyer Royall, constructed by a patriarchal order that forces her to renounce what might be more 'natural' desires – for lover/brother, for mother, for self.[44] But as the ambiguous allegory of Charity's name suggests, the father's desire for the daughter is inevitable, a desire not only to give but to receive charity. Standing outside the girl's room after proposing to her (and being rejected) for the second time, Lawyer Royall seems to understand this: 'His hand on the door knob[,] "Charity!" he plead[s]' (*S*, p. 119). For not only is the 'daughter' a milk-giving creature, a suitably diminished and dependent mother, she is also, as a living manifestation of the father's wealth, the charity to which he is culturally entitled.

Finally, therefore, from Charity's point of view, *Summer* is very much a novel about both renunciation and resignation. When her last hope for escape is buried with her mother, she must resign herself, or, rather, reassign herself, to her symbolic father.[45] After her marriage she will be Charity Royall Royall, a name whose redundancy emphasizes the proprietorial power by which her guardian/husband commands her loyalty. But from Lawyer Royall's point of view or, for that matter, from Lucius Harney's, *Summer* is a novel about assignment – that is, about the roles of cultural authority to which men are assigned and about the women who are assigned – marked out, given over – to them to signify that authority. No wonder, then, that Lawyer Royall's first gesture after his marriage to Charity is to give his new bride the munificent sum of forty dollars to buy clothes so that, like an illustration from Thorstein Veblen's *Theory of the Leisure Class*, she will prove his wealth by 'beating' all the other girls 'hollow' (*S*, p. 285). 'Of course, *he's* the book', said Wharton enigmatically about Lawyer Royall.[46] Consciously, she no doubt meant that he is the novel's most complex personality – indeed, its only Jamesian adult – and therefore the only character whose redemption is worth tracing in detail. But, less consciously, she might have meant that, as law-giving patriarch, he is the 'book' in which Charity's fate must be inscribed; for it is, after all, the text of his desire that determines the destiny of hers.

Apart from fictions like *Silas Marner* and *Summer*, what evidence have we that father–daughter incest is a culturally constructed paradigm of female desire? Equally to the point, what proof is there that the father may need, even desire, the daughter at least as much as she needs him? Though psychoanalytic and sociological replies to both these questions have been disputed, many answers have been offered, particularly in recent years. From Phyllis Chesler to Judith Lewis Herman, for instance, feminist theorists have argued that in a patriarchal culture women are encouraged by society, in Chesler's words, 'to commit incest as a way of life'. 'As opposed to marrying our fathers, we marry men like our fathers', Chesler declares, 'men who are older than us, [and] have more money [and] more power [and are taller]'. Similarly, in her study of literal father–daughter incest, Herman claims that 'overt incest represents only the furthest point on a continuum – an exaggeration of patriarchal family norms, but not a departure from them'.[47] Less extravagantly but along the same lines, Nancy Chodorow has observed, following Talcott Parsons, that 'father–daughter incest does not threaten a daughter [with a return to infantile dependency] in the same way' in which 'mother–son incest . . . threatens a son', so that 'mother–son and mother–*daughter* [not father–daughter] incest are the major threats to the formation of new families (as well as to the male-dominant family'.[48]

Nor are any of these views incompatible with Freud's own belief that what he called the 'female Oedipus complex' – the process through which the little girl relinquishes her earliest mother-attachment and transfers her affection to her father – is both the end result of an extraordinarily difficult procedure and, as he puts it, a 'positive' development. Only by a 'very circuitous path', he admits in his late essay 'Female Sexuality' (1931), does the girl 'arrive at the ultimate normal feminine attitude in which she takes her father as love-object'. And because *her* Oedipus complex (unlike the boy's) represents the 'final result of a lengthy process,

. . . it escapes the strong hostile influences which, in men, tend to its destruction' – that is, because the female Oedipus complex is not destroyed but created by the 'castration complex' (which signifies the recognition of sexual difference), many women, in Freud's view, never surmount the female Oedipus complex at all and perhaps never should ('FS', p. 199).

As the researches of Judith Herman and Lisa Hirschman have shown, however, and as Deutsch argued, the desire of the father for the daughter is frequently complicitous, even essential in constructing the desire for him that she manifests in the 'positive' female Oedipus complex. Proposing a theory of what has come to be called 'reciprocal role learning', Deutsch suggested in *The Psychology of Women* that the father functions 'as a seducer, with whose help the girl's aggressive instinctual components are transformed into masochistic ones'.[49] Recent investigators have suggested that girls do 'learn to behave in a feminine fashion through complementing the masculine behavior of their fathers'. Tellingly, though, 'there is no evidence that reciprocal role learning is of any significance in the development of masculinity'.[50] In other words, boys are not encouraged to learn to be boys by responding with precocious virility to seductive behavior by their mothers. This last point, however, leads to my second question – What proof is there that the father needs the daughter at least as much as she needs him? – and to a related query – Why *should* the father desire the daughter? If men have not developed masculinity through reciprocal role learning with mothers, why should they interact 'reciprocally' with their daughters? I have extrapolated from my readings of *Silas Marner* and *Summer* the idea that the father needs the daughter because she is a suitably diminished 'milk-giver', a miniaturized version of the mother whom patriarchal culture absolutely forbids him to desire. Beyond the often ambiguous configurations that shape literary texts like Eliot's and Wharton's, there is considerable evidence that this is so.

The empirical investigations of Herman and Hirschman, for instance, have yielded crucial information: in studying surveys of 'white, predominantly middle-class, urban, educated women', these clinical psychologists discovered that 'between four and twelve percent of all women reported a sexual experience with a relative, and one woman in one hundred reported a sexual experience with her father or stepfather.' Examining individual incest cases, moreover, they learned that, often because of a wife's illness, absence, or alleged frigidity, a father had transferred his affections to his daughter in an attempt 'to continue to receive female nurturance'. More generally, they observed that 'in the father's fantasy life, the daughter becomes the source of all the father's infantile longings for nurturance and care. He thinks of her first as the idealized childhood bride or sweetheart, and finally as the all-good, all-giving mother.' Reasoning both from anthropological studies and from the Bible, they conclude that 'in patriarchal societies [where] the rights of ownership and exchange of women within the family are vested primarily in the father [, t]hese rights find their most complete expression in the father's relationship with his daughter' because – of all female relatives – 'the daughter belongs to the father alone.' They then cite a key passage from Leviticus in which, while forbidding sexual union with every other female blood relative or in-law, 'the patriarchal God sees fit to pass over father–daughter incest in silence.'[51]

Freud's theories of psychoanalysis began, of course, with the hypothesis that just such incest was the root cause of the hysteria manifested by the female patients he and Josef Breuer treated in the 1890s. But traditional interpretations of the history of psychoanalysis propose that, as Dianne Sadoff puts it, 'Freud realized that his female patients' stories of remembered paternal seduction did not necessarily report reality and may have reported fantasy [so that] the scene of paternal seduction retroactively seeks to represent and solve a major enigma confronting the daughter: the origin or upsurge of her sexuality.'[52] In fact, explains O. Mannoni, 'the theory of trauma, of the seduction by the father . . . served as [Freud's] defense against knowledge of the Oedipus complex'.[53] Even the feminist theorist Juliet Mitchell acquiesces in this view, observing that 'the fact that, as Freud himself was well aware, *actual* paternal seduction or rape occurs not infrequently, has nothing to do with the essential concepts of psychoanalysis' (which are, after all, founded on the hypothesis of filial rather than paternal desire) (*PF*, p. 9). Yet, interestingly enough, we have from the Father of Psychoanalysis himself strikingly direct evidence of the reality of paternal desire.

In May 1897, shortly before abandoning his theory that hysteria was caused by paternal seduction or rape, Freud had a dream about 'feeling over-affectionately towards' his oldest daughter, Mathilde. 'The dream', he wrote to his friend Wilhelm Fliess, 'of course fulfills my wish to pin down a father as the originator of neurosis and put an end to my persistent doubts.'[54] Yet, on the one hand, the experience clearly troubled him, while, on the other hand, it does seem to have functioned as a screen for what troubled him even more: the sequence of dreams and memories Freud recorded in the letters of spring–summer 1897 shows that many of the psychic events he examined as part of the self-analysis he was conducting at this time had to do with desires for or anxieties about mature women – his mother or figures for her. The sequence culminated in his crucial speculation that '(between the ages of two and two-and-a-half) libido towards *matrem* was aroused' at a time when he 'had the opportunity of seeing her *nudam*'.[55] Embedded in this dramatic series of reveries is his equally dramatic decision that though 'in every case [of female hysteria] blame was laid on perverse acts by the father . . . it was hardly credible that perverted acts against children were so general', a decision that, despite its negative implications for a career he had been building on theories about paternal seduction, left him feeling inexplicably exhilarated.[56]

Careful analysis of these materials suggests that Freud's brilliant self-interrogations both reveal and conceal a slippage in his thinking. His no doubt accurate discovery of feelings for his mother is quite unaccountably associated with the notion, which he later repudiated, that his female patients would naturally have had equivalent desires for their *fathers*. That even as he surfaced his own Oedipal wishes, he may have disguised them (for instance, reporting awful dreams about an ugly elderly nurse who washed him in 'reddish water') implies his own *resistance* to these wishes, however, a resistance also expressed in his dream of Mathilde. As Mitchell observes, even 'Freud . . . found it more acceptable to be the father than the incest-desiring or rival-castrating son – as do most men' (*PF*, p. 75). Thus the theory of paternal seduction appropriately led to Freud's understanding of the son's desire for the mother, of which the father's desire for the daughter is a belated but more socially acceptable transformation. Nevertheless, the father's desire for the daughter was not so acceptable to Freud that he could persist in his 'wish to pin down a father as the originator of neurosis'.[57] Rather, having admitted his own filial desire, he seems to have wished to 'pin down' daughters as equivalent sources of desire. Yet as his later formulations of female psychosexual development were to suggest, erotic feelings of daughters for fathers symmetrical with those of sons for mothers were not necessarily implicit in the accounts of paternal seduction that he called his patients' 'fantasies'. In fact, as recent reports about the unpublished portions of his letters to Fliess, along with analyses of the alterations and evasions in *Studies on Hysteria* have suggested, Freud himself was, in Mitchell's phrase, 'well aware' that many of these patients were not fantasizing, that they actually had been seduced or in some sense seductively manipulated by their fathers or by father figures. Their 'hysteria' may therefore have constituted not a rejection of their own desire but a refusal of the paternal demands that not only their own families but also their culture defined as psychologically 'right'.[58] Even so early in his career, in other words, Freud's fruitful transformation of speculations about father–daughter seduction into a theory about son–mother incest, with its corollary evasion of a theory of father–daughter desire, expresses his proleptic awareness that he would eventually have to construct a far more complicated model of female psychosexual development in order to trace the girl's 'circuitous path' to what he was to define as mature (heterosexual) femininity.

That path, with its obstacles, its terrors and its refusals, is the road studied in *Silas Marner* and *Summer* – in *Silas Marner's* exploration of the powers the daughter gives the father and in *Summer's* examination of the powers the father takes away from the daughter. But of course countless other literary texts – written by both men and women – focus on the submerged paradigm of father–daughter incest that shapes the plots and possibilities inscribed in these novels. From *The Oresteia*'s repudiation and repression of the matriarchal Furies and its concomitant aggrandizement of Athene, the dutiful father's daughter, to *Oedipus at Colonus*' praise of Antigone and Ismene, the two loyal daughters who have been their father's sole guardians in the blinded exile to which his incestuous marriage with his mother condemned him, Greek literature consistently valorizes such a paradigm. That Oedipus' daughters, in particular, functioned as their father's 'eyes' reminds us, moreover, that 'the word for daughter in Greek is *Kore*, the literal meaning of which is pupil of the eye.'[59] Similarly, the violent obliteration of the mother in these works and many others recalls one version of the story of Athene's origin: after raping Metis the Titaness, the father-god *swallowed her*, having heard that, though she was now pregnant with a daughter, she would bear a son who would depose him if she had another child; then, 'in due time . . . seized by a raging headache', he himself gave birth to Athene, who 'sprang fully armed' from his skull.[60] In just the way that Antigone and Ismene properly replace Jocasta as Oedipus' helpmeets – indeed, as the 'eyes' who, according to Freud, would signify his continuing sexual potency – so Athene supplants Metis as Zeus' true child/bride.

To be sure, these archaic texts enact the prescriptions and proscriptions of patriarchal culture with exceptional clarity; yet such imperatives also underlie a surprising number of other, later works, ranging from Shakespeare's *King Lear* to Percy Bysshe Shelley's *Cenci*, from Mary Shelley's *Mathilda* to Christina Stead's *Man Who Loved Children*, from some of Sylvia Plath's and Anne Sexton's most striking poems to Toni Morrison's *Bluest Eye*. Whereas the stories of such heroines as Antigone and her later, more angelically Victorian avatar Eppie Marner – the creation of a novelist long haunted by Antigone – had recounted the daughter's acquiescence in her filial destiny, however, these works, like Wharton's *Summer*, record her ambivalence toward a fate in which, as Beatrice Cenci cries, 'all things' terrifyingly transform themselves into 'my father's spirit, / His eye, his voice, his touch surrounding me'.[61] Specifically, in each of these works a father more or less explicitly desires a daughter. His incestuous demands may be literal or they may be figurative, but in either case the heroine experiences them as both inexorable and stifling. Thus, in each work the girl struggles with more or less passion to escape, arguing that 'I love your Majesty according to my bond, no more, no less'. And in almost all these works, she discovers, finally, just what the nature of that bond is: no more, no less, than – on the one hand – death or – on the other hand – a surrender to the boundless authority of paternal desire that governs the lives of mothers and daughters in what Adrienne Rich has called 'the kingdom of the sons' and the fathers.[62] Indeed, in the few works (for instance, Plath's 'Daddy' and Stead's *Man Who Loved Children*) where the daughter neither dies nor acquiesces, she becomes a murderess and an outlaw.

Reducing the plot, as fairy tales so often do, to its most essential psychic outline, a narrative recorded by the brothers Grimm provides a resonant summary of the father–daughter 'story' I have been exploring here. The fairy tale 'Allerleirauh' (which means 'many different kinds of fur') introduces us to a king whose dying wife has made him promise not to remarry unless he can find a new bride who is a beautiful as she is and who has 'just such golden hair as I have'.[63] Grief-stricken, the king keeps his word until one day he looks at his growing daughter, sees that she is 'just a beautiful as her dead mother, and ha[s] the same golden hair', 'suddenly [feels] a violent love for her', and resolves to marry her. Shocked, the daughter tries to escape by setting him impossible tasks – she asks for three magical dresses and 'a mantle of a thousand different kinds of fur' – but when he fulfills her requests, she has no choice but to run away. Taking her three dresses and three tiny domestic treasures, she wraps herself in her fur mantle and escapes to a great forest. There she is asleep in a hollow tree when 'the King to whom this forest belong[s]' passes through with some huntsmen who capture her, thinking she is 'a wondrous beast'. When she tells them she is simply a poor orphan child, they bring her to this king's palace, where they set her to work, like Cinderella, in the kitchen ('A', pp. 327, 328).[64]

Of course, however, the king at this palace soon manages to discover her identity. He gives a series of three feasts, at each of which she appears in one of her magic dresses; he admires the soup she cooks while she is disguised in her furry Cinderella garb; and he finally manages to tear off her protective mantle, revealing her magic dress and her golden hair so that, in the words of the story, 'she [can] no longer hide herself', and the pair are wed soon after this epiphany ('A', p. 331). Like such texts as *Summer*, *Mathilda* and *The Cenci*, then, this tale records the case history of a daughter who tries to escape paternal desire, and like the heroines of many such works (for instance, Charity Royall journeying to the Mountain), the 'fair princess' who becomes 'Allerleirauh' flees from culture (her father's palace) to nature (the great wood), trying to transform herself into a creature of nature (a 'hairy animal') rather than acquiesce in the extreme demands culture is making upon her ('A', pp. 329, 330).[65] Like a number of the other protagonists of these stories and case histories, however, Allerleirauh cannot altogether abandon the imperatives her culture has impressed upon her: she brings with her the three magical dresses and the three domestic tokens which will eventually reveal her identity and knit her back into society. Like countless other heroines in such tales, moreover, she is motherless, a fact which, the story emphasizes, has brought about the seductive paternal persecution she is trying to evade. Finally, like that of so many of these heroines – perhaps most notably *Silas Marner's* Eppie – her function as a 'treasure' to both kings is manifested by the golden hair that she is at last unable to conceal.

That there are in fact two kings in 'Allerleirauh' may at first seem to controvert my argument that this tale offers us a paradigm of the prescription for father–daughter incest that lies at the heart of female psychosexual development in patriarchal society. Not just the princess but also the first king's courtiers, after all, express dismay at his desire to marry his daughter. In addition, the second king is distinguished from the first by a restrictive clause: he is not 'the king, who owns his forest' – that is, the king from whose palace Allerleirauh has just fled – but, rather, 'the king who owns this forest'. Yet structurally and psychologically, if not grammatically, the two kings are one: paternal figures from both of whom the 'fair princess' tries to escape, though not, perhaps, with equal vigor. In fact, for all practical purposes, the distinction between the two is best expressed by a single comma, the linguistic mark that marks the difference between illegitimate and legitimate incest, a difference Allerleirauh herself involuntarily acknowledges by the ambivalence with which at one moment she decks herself in glorious apparel and then, soon after, retreats into her old life as a wild child.

To be sure, given such ambivalence, some readers might see this tale simply as an account of the advances and retreats through which an adolescent girl comes to terms with her own mature desires. At the same time, however, what gives the tale a good deal of its force is the fatality it shares with subtler works like *Silas Marner* and *Summer* – specifically, a fatality provided by the *mother's* complicity in her daughter's destiny. For it is, after all, Allerleirauh's mother who has set the girl's story going with her admonition to the father that he must marry only a bride as beautiful as she. Lost to the daughter, like Molly Farren Cass and Mary Hyatt, she nevertheless rules her daughter's life with the injunctions of the culture-mother: 'You must bury your mother, you must give youself to your father.' In such novels as *Silas Marner* and *Summer*, the authors themselves replace her, splitting the maternal function between the ignominy of the dead mother and the qualified triumph of the male-identified maternal authority. But in all these stories, as even in more apparently rebellious works, the text itself discovers no viable alternative to filial resignation. Certainly, paradigmatic culture-mothers like Eliot and Wharton do not suggest (at least not in works like *Silas Marner* and *Summer*) that the daughter has any choice but that of acquiescence.[66] Though the 'empty Pack' of daughteronomy may be heavy, as Dickinson saw perhaps more clearly than they, it is vain to 'punish' the cultural 'Honey' it manufactures; for the daughter who understands her duty and her destiny, such honey 'only sweeter' grows. Under 'a blue sky out of the Oresteia', Eppie Marner, Charity Royall and the fair princess Allerleirauh, along with many others, and each in her own way, obey the implicit command of patriarchal society and marry the winter of the Father's year.

Notes

1. See SANDRA M. GILBERT and SUSAN GUBAR, 'Tradition and the Female Talent', *Proceedings of the Northeastern University Center for Literary Studies* 2 (1984), and '"Forward Into the Past". The Complex Female Affiliation Complex', in *Historical Studies in Literary Criticism*, ed. Jerome J. McGann (Madison, Wisconsin, 1985).
2. VIRGINIA WOOLF to Lady Robert Cecil (26 Jan.? 1919), (no. 1010), *The Letters of Virginia Woolf*, ed. Nigel Nicolson and Joanne Trautmann, 6 vols (New York, 1975–80), 2; p. 322; the historian Shelton Rothblatt called George Eliot a 'Man of Ideas' (paper delivered at the George Eliot Centenary Conference, Rutgers University, Sept. 1980); and see Leslie Stephen, *George Eliot*, English Men of Letters Series (London and New York, 1902).
3. ELAINE SHOWALTER, *A Literature of Their Own: British Women Novelists from Brontë to Lessing* (Princeton, NJ, 1977), p. 108; Elizabeth Robins, George *Mandeville's Husband*, quoted in *A Literature of Their Own*, p. 109.
4. ELIOT had said that *Silas Marner* 'came to me first of all, quite suddenly, as a sort of legendary tale' (Eliot to John Blackwood, 24 Feb. 1861, quoted in Gordon S. Haight, *George Eliot: A Biography* (New York, 1968), p. 341).
5. EMILY DICKINSON to Thomas Niles, April 1883 (no. 814), *The Letters of Emily Dickinson*, ed. Thomas H. Johnson, 3 vols (Cambridge, Mass, 1965), 3, pp. 769–70; and see Dickinson, *The Complete Poems of Emily Dickinson*, ed. Johnson (Boston, 1960), no. 1562, p. 650.
6. EDITH WHARTON, review of *George Eliot* by Stephen, *Bookman* 15 (May 1902); p. 251, 250.
7. ELIOT, 'Prelude', *Middlemarch*, ed. W. J. Harvey (Harmondsworth, 1965), p. 26.
8. JACQUES LACAN, 'On a Question Preliminary to Any Possible Treatment of Psychosis', *Ecrits: A Selection*, trans. Alan Sheridan (New York, 1977), p. 199. Anika Lemaire succinctly summarizes this Lacanian position:

   > Society and its structures are always present in the form of the family institution and the father, the representative of the law of society into which he will introduce his child by forbidding dual union with the mother (the register of the imaginary, of nature). By identifying with the father, the child receives a name and a place in the family constellation; restored to himself, he discovers that he is to be made in and by a world of Culture, language and civilization.
   >
   > (*Jacques Lacan*, trans. David Macey (London, 1977), p. 92)

Elsewhere, Lacan observes: 'That the woman should be inscribed in an order of exchange of which she is the object, is what makes for the fundamentally conflictual, and, I would say, insoluble character of her position: the symbolic order literally submits her, it transcends her' (Lacan; 'Seminar 2' (1954–55), quoted in Jacqueline Rose, introduction to *Feminine Sexuality: Jacques Lacan and the 'école freudienne'*, ed. Juliet Mitchell and Rose, trans. Rose (New York, 1983), p. 45.

9. For female 'anxiety of authorship' and women's corollary need for matrilineal legitimation, see Gilbert and Gubar, *The Madwoman in the Attic: The Woman Writer and the Nineteenth-Century Literary Imagination* (New Haven, Conn., 1979), chapter 2.

10. Eliot, 'Silly Novels by Lady Novelists', *The Writings of George Eliot*, 25 vols (Boston and New York, 1907–8), 22; p. 209. In a study of Eliot's stance toward paternal authority, Dianne F. Sadoff makes a point similar to this one, noting that Eliot seeks 'to usurp [paternal authority] as the discourse of a male narrator, the authority of a male author' (*Monsters of Affection: Dickens, Eliot, and Brontë on Fatherhood* Baltimore, 1982, p. 3).

11. Eliot to Blackwood, 12 Jan. 1861, quoted in Ruby V. Redinger, *George Eliot: The Emergent Self* (New York, 1975), p. 436. As Susan Gubar has suggested to me, the resonant image of the 'packman' may be associated with the figure of Bob Jakin in *The Mill on the Floss* (which Eliot had just completed), the itinerant pack-bearing peddler who brings Maggie Tulliver a number of books, the most crucial of which is Thomas à Kempis' treatise on Christian renunciation (so that its subject metaphorically associates it with Silas Marner's pack full of emptiness).

12. Redinger, *George Eliot*, p. 439; Eliot, 'Finale', *Middlemarch*, p. 896.

13. For 'liminal zone', see Victor Turner, 'Passages, Margins, and Poverty: Religious Symbols of Communitas,' *Dramas, Fields, and Metaphors: Symbolic Action in Human Society* (Ithaca, N.Y., 1974), pp. 231–71, and 'Betwixt and Between: The Liminal Period in *Rites de Passage*', *The Forest of Symbols: Aspects of Ndembu Ritual* (Ithaca, NY, 1967), pp. 93–111.

14. Eliot, *Silas Marner: The Weaver of Raveloe*, ed. Q. D. Leavis (Harmondsworth, 1967), pt 1, chapter 1, pp. 51, 52; all further references to this work, abbreviated *SM*, will be included in the text, with only part and chapter numbers (or chapter title) for convenience of those using other editions.

15. Eliot herself consciously exploits the text–textile analogy in *Silas Marner*, referring to the 'tale' of cloth Silas weaves and letting Silas accuse William Dane of having 'woven a plot' against him (*SM*, 1. 2, 1). For discussions of her more general use of webs, weaving, and spinning as metaphors, see Gilbert and Gubar, *The Madwoman in the Attic*, pp. 522–8; Reva Stump, *Movement and Vision in George Eliot's Novels* (Seattle, 1959), pp 172–214; and J. Hillis Miller, 'Optic and Semiotic in *Middlemarch*', in *The Worlds of Victorian Fiction*, ed. Jerome H. Buckley (Cambridge, Mass, 1975), pp. 125–45. On Eliot's own tendency to avarice – an inclination that, at least in the view of Blackwood, her publisher, became problematic just at the time she was composing *Silas Marner* – see Lawrence Jay Dessner, 'The Autobiographical Matrix of *Silas Marner*', *Studies in the Novel* 11 (Fall 1979), pp. 258–9.

16. See Sherry B. Ortner, 'Is Female to Male as Nature Is to Culture?', in *Women, Culture, and Society*, eds. Michelle Zimbalist Rosaldo and Louise Lamphere (Stanford, California, 1974), pp. 67–87. In connection with Silas' 'female' qualities, it is interesting that the villagers respond to his herbal knowledge by trying to make him take the place of 'the Wise Woman', a role he at first vigorously resists (see *SM*, 1. 2).

17. Eliot, quoted in Haight, *George Eliot*, p. 336. U. C. Knoepflmacher has pointed out that Silas, like Shakespeare's Pericles, will become 'another passive Job . . . redeemed through the miraculous gift of a daughter' (*George Eliot's Early Novels: The Limits of Realism* Berkeley and Los Angeles, 1968, p. 229).

18. In a psychoanalytic study of Eliot's work, Laura Comer Emery points out 'the connection of [Silas'] guineas' to a solipsistic 'anality' (*George Eliot's Creative Conflict: The Other Side of Silence* (Berkeley and Los Angeles, 1976), pp. 62, 63).

19. See Sigmund Freud's observation that, as the girl enters the Oedipal stage, her 'libido slips into a new position by means – there is no other way of putting it – of the equation "penis = child". She gives up her wish for a penis and puts in place of it a wish for a child' ('Some Psychological Consequences of the Anatomical Distinction between the Sexes' (1925), trans. James Strachey, *Sexuality and the Psychology of Love*, ed. Philip Rieff (New York, 1963, p. 191). On the special qualities of a boy-child, see Nancy Chodorow, *The Reproduction of Mothering: Psychoanalysis and the Sociology of Gender* (Berkeley and Los Angeles, 1978), pp. 107 and 131–2.

20. See Claude Lévi-Strauss: 'Even with regard to our own society, where marriage appears to be a contract between persons, . . . the relationship of reciprocity which is the basis of marriage is not established between men and women, but between men by means of women, who are merely the occasion of this relationship' (*The Elementary Structures of Kinship*, trans. James Harle Bell, John Richard von Sturmer and Rodney Needham, ed. Needham Boston, 1969, pp. 115–16).

21. See Eliot, *A Writer's Notebook, 1854–1879*, and *Uncollected Writings*, ed. Joseph Wiesenfarth (Charlottesville, Va., 1981), p. 98, where Eliot looks at Grimm's law, which traces the evolution of *dhugh* into 'daughter'. The theme of the daughter as treasure is, in addition, one that Eliot might have picked up from Honoré de Balzac's *Eugénie Grandet* (1833), a novel which treats the relationship of a miserly father and a 'treasured' only daughter far more cynically than *Silas Marner* does; also, in an unpublished discussion of *Romola*, Robin Sheets has proposed to analyze this theme.

22. It is arguable that the very name 'George Eliot' represents Marian Evans' own concern with this question. Unable legally to marry the man to whom she felt herself to be married, she still wanted, like a dutiful wife, to 'take' his name. Since George Henry Lewes' surname was not available to her – his first 'wife' had preempted it – she had to content herself with his Christian name. In this way, though she was ostensibly a lawbreaker, she was able symbolically to signal that even 'so substantive and rare a creature' as Marian Evans had been properly (if only partially) 'absorbed into the life of another', as, according to the laws of her society, every woman ought to be (Eliot, 'Finale', *Middlemarch*, p. 894).

23. Emery observes that at the end of *Silas Marner* 'it is almost as though Eppie and her father were being married' (*George Eliot's Creative Conflict*, p. 70). Similarly, Sadoff suggests that Eliot 'portrays . . . daughterly desire as fabled fantasy in *Silas Marner* and *Felix Holt*', adding in a general analysis of the (father–daughter) 'scene of seduction' that 'the story the daughter relates about this scene, this moment in her history, symbolizes the emergence of her sexuality expressed as desire for her father and represents her attempt to solve this enigma of childhood history' (*Monsters of Affection*, pp. 78, 104). Although Sadoff cites an early, unpublished version of my 'Life's Empty Pack' essay as making some of the same points she makes, we differ radically in our interpretation of the meaning that the female Oedipus complex has for Eliot and other culture-mothers. Sadoff takes as a given the 'emergence' of female sexuality and its inevitable expression as 'daughterly desire'; I am interested in the coercive cultural construction of 'daughterly desire', a point Mitchell emphasizes when she remarks that 'the father, so crucial for the development of femininity, and the men that follow him, so essential for the preservation of "normal" womanhood, are only secondary figures, for pride of place as love-object is taken by the mother – for both sexes [so that] in a sense, the father is only second-best anyway' (*Psychoanalysis and Feminism* New York, 1975, p. 111; all further references to this work, abbreviated *PF*, will be included in the text).

24. Haight, *George Eliot*, p. 49.

25. Eliot, 'Brother and Sister', *The Poems of George Eliot* (New York, n.d.), pp. 356, 357.

26. James Joyce, *Ulysses* (New York, 1934), p. 205; on the significance of the name 'Cass', see Knoepflmacher, *George Eliot's Early Novels*, p. 239.

27. Because of her metonymic as well as coincidental connection with the gold stolen by Godfrey Cass' brother Dunstan, Eppie represents the law in yet another way, reinforcing our sense that its curses as well as its blessings cannot be averted. The place in society that Silas' false brother, William *Dane*, stole from him is ironically restored to him through an act of theft perpetrated by Godfrey's false brother, *Dunstan* Cass. Though he has tried to flee culture on the horse Wildfire, moreover, Dunstan falls inexorably into the Stone-pits of damnation – the abyss the law has prepared for him. Similarly, his God-free brother, who tries to flee his cultural responsibility as father, loses not one but all children and inherits an empty house, a mere shell or box (a 'case', so to speak) devoid of meaning because devoid both of sons who can carry on its name and daughters who can link it into society. Even his refusal to be his prodigal brother's keeper eventually brings about Godfrey's nemesis, for it is the discovery of Dunstan's skeleton in the Stone-pits that causes this rejecting father to make his rejected proposal to Eppie. In all these cases, essentially, the machinations of murderous brothers dramatize failures of just those Mosaic Laws of the Father which should make transactions between man and man both orderly and faithful.

28. Freud, 'Female Sexuality' (1931), trans. Joan Riviere, *Sexuality and the Psychology of Love*, p. 195; all further references to this work, abbreviated 'FS', will be included in the text.

29. According to Freud, the Oedipus complex means for the girl an attachment to

the father which parallels the boy's attachment to his mother; but for the girl, her attachment to the father is a 'positive' phenomenon that succeeds an earlier 'negative' phase in which she experiences the same 'first mother-attachment' that the boy feels. When the girl learns that her mother has not 'given' her a penis, however – i.e., in Lacan's sense, that the mother has not given her the power represented by the 'Phallus' – she turns in disgust and despair to the father, the one who has the phallus and may therefore be able to give her some of its power (see Freud,'FS', pp. 195,199, and passim, and 'Some Psychological Consequences of the Anatomical Distinction between the Sexes'). Interestingly in this regard, Sadoff observes that a 'pattern of the displaced mother occurs throughout Eliot's novels and serves the story of father–daughter seduction' (*Monsters of Affection*, p. 69).

30. Observing that 'a boy's repression of his Oedipal maternal attachment (and his pre-oedipal dependence) seems to be *more* complete than a girl's' – in part, no doubt, because the boy can look forward to a future in which he will 'have' at least a figure of the mother, Chodorow quotes Alice Balint's assertion that 'the amicable loosening of the bond between daughter and mother is one of the most difficult tasks of education' (*The Reproduction of Mothering*, p. 130).

31. Aeschylus, *The Eumenides, The Oresteian Trilogy*, trans. Philip Vellacott (Harmondsworth, 1959), p. 169; this is Apollo's argument.

32. Hélène Cixous, 'Sorties', trans. Ann Liddle, in *New French Feminisms: An Anthology*, eds. Elaine Marks and Isabelle de Courtivron (Amherst, Mass., 1980), p. 92.

33. Henry James to Wharton, Dec. 1912, quoted in Millicent Bell, *Edith Wharton and Henry James: The Story of Their Friendships* (New York, 1965), p. 274.

34. On the analogy between nature ('raw') and culture ('cooked'), see Lévi-Strauss, *Introduction to a Science of Mythology*, vol. 1, *The Raw and the Cooked* (New York, 1969).

35. Sylvia Plath, 'The Colossus', *The Collected Poems*, ed. Ted Hughes (New York, 1981), pp. 129; 'The Beekeeper's Daughter', *Collected Poems*, p. 118; and see 'Electra on Azalea Path', pp. 116–17.

36. Wharton, *Summer* (with an introduction by Cynthia Griffin Wolff), (New York, 1980), p. 44; all further references to this work, abbreviated S, will be included in the text.

37. See Maria Cummins, *The Lamplighter* (Boston, 1854); a major best-seller in its day, it tells the story of orphaned Gerty's daughterly devotion to the adoptive father, Trueman Flint, who rescued her from poverty and starvation. For a discussion of the book's appeal in its day, see Nina Baym, *Woman's Fiction: A Guide to Novels by and about Women in America, 1820–1870* (Ithaca, N.Y., 1978), pp. 164–9.

38. Andrea Hammer's remark was made in an unpublished paper on *Summer*. Wolff notes that Charity Royall's feelings for Lucius Harney are 'explicitly sexual' and her view of him 'inescapably phallic' (introduction to *Summer*, p. xi).

39. It is possible that in recounting Charity's desire for Lucius Harney, Wharton is recording nostalgic details of her affair with Morton Fullerton (see

R. W. B. Lewis, *Edith Wharton: A Biography* (New York, 1975), pp. 203–328). In addition, by implying that Charity at first experiences her passion for Lucius Harney as a desire for a brotherly equal, she may be meditating on Fullerton's long erotic relationship with his cousin Katherine, who had been brought up to believe she was his half-sister (see pp. 200–3). Further resonance might have been added to the relationship by the brother–sister romance of Siegmund and Sieglinde in Richard Wagner's *Die Walküre*, a work Wharton surely knew.

40. Wharton, 'Beatrice Palmato', in Lewis, *Edith Wharton*, p. 548; and see pp. 544–8. For a related analysis of father–daughter incest in *Summer* and 'Beatrice Palmato', see Elizabeth Ammons' suggestion that *Summer* is 'Wharton's bluntest criticism of the patriarchal sexual economy' and her ensuing discussion of the two texts; *Edith Wharton's Argument with America* (Athens, Ga., 1980), p.133; and see pp. 133–43. I agree with many points in Ammons' reading of *Summer* but do not believe that Wharton was consciously 'criticizing' the 'patriarchal sexual economy'; rather, like Eliot, she was transcribing a myth that nonjudgmentally (if painfully) 'explains' woman's position in patriarchal culture.

41. Aeschylus, *The Eumenides*, p. 169; and see Lewis, *Edith Wharton*, p. 397.

42. Elizabeth Barrett Browning, *Aurora Leigh, 'Aurora Leigh' and Other Poems* (London, 1978), bk. 1, ll. 622–3, p. 57; Dickinson, *Complete Poems*, no. 722, p. 354. For a more general discussion of maternal images in the works of Barrett Browning, see Gilbert, 'From *Patria* to *Matria*: Elizabeth Barrett Browning's *Risorgimento*', Publications of the Modern Language Association (*PMLA*) 99 (March 1984): 194–211; for a discussion of Dickinson's use of such imagery, see Gilbert and Gubar, *The Madwoman in the Attic*, pp. 642–50.

43. Christiane Olivier, *Les enfants de Jocaste: L'empreinte de la mère* (Paris, 1980), p. 149; my translation ('Or dans (le miroir tendu par l'homme) la femme ne voit pas son image mais celle que l'homme a d'elle. Jocaste a imprimé au coeur de l'homme sa trace indélébile car ce miroir ne contient que l'image d'une femme "morte" ').

44. Helene Deutsch, *The Psychology of Women: A Psychoanalytic Interpretation*, 2 vols (New York, 1944–45), 1, p. 252.

45. In his essay 'Fathers and Daughters', the psychoanalyst Joseph H. Smith makes a similar case for the inevitability of what I am calling 'resignation' in women; see 'Fathers and Daughters', *Man and World: An International Philosophical Review* 13 (1980): especially pp. 391 and 395. For a different formulation of the same point, see Freud, 'Analysis Terminable and Interminable' (1937), trans. Riviere, *Therapy and Technique*, ed. Rieff (New York, 1963), especially pp. 268–71. Freud's n. 14, a quotation from Sandor Ferenczi, is particularly telling in this regard: 'In every male patient the sign that his castration-anxiety has been mastered . . . is a sense of equality of rights with the analyst; and every female patient . . . must have . . . become able to *submit without bitterness* to thinking in terms of her feminine role' (p. 270 n. 14; italics mine).

46. Wharton, quoted in Wolff, introduction to *Summer*, p. xv.

47. Phyllis Chesler, 'Rape and Psychotherapy', in *Rape: The First Sourcebook for Women*, eds. Noreen Connell and Cassandra Wilson (New York, 1974), p. 76;

Judith Lewis Herman, with Lisa Hirschman, *Father–Daughter Incest* (Cambridge, Mass., 1981), p. 110.

48. CHODOROW, *The Reproduction of Mothering*, p. 132. Chodorow also notes that 'sociologist Robert Winch reports that marked attachment to the opposite gender parent retards courtship progress for male college students and accelerates it for females' (p. 133); thus, the father–daughter bond is actually 'healthful' for women while the mother–son bond is 'unhealthy' for men.

49. DEUTSCH, *The Psychology of Women*, 1, p. 252.

50. MICHAEL E. LAMB, MARGARET TRESCH OWEN and LINDSAY CHASE-LANSDALE, 'The Father–Daughter Relationship: Past, Present, and Future', in *Becoming Female: Perspectives on Development*, ed. Claire B. Kopp, in collaboration with Martha Kirkpatrick (New York, 1979), p. 94.

51. HERMAN, with Hirschman, *Father–Daughter Incest*, pp. 12, 87, 60, 61.

52. SADOFF, *Monsters of Affection*, p. 68.

53. O. MANNONI, *Freud*, trans. Renaud Bruce (New York, 1971), p. 45.

54. FREUD to Wilhelm Fliess, 31 May 1897 (no. 64), *The Origins of Psycho-Analysis: Letters to Wilhelm Fliess, Drafts and Notes: 1887–1902*, ed. Marie Bonaparte, Anna Freud, and Ernst Kris, trans. Eric Mosbacher and Strachey (New York, 1977), p. 206.

55. FREUD to Fliess, 3 Oct. 1897 (no. 70), *Origins*, p. 219; and see the dreams and memories reported on pp. 215–25.

56. FREUD to Fliess, 21 Sept. 1897 (no. 69), *Origins*, pp. 215–16.

57. An article in *Newsweek* in 1981 reported interviews with a number of scholars who speculated, on the basis of recently discovered documents relating to the Freud family and unpublished portions of the letters to Fliess, that Freud's anxiety about his own father 'prevented him from recognizing the primal guilt of Laius' – that is, of all fathers (David Gelman, 'Finding the Hidden Freud', *Newsweek*, 30 Nov. 1981, p. 67; and see pp. 64–70).

58. As Kris points out in a footnote to the Fliess letters, Freud later observed that 'seduction still retains a certain aetiological importance, and I still consider that some of the psychological views expressed [in the first theory] meet the case' (*Origins*, p. 217, n. 1). Herman declares that 'Freud falsified his incest cases', that he named uncles instead of father as seducers in several instances, because he wanted to exercise 'discretion' (*Father–Daughter Incest*, p. 9). The *Newsweek* article asserts that 'in unpublished passages of the Fliess letters [Freud] continued to describe cases of sexual brutality by fathers' ('Finding the Hidden Freud', p. 67). In a pioneering essay on this subject, Robert Seidenberg and Evangelos Papathomopoulos discuss the pressures put on late-Victorian daughters by ill or tyrannical fathers and the implications of those pressures for *Studies on Hysteria* (see 'Daughters Who Tend Their Fathers: A Literary Survey', *Psychoanalytic Study of Society* 2 (1962); especially pp. 135–9).

59. SEIDENBERG and PAPATHOMOPOULOS, 'Daughters Who Tend Their Fathers', p. 150. They observe, in addition, that 'the word, *Kore*, is also used to designate the female figures who act as supports, the Caryatids of the Holy Temples' (p. 150).

60. Robert Graves, quoted in ibid., p. 151.

61. Percy Bysshe Shelley, *The Cenci, Poetical Works*, ed. Thomas Hutchinson (New York, 1967), act 5, sc. 4, ll. 60–1, p. 332. For discussions of Eliot's views of Antigone, see Gilbert and Gubar, *The Madwoman in the Attic*, p. 494, and Redinger, *George Eliot*, pp. 314–15 and 325; both these analyses emphasize the rebellious heroine of *Antigone*, but, significantly, Eliot had the eponymous heroine of *Romola* sit for a portrait of Antigone at Colonus – the dutiful daughter.

62. Adrienne Rich, 'Sibling Mysteries', *The Dream of a Common Language: Poems, 1974–1977* (New York, 1978), p. 49.

63. 'Allerleirauh', *The Complete Grimm's Fairy Tales*, trans. Margaret Hunt and James Stern, rev. edn (New York, 1972), pp. 326–7; all further references to this work, abbreviated 'A', will be included in the text.

64. In a brief discussion of this tale, Herman argues that 'Allerleirauh' is a version of 'Cinderella'; see *Father–Daughter Incest*, p. 2. Even more interestingly, the folklorist Alan Dundes argues a connection between the plot of this story ('tale type 923, Love Like Salt'), 'Cinderella', and *King Lear*, although he claims – as perhaps Sadoff would – that this basic plot functions as *'a projection of incestuous desires on the part of the daughter'*) ('"To Love My Father All": A Psychoanalytic Study of the Folktale Source of *King Lear*', *Southern Folklore Quarterly* 40 (Sept.–Dec. 1976); pp. 355, 360; italics his).

65. Psychologically speaking, in fact, Allerleirauh's flight could even be compared to the seizures of hysteria suffered by so many of Freud's and Josef Breuer's patients, daddy's girls who sought to escape the imprisonment of the father by rejecting not only the modes and manners but also the language of 'his' culture and speaking instead through a more 'natural' body language.

66. To be sure, in, e.g., *Romola* and *Middlemarch* and in, e.g., *The Age of Innocence*, Eliot and Wharton, respectively, embed fantasies of female, and sometimes even matriarchal, autonomy, fantasies which clearly function as covertly compensatory gestures toward liberation from the father–daughter scripts elaborated in works like *Silas Marner* and *Summer*.

8 *Romola*: Trauma, Memory and Repression*

DIANNE F. SADOFF

Dianne F. Sadoff, a psychoanalytic critic, argues that the Freudian primal scene of seduction, in which the child has been or imagines that she has been seduced by her father, operates as 'metaphor' in George Eliot's fiction. It is particularly crucial in *Romola*, which she sees as George Eliot's most confessional novel, since Romola rejects the law of the father but cannot bring herself to break with father figures, thus creating an unresolved tension in the novel between 'paternal authority and daughterly desire' (see Introduction, pp. 23–4).

The languages of tenderness and passion have their initial encounter in childhood, and it is that clash which is at the origin of trauma.

(Jean Laplanche, *Life and Death in Psychoanalysis*)

Romola's composition appears to have been a unique process in Eliot's career.[1] At the same time, however, it is characteristic of a difficult period in that career, a period that began with the idea for the Florentine romance and ended with the completion of *The Spanish Gypsy*.[2] While researching the Florentine novel, Eliot suddenly experienced an over-whelming urge to write another story. Eliot described this interruption almost as a penetrating need: the desire to write this story 'came across my other plans by a sudden inspiration' which 'thrust itself between me and the other book I was meditating' (*Letters*, 3: 371, 360).[†] Eliot's metaphors for the conception of *Silas Marner* indicate that planning and meditating the narrative material of *Romola* proved too painful for continuation. It demanded to be deferred, and the inspired interruption *Silas Marner* provided effectively put off beginning the historical romance.

---

* Reprinted from Dianne F. Sadoff, *Monsters of Affection: Dickens, Eliot and Brontë on Fatherhood* (Baltimore: Johns Hopkins University Press), pp. 88–99; footnotes renumbered from the original.

[†] *The George Eliot Letters*, ed. Gordon S. Haight, 9 vols (New Haven: Yale University Press, 1954–56, 1978).

This dialectic of interruption and deferral, of course, appeared elsewhere in Eliot's career. Composition of 'The Lifted Veil' interrupted the slow and painful initiation of *The Mill on the Floss*; work on *Felix Holt* followed the illness-ridden writing of *The Spanish Gypsy*, after Lewes took the poem's manuscript away from Eliot in February 1865. Yet Cross reports Eliot's own understanding of *Romola*'s singular function in her career: 'She could put her finger on it', he wrote, 'as marking a well-defined transition in her life. In her own words, "I began it a young woman – I finished it an old woman."'[3] *Romola* marks a well-defined transition in a career as well as in a life, a transition for which the interruptions of writing *The Mill* prepared and the apparent ending of *The Spanish Gypsy* before its completion fulfilled. Like Felicia Bonaparte, I believe *Romola* occupies a 'pivotal place in the evolution of Eliot's fiction';[4] Eliot herself accords that novel its place as turning point.

Eliot's letters and journal entries attest to the difficulty of beginning *Romola*. During the period of research in Florence, the author appears to have enjoyed visiting prospective narrative settings and reading old Florentine manuscripts. In London, however, Eliot later found herself unable to stop researching and begin writing. Lewes metaphorically described her state as a kind of death: she was 'buried in old quartos and vellum bound literature' (*Letters*, 3: 430). Eliot admitted she suffered 'greatly from despondency and distrust' of herself during this time; in her journal she wrote, 'Got into a state of so much wretchedness in attempting to concentrate my thoughts on the construction of my story, that I became desperate, and suddenly burst my bonds, saying I will not think of writing!' (*Letters*, 3: 448). Eliot began the novel, then stopped writing. In her journal, Eliot wrote, 'So utterly dejected that, in walking with G. in the Park, I almost resolved to give up my Italian novel'.[5] Lewes described Eliot's 'immovable . . . conviction that she *can't* write the romance because she has not knowledge enough. Now as a matter of fact I know that she has immensely more knowledge of the particular period than any other writer who has touched it; but her distressing diffidence paralyses her' (*Letters*, 3: 473–4). Eliot deferred writing by researching; the need to know everything about fifteenth-century Florence represented an exaggerated version of a writer's normal rituals for beginning a project. Given the great struggle with her material in *Romola* and immediately following it with *The Spanish Gypsy*, however, Eliot's deferring strategies appear reasonably self-protective. Yet Lewes identified 'her singular diffidence' as 'exaggerated in this case' (*Letters*, 3: 446). Eliot's despair over writing her historical romance eventually made her ill; in several journal entries she reported she had been ailing all week, with an 'oppressive sense of the far-stretching task' of writing the narrative. 'Will [the romance] ever be finished? – ever be worth anything?' she queried (*Letters*, 4: 15, 17). The pain, suffering, even illness that appear characteristic of Eliot's writing process seem to have abated somewhat after she began *Felix Holt*. Lewes never again took a manuscript away from the genius he felt he must protect and nurture, and the dialectic of interruption and deferral became immensely fruitful in the composition of *Middlemarch*'s several plots. *Romola*, that 'well-defined transition in her life', that 'exaggerated' case of diffidence and paralysis, appears to have made a difference to its writer.

Despite suffering, interruption and deferral, then, Eliot wrote *Romola*. In justifying to Sara Hennell her desire to write a novel she knew would not be popular, Eliot admitted how personal that historical romance had become to her: 'If one is to have freedom to write out one's own varying unfolding self, and not be a machine always grinding out the same material or spinning the same sort of web, one cannot always write for the same public' (*Letters*, 4: 49). The distancing impersonal pronoun, like the historical setting and research for the novel, protected Eliot from what appears true of *Romola*: that it indeed unfolded herself. In Cross's quotation about its having aged his famous wife, he also reported the writing of *Romola* 'ploughed into her' – provided the possibility of new growth as well as the harrowing of the ground of her self-esteem. Although critics usually consider *The Mill on the Floss* Eliot's most autobiographical novel, *Romola* is clearly more confessional than is the earlier narrative. The distance in time and setting of the romance allowed Eliot to include yet disguise her most painful personal memories and meditations.[6] The pain, the welcome, thrusting interruption of *Silas Marner*, and the deferral of *Romola*'s beginning suggest the difficulty of confronting those harrowing memories and suggest as well that writing *Romola* was nothing short of traumatic for its author. Eliot herself unconsciously figured that writing process as traumatic; it combined a sudden, thrusting inspiration with the pain of planning and meditation. As Jean Laplanche and J.-B. Pontalis point out, psychoanalysis adopts the term 'trauma' from the Greek word for 'wound', which itself derives from the Greek 'to pierce'.[7] The 'exaggerated case' of interruption and deferral, of pain and piercing imagination, demands interpretation and makes most sense when read as a traumatic process of recollection and self-defense.

When I use the term 'traumatic', I intend a particular psychoanalytic meaning. Freud defines trauma as an event that arouses psychical excitation too powerful to be dealt with or worked off in a normal way.[8] The psychical apparatus attempts to eliminate or bind these excitations by the principle of constancy, which achieves a balanced state of stimulation or a lowered level of tension. In his early theories, Freud formulated the essentially sexual nature of trauma and linked it in his theory of seduction with temporality and repression, as I mentioned in the first section of this chapter. Freud also postulates trauma as a double event, one with two scenes. The actual adult sexual advance takes place when the subject is a prepubertal child, and so she experiences no sexual excitation; after puberty, however, a second scene, often of a specifically non-sexual nature, evokes to the subject the first scene, and sexual excitation now associated with the first scene overwhelms the subject's ability to defend against it. This theory's mainspring is temporality: the discontinuous nature of human sexual development plus the function of retrospection make the memory itself rather than the adult sexual advance traumatic. Thus by deferral, or retroactivity, the postpubertal child must reconstruct events of the present in the light of a past event; to do so, she must defend against sexual excitation, bind the stimulus evoked by the deferred memory, or repress memory of the first scene. And just as Freud later disavowed the reality of the first scene of seduction, he also broadened his conception of trauma to include a variety of internal and external excitations as well as the larger events of a particular childhood history; he moved from a simple model of repression built on the two scenes of seduction to a complex model of primal repression, repression proper and the return of the repressed. Yet Freud never totally abandoned the terms for temporality, repression, and sexuality he adopted in the early theory of seduction; I will generalize these terms and will also use them in discussing seduction, although not always in Freud's necessarily schematic early theoretical sense.[9] When I use the term 'repression', I refer to the mechanism by which the mind banishes to the unconscious memories, images, and ideas – signifiers – that can arouse painful excitation. Repression, however, is only one of Freud's mechanisms of defense; when I use the terms 'defense' or 'binding', I refer to a general designation for the ways the mind controls excitation aroused by deferred memory or retroactivity.

When I identify Eliot's writing of *Romola* as traumatic, then, I refer to its ability to arouse in the author's conscious mind memories that by the mechanism of deferred action or retroactivity appear linked to the scene of seduction. I do not mean, however, to identify implicitly a first scene in which seduction actually occurred in Eliot's childhood; such biographical speculation would be purely conjectural. Freud's initial concept of 'first scene' in fact became less schematic in his later speculation about seduction, primarily because his patients' originating scenes of seduction disappeared in analysis further backward into their childhoods. I intend here to articulate Freud's theory of trauma and temporal deferral with his later structural theory of oedipal desire; together, the two constitute a childhood history. In writing *Romola*, Eliot tapped the material of Mary Ann Evans's childhood history, material she had been unable fully to integrate into a conception of herself because it was linked to the scene of seduction, to issues of desire and prohibition. The traumatic memory of this first generalized childhood scene forced Eliot to reinterpret the events of her experience and to repress those memories or to control and bind them in order to go forward in her life and in her career. A psychoanalytic model, then, allows us to interpret Eliot's struggles with *Romola* as a traumatic confrontation with unassimilated material she must retroactively reinterpret in a 'second scene' in which language symbolizes the memories of the 'first'.

In *Romola,* Eliot specifically confronts the complex memories of her struggles with father and brother. Every major male character in the novel represents a father or brother; Romola herself is a figure for the young Mary Ann Evans. Savonarola's triple message to the people of Florence stands as metaphor for the function of the narrative for its writer. Because of pestilence and moral corruption, God will scourge the city with His avenging wrath; He will purge of sin and so purify the people; this will happen in our days.[10] In the novel as a whole, Eliot scourges Romola and so a figure for herself for daring to have her own desires; she purges fathers and brothers from the narrative and so achieves a purified virtually female society; this happens because Eliot retroactively reconstructs the events of her past as memory becomes traumatic. *Romola* demonstrates that for Eliot, the scene of seduction must be remembered with certain self-protection: the distance and artifice of historical romance, for example; the displacement of desire from its rightful subject, Romola; the invoking of extreme prohibition from within and without the subject; the binding of the subject to her own law or self-prohibition. *Romola* replays the Holy Wars (a generalized version of Freud's 'first scene') in a fictional arena. *Romola* performs for its author the 'work of recollection' and so can later be spoken of by her as a 'well-defined transition' in her life.

In this transitional narrative, Romola binds herself to the law of fathers, discovers the inauthentic authority of each, and so proceeds to bind herself to her own law. Romola's relationship with her old scholarly father stands midway between Maggie's with Mr Tulliver and Dorothea's with Casaubon. Bardo resembles Mr Tulliver already fallen into paralysis at the beginning of the novel; Bardo prophesies what Casaubon will become when the daughter blindly devotes her life to the father as husband. According to the narrator, Romola lives a 'self-repressing' life in which all her ardor and affection have been spent on sympathy with her father's 'aged sorrows, aged ambition, aged pride and indignation' (1: 196). Her symbolically blind father fails to see his daughter's affection and pity, her passionate tenderness, just as will Dorothea's self-protective father–husband (1: 87–88). Like Dorothea's uncle and Miltonic husband, Romola's father belittles his daughter for her gender, her feminine imagination, and her failure to be a son (1: 104–5). Nonetheless, Romola devotes herself to this old patriarch simply because he is her father and promises to marry a scholar who will take her abandoning brother's place in the father's research project about antiquity: family ties indeed bind. Romola never questions her devotion to Bardo but the narrator interprets the father–daughter scene and speaks Eliot's judgment of the patriarch. Eliot's portrait of Romola and Bardo represents her bitter resentment of the time she voluntarily spent as her father's housekeeper. This anger can be narrated only after the fact and only by a narrator clearly differentiated from either George Eliot or Mary Ann Evans. *Romola* retroactively reinterprets Mary Ann Evans's struggle with paternal law and incorporates into a figure for the young housekeeping daughter as subject a meaningful interpretation of that life with her father.

Although *Romola* explicitly represents the father's law, as I will discuss later, the narrative also symbolizes desire and, at its beginning, clearly displaces desire from its rightful subject, the daughter. Tito, the scholar Romola marries to replace the brother, calls forth Romola's first expression of desire. Yet as the novel's symbols prophesy, Romola's wedding is also a funeral, a nunlike renunciation of desire. For Tito, Romola's symbolic brother and figure for her own desires, immediately follows his impulses, obeys no law but his own 'irresistible desire', and in a 'lawless moment' marries Tessa at a carnival during the ironic Festival of the Nativity of the Virgin. This marriage, performed by a conjurer, parodies the lawful ceremony to which Romola binds herself and from which, soon enough, she wishes to escape (1: 223, 209). Romola soon desires voluntarily to leave her husband; this desire, Savonarola tells her, represents the urge to follow her 'own blind choice', her 'own will' (2: 105). In her well-known letter to her father during the 'Holy Wars', Mary Ann Evans linked desire with choice and separation; she feared nothing but 'voluntarily leaving' her father, but would do so, she wrote, should he prohibit her return to Foleshill (*Letters*, 1: 129).

Romola's narrative, however, refuses to allow her voluntarily to leave her husband. She returns to her loveless marriage in a state of 'yearning passivity' (2: 112). Desire is then metonymically displaced onto brothers (or sons) real and symbolic in the narrative; Dino and Tito act out Romola's desire to abandon her closest tie and kinship, and this desire symbolizes the narrative desire voluntarily to leave fathers as Eliot displaces the struggles of filiation onto affiliation, descent onto consanguinity. Romola's brother, Dino, abandons his father for a 'higher love' and counsels Romola to follow his example. Fra Luca accuses his father of 'worldly ambitions and fleshly lusts'; he tells Romola of his new religious life of 'perfect love and purity for the soul' in which he experiences 'no uneasy hunger after pleasure, no tormenting questions, no fear of suffering'. Yet Luca's rhetoric reveals this purified love as a traditional religious metaphor for desire: he understands the saints' 'ecstasy', which truth 'penetrates' even pagan philosophy; he understands the 'bliss' of living with God; he feels 'no affection, no hope . . . wed[s]' him to 'that which passeth away' (1: 236–9). In pursuit of this life of purified or repressed desire, God calls upon Dino to flee his father, and the son obeys; only when commanded to abandon an earthly father by a heavenly Father can the son represent his flight from filial duty as a higher form of obedience. Eliot justifies this filial abandonment and represents it as a spiritual adherence, exonerating the desires of her young self.

If Fra Luca correctly abandons father for Father, however, Tito Melema does not. Tito's adoptive father, Baldassarre, chose through love to be his father rather than was destined through biological necessity, and as a result the narrative exaggerates Tito's crime as it exonerates Fra Luca's. After arriving in Florence, Tito chooses not to seek his adoptive father but to believe him dead, and by so choosing demonstrates his 'desire' it 'be the truth that his father was dead' (1: 152–3). Throughout the narrative, when confronted by his still-living father, Tito refuses to recognize him: he calls his father 'mad' in a Florentine square; he renounces his father at a public dinner as Judas renounced Christ; he fails to heed the repeated and symbolic motif of the 'hand on the shoulder' which brings him from Luca news of his father and finally brings his father to kill him. In fact, as Felicia Bonaparte points out, Tito Melema betrays all the novel's fathers: he refuses to save his adoptive father, Baldassarre; he denies Romola the opportunity to create Bardo's library; he conspires against Savonarola and later against Bernardo del Nero.[11] This lawless, desiring son enacts all the narrative's unjustified desires voluntarily to abandon fathers. Tito and Luca, the two abandoning sons, represent Eliot's narrative ambivalence about leaving fathers.

Such abandonment of fathers inevitably appears dangerous. Fra Luca conveniently wastes away after devoting his life to purifying the worldly desires of his earthly father. But another earthly father refuses to tolerate filial abandonment. Baldassarre enacts not the displaced rebellion of the son, as Carole Robinson suggests, but rather the punishment the father deals out for the child's abandonment.[12] Like his adoptive son, Baldassarre is passionate and lawless. Tito wears armor and buys a dagger because he understands his father will revenge a son's abandonment and will attempt to kill the son who metaphorically desires to kill him. When Tito attempts repentance, Baldassarre indeed tries to stab his son: 'I saved you – I nurtured you – I loved you', he cries; 'you forsook me – you robbed me – you denied me' (2: 29). The father's revenge, figured as a Christlike suffering, appears justifiable, even just.

If sons act out the narrative's desire to abandon filial ties, Romola must learn to act otherwise. She, like the narrator, comes to believe that the 'sanctity attached to all close relations, and, therefore, pre-eminently to the closest, was but the expression in outward law of that result towards which all human goodness and nobleness must spontaneously tend; that the light abandonment of ties, whether inherited or voluntary, because they had ceased to be pleasant, was the uprooting of social and personal virtue' (2: 272). Romola learns this moral lesson from Savonarola, a figurative father. After the death of her father, Bardo, Romola is left 'lawless', a worshiper of 'beauty and joy' (2: 60). When she desires impulsively to abandon her closest tie, feels the 'instinct to sever herself from the man she loved no longer' (2: 48), Savonarola waylays her outside the city gates and so replaces her dead father as the figure of law in her life. He demands absolute submission to the earthly law of marriage: Romola must not forsake her duty as wife, her place in the community for which the affiliated tie of marriage is metaphor. Savonarola teaches Romola to bind herself to his law, the 'Divine law' for which he stands. Marriage, the father tells this daughter, is not 'carnal only, made for selfish delight', but represents the 'bond of a higher love'. Romola must quench the 'sense of suffering Self in the ardours of an ever-growing love' (2: 110–11). Accepting the divine law, binding herself to a higher love, signifies according to this father a repression of selfish desire and a devotion to fellow-feeling rather than personal happiness. In deciding not to abandon her closest tie, Romola dedicates herself to such self-repression; she binds her desire by the prohibitive word of a father and accepts his law as final.[13]

In psychoanalytic terminology, 'binding' signifies a psychical operation that restricts the free flow of excitations, links ideas together, and constitutes and maintains relatively stable forms of energy. Freud often associated 'binding' with the notion of trauma or memory as displeasure: the memories associated with trauma – excitations connected with the scene of seduction which have not been integrated into the subject's conception of herself – demand to be bound to previously established psychic structures. The energy associated with trauma must be related to or integrated with forms that have specific limits or boundaries, must therefore be fixed or controlled.[14] *Romola* performs this task for its heroine, binds her to social structures that compensate for or control the energy associated with desire in the scene of seduction: the marriage bond, the communal good. Desire must be controlled because it is unstable. The young Mary Ann Evans found her affections 'disturbing forces'; she yearned for more love 'than in sober reason and real humility' she thought she 'ought to desire', until that yearning became her 'curse' (*Letters*, 1: 142, 137, 70). The evangelical girl failed to understand her desire as a result of deprivation; instead, she believed it 'egoistic', a sign of self-involvement and failure to relate well to others. Eliot's traumatic adult analysis of desire confirms and extends this definition. *Romola*'s narrator instructs: 'It is in the nature of all human passion . . . that there is a point at which it ceases to be properly egoistic, and is like a fire kindled within our being to which everything else in us is mere fuel' (1: 413). The novel's characters destroy themselves because they desire: Baldassarre takes revenge against Tito with 'a thirst . . . like that which makes men open their own veins to satisfy it' (1: 416), a 'supreme emotion, which knows no terror, and asks no motive, which is itself an ever-burning motive, consuming all other desire' (2: 70); Tito 'sacrifice[s] himself to his passion as if it were a deity to be worshipped with self-destruction' (1: 339). Such passion, revenge and self-destruction clearly endanger other members of the community and so must be repressed.

Yet Eliot's ambivalence about such repression appears in the abstract terminology of the novel's morality. As Carole Robinson points out, Romola's duties to the community seem remarkably unpleasant to her:

> She had no innate taste for tending the sick and clothing the ragged. . . . Her early training had kept her aloof from such womanly labours; and if she had not brought to them the inspiration of her deepest feelings, they would have been irksome to her;
>
> . . . all that ardour of her nature which could no longer spend itself in the woman's tenderness for father and husband, had transformed itself into an enthusiasm of sympathy with the general life,

despite its 'miserabl[e] narrow[ness]' (2: 146–7). Romola commits her sympathy outward for lack of center at home. 'Enthusiasm of sympathy' appears to be Eliot's euphemism for repression of love for father and husband.

Romola must free herself from her prohibitive fathers and husband–brother precisely because they fail to reciprocate affection. Yet she refuses 'voluntarily to leave' either, and so the narrative machinery creaks as it casts off fathers for its passive heroine. The spiritual father, Savonarola, handily betrays Romola by refusing to save her godfather from execution and therefore provokes her rebellion against him. The struggle between the father and the woman he calls 'my daughter' (2: 99–110) centers on authority and signification. In a chapter entitled 'Pleading', Romola asks Savonarola to intercede politically so that her godfather, Bernardo del Nero, may be granted appeal against the death sentence for treason. Savonarola himself created the procedure for appeal which he now refuses to allow Bernardo and the other Mediceans. Romola and Savonarola argue about 'law and justice': Savonarola declares the city's welfare demands 'severity' rather than 'mercy' in this case.[15] The father's law resides, as this scene demonstrates, in his word, his promise of mercy. Romola begs Savonarola's lenience, saying, 'You know that your word will be powerful' (2: 305). She believes the father gave his 'word' that appeal would be granted any political prisoner regardless of his crime. Indeed, when Savonarola urges Romola not to flee Florence and her marriage, he identifies one's word as the basis of law: 'Of what wrongs', he asks Romola, 'will you complain, when you yourself are breaking the simplest law that lies at the foundation of the trust which binds man to man – faithfulness to the spoken word?' (2: 102). Savonarola binds Romola to his law by demanding she not break her word – her marriage vow– as Tito has broken his word to create her father's library. In the case of Romola's godfather, however, Savonarola himself breaks his word and so the law that binds man to man. In this chapter, Romola speaks out against her father and defines her rebellion against his law as a verbal act. She senses her words in 'painful dissonance' with her past relationship to him saying, 'Forgive me, father; it is pain to me to have spoken those words – yet I cannot help speaking' (2: 301–9). When the father's word proves duplicitous and inauthentic, the daughter feels forced to speak against him. Although Romola waits at Savonarola's execution for his 'last word' of self-justification, the father's silence implies and in fact confirms his guilt (2: 436–40).

Romola successfully rebels against one father only because in doing so she dedicates herself to another. Romola decides to walk to the scaffold in identification with her godfather's shame. Earlier in the novel, this godfather symbolically replaced and transformed Romola's unloving real father. This 'second father' offers Romola a 'father's home' and a 'father's ear' for the words of her suffering; he tells her after Bardo's death, 'I am your father' (2: 247–8). Romola's dedication to her 'padricullo' reunites her with love for her dead father: her 'affection and respect were clinging with new tenacity to her godfather, and with him to those memories of her father' (2: 235); Romola pledges to remember her godfather, 'the man who alone in all the world had shared her pitying love for her father' (1: 318). Romola's public display of love for her godfather signifies her refusal to forsake fathers, despite her verbal rebellion against and ultimate forsaking of her spiritual father. This narrative trick justifies voluntarily leaving fathers while at the same time enforcing false and sentimental sympathy with them. This narrative justification, like so much of *Romola*, proves terribly contradictory. Romola identifies herself with Bernardo in an act of 'sympathy with the individual lot' (2: 317). But Bernardo is guilty of treason against the government: Romola's sympathy with this individual father signifies a failure of sympathy with the community, a sympathy the novel elsewhere defines as its narrative ideal. This contradiction identifies Eliot's failure to resolve her feelings about paternal authority and daughterly desire.

Once Romola dedicates herself to the memory of her father, other fathers may be purged from the narrative. By the end of the novel, Lorenzo de' Medici, Bardo, Baldassarre, Savonarola, and Bernardo del Nero are dead. Lorenzo's death at the novel's opening and Bernardo's at its close represent the public death of fathers, the decline of paternal authority in fifteenth-century Florence, which initiates corruption, plague and pestilence. Baldassarre dies while killing Tito. Savonarola, who fears to prove his innocence by walking through fire – symbol of his passion and his scourge – is executed. The apparently innocent daughter participates in this structural scapegoating of fathers. Romola's seemingly unmotivated guilt about her father's death and her desire to institutionalize Bardo's library spring from her unspoken wish to live happily alone with Tito – and therefore clearly without her father. Like Tito, Romola metaphorically wishes her father dead. Romola's rescue of her starving father-in-law from the streets of Florence enables his own and Tito's embracing deaths. Baldassarre identifies himself and tells Romola, 'You would have been my daughter'; but, he confides, 'we will have our revenge' (2: 239, 245). When Baldassarre kills Tito, and with his son himself, he acts out Romola's revenge as well as his own. Finally, the narrative also implies Romola's guilt for her godfather's death. Fearing she has hardened Savonarola against Bernardo by pleading for his life, Romola cries out to her padricullo, 'If any harm comes to you, it will be as if I had done it' (2: 249). The narrative surreptitiously attributes these deaths to its otherwise dutiful heroine and identifies the desire for parricide as belonging rightfully to her.

Romola decides at the end of the novel to obey only her own law, to 'act on her own warrant'. She decides voluntarily to leave her husband not only because he has taken another wife but because he has forsaken his father. The 'demands of inner moral facts' now outweigh those of an 'outward law'. Although the marriage law is sacred, 'rebellion might be sacred too' (2: 273–4). Romola's now rightful desire to leave her husband and fathers takes the metaphorical form of her deathlike drift to Spain and her dreamlike salvation of its people from the plague. Without fathers, without male relation, Romola becomes the desireless 'Visible Madonna'.[16] On the eve of the eleventh anniversary of Savonarola's death, Romola tells her little figurative family sentimental stories about the deaths of her father and spiritual father, moralistic fables about the lawless desire and necessary death of her husband. As 'ideal' figure for the young writer, Romola's binding herself to her law facilitates Eliot's binding herself to her own law, her authoritative narrative word, her career as storyteller (*Letters*, 4: 104). When memory of desire and prohibition becomes traumatic, George Eliot retroactively interprets the first scenes of a history in the symbols of a second. *Romola* indeed marks a 'well-defined transition' in the life of its writer.

As I intend to argue in this discussion of *Romola*, although Eliot's material forced her to confront her traumatic memories of father and brother, the concepts of retroactive reconstruction and of the 'work of recollection' do not imply that the woman who remembers necessarily resolves the trauma memory creates. In symbolizing her memory, in binding and repressing desire and calling it 'sympathy' or 'fellow-feeling', Eliot controls her memory and so its traumatic effects. Yet she also ensures this repressed material will reappear in her later novels. Indeed, Eliot's final narratives, *Middlemarch* and *Daniel Deronda*, carry the trace of *Romola*'s bindings, its repressions. In both novels, the uncle replaces the scapegoated father as a figure of failed and apparently illegitimate authority, although the figurative 'shadow of the father' nonetheless haunts both narratives.[17] The 'ploughing up' and 'scourging' of herself the writing of *Romola* performed enables Eliot to view Dorothea and Gwendolen with an irony that intends to declare the writer's difference from her two heroines, one blinded by her idealistic, the other her egoistic, ambition. Both narratives, however, place the daughter as desiring subject in a repressed scene of seduction, and both narratively blame that daughter for her desire. After having bound the daughter to her own law in *Romola*, Eliot nevertheless portrays her last heroines struggling to bind themselves to a community's law. Eliot condemns Dorothea and Gwendolen to learn sympathy through suffering, a fate once reserved for the 'hard' fathers of the early novels.

Notes

1. Ruby V. Redinger, *George Eliot: The Emergent Self* (New York: Alfred A. Knopf, 1977), pp. 440–59, also defines *Romola*'s publication as unique.
2. Redinger, ibid., p. 433, defines this 'strange sequence of fiction' as beginning with 'Brother Jacob' and extending through *Romola*: I see this period of struggle as slightly longer.
3. John W. Cross, *George Eliot's Life as Related in Her Letters and Journals*, 3 vols (Edinburgh and London: William Blackwood and Sons, n.d.). 2, p. 255.
4. Felicia Bonaparte, *The Triptych and the Cross: The Central Myths of George Eliot's Poetic Imagination* (New York: New York University Press, 1979), p. 10.
5. Quoted by Redinger, *George Eliot*, p. 442.
6. Bonaparte, *The Triptych and the Cross*, pp. 1–33, makes some of these same points about *Romola*'s importance and Eliot's process of composition.
7. Jean Laplanche and J.-B. Pontalis. *Language of Psycho-Analysis.* trans. Donald Nicholson-Smith (London: Hogarth Press, 1973), pp. 465–9.
8. Sigmund Freud 'Fixation to Traumas: The Unconscious', *The Standard Edition of the Complete Psychological Works of Sigmund Freud.* 24 Vols, ed. James Strachey (London: Hogarth Press, 1953–74), 16 (1963), pp. 273–85, especially p. 275.
9. Laplanche and Pontalis, 'Fantasy and the Origins of Sexuality', *International Journal of Psychoanalysis*, 49 (1968): pp. 3–11; Laplanche and Pontalis, *Language of Psycho-Analysis*, pp. 404–7; Laplanche, *Life and Death in Psychoanalysis*, trans. and intro. Jeffrey Mehlman (Baltimore: Johns Hopkins University Press, 1976), pp. 25–47: Sigmund Freud, 'Studies in Hysteria', *SE*, 2 (1955), 162.

10. George Eliot, *Romola*, 2 vols (Edinburgh and London: William Blackwood and Sons, n.d.). 1, pp. 343–52. All references in my text are to the Cabinet Edition.

11. Bonaparte, *The Triptych and the Cross*, p. 116.

12. Carole Robinson, '*Romola*: A Reading of the Novel', *Victorian Studies*, 7 (1962): 29–42.

13. Bonaparte, *The Triptych and the Cross*, pp. 188–93, believes Eliot discriminates in *Romola* between the Bacchic law of the aggregate, which protects the individual against the encroachments of others on his freedom, and the Christian law of the community, which binds the individual to concern for the welfare of all. Although Bonaparte discusses Eliot's faith in this Christian law as moral but nondidactic, as descriptive but not normative, I think *Romola* is Eliot's most didactic and normative novel primarily because it taps dangerous memories that must be controlled or repressed to allow its author to go forward in her life and career as a writer.

14. Laplanche and Pontalis, *Language of Psycho-Analysis*, pp. 50–2.

15. As Felicia Bonaparte points out, the public handbills titled 'Justice' (which demands execution of the traitors) and 'Law' (which urges the appeal be granted) define Savonarola's law as lawless and opposed to the community's interest and mortality. See *The Triptych and the Cross*, p. 221.

16. See Robinson, '*Romola*', p. 41, and Bonaparte, *The Triptych and the Cross*, pp. 229–39.

17. For discussions of uncles in Eliot's novels, see U. C. Knoepflmacher, '*Middlemarch*: An Avuncular View', *Nineteenth-Century Fiction*, 30 (1975), pp. 53–81; Joseph Wiesenfarth, 'Commentary', *Nineteenth-Century Fiction* 30 (1976), pp. 572–3, explicates the allusion in *Middlemarch*: 'Der Neffe als Onkel'.

9 The Failure of Realism: *Felix Holt**

CATHERINE GALLAGHER

Catherine Gallagher is one of the growing number of critics who are applying New Historicist critical approach to nineteenth-century fiction. Unlike post-structuralist critics such as J. Hillis Miller and Jonathan Arac, she sees George Eliot's realism as beset by irresolvable contradictions and argues that these utimately derive from the failure of George Eliot and other nineteenth-century intellectuals to find a way of overcoming the contradictions in the ideology of liberalism (see Introduction, pp. 18–19).

In a London art gallery in 1861, two middle-aged women stand before a painting of a stork killing a toad. The painting provokes a short, sharp argument. The older woman dislikes it intensely, calling it coarse and amoral; the younger woman admires it, explaining, somewhat condescendingly, that the purpose of art is a careful delineation of the actual. Good art, she insists, must show the world as it is. The older woman then pointedly asks whether it would be good art to delineate carefully men on a raft eating a comrade. According to the older woman's later report, the question silences her companion.[1]

In itself, the exchange is hardly remarkable. It seems still another iteration of a debate that was already wearing thin by 1861, the controversy between aesthetic idealists and realists. If the followers of the one orthodoxy required art to imbue reality with value, to show the world as it could be, followers of the other orthodoxy required art to record facts and show the world as it is. The two debaters, however, were more than followers of established orthodoxies. As an exchange between Harriet Martineau and George Eliot, women whose opinions had a profound effect, the dispute deserves closer attention.

George Eliot's insistence, in 1861, on a totally unembellished rendering of reality might surprise not only those turn-of-the-century detractors

---

* Reprinted from *Nineteenth-Century Fiction*, 35 (1980), pp. 372–84.

who called her work tediously didactic, but also all those more recent critics who have rightly insisted that even early works such as *Adam Bede* present a world at once probable yet 'shaped through and through by moral judgment and moral evaluation'.[2] Martineau's remarks, too, might seem puzzling: certainly no early-Victorian writer seems more comfortable with unpleasant facts than the writer who – long before George Eliot professed to find 'few sublimely beautiful women' and even fewer real 'heroes'[3] – had introduced English readers to truly plebeian and unpicturesque protagonists, to dismal quotidian destinies, to an unflinching (at times even unfeeling) scrutiny of the harshest realities. Indeed, many of her contemporaries would have considered 'men on a raft eating a comrade' an accurate emblem for Martineau's own social vision.[4]

The argument between the two women, then, was not, as it might have seemed to a casual eavesdropper, an argument between an aesthetic idealist and a realist, but rather a debate between two realists eager to settle the right relationship between facts and values. Their debate illustrates an essential tension within the tradition of English realism. Moreover, it also points to a tension within George Eliot's own realistic fiction – a tension which results in contradictions and shifts that become most marked in her productions of the 1860s, especially in *Romola, The Spanish Gypsy* and *Felix Holt*, the 1866 novel which will serve as this essay's prime illustration of George Eliot's break with the notions of realism to which she still paid lip service in her debate with Martineau.

Theoretically at least, Harriet Martineau and George Eliot were equally dedicated to the desire to keep facts and values continuous and inseparable. Martineau's objection to 'mere delineation' grows out of her belief that all facts emanate from values inherent in a God's benign purpose. The parabolic stories in her *Illustrations of Political Economy* (1834) yield facts that supposedly leave behind a sedimented deposit of meanings and morals, the principle of political economy that can be tallied at the end of each tale.[5] Reality itself thus furnishes an illustration of principles, at once material and moral. For Martineau, a morally neutral realism was a contradiction in terms; her own didactic fiction was simply the most efficient form of realism, deducing facts from principles she knew to be true.

George Eliot's narrative method purports to be inductive rather than deductive like Martineau's. Unable to share the older woman's belief in a benign providential necessity, the younger adopts, as critics have shown, the methodology and diction of those who scrutinize a more impersonal process of evolution. Still, like Martineau, George Eliot assumes a bond between facts and values. Indeed, her insistence that art need only 'delineate the actual' would appear, superficially at least, to express a greater faith than Martineau's in the necessary connection between 'is' and 'ought'. Despite the doubts expressed in such early works as 'The Lifted Veil', George Eliot continued to cling to the hope that a detailed recording of everyday life might ineluctably lead to moral progress. This, at least, is the faith professed in the much-analyzed seventeenth chapter of *Adam Bede*, where the narrator defends herself against an imagined idealistic reader by claiming that realistic fiction could increase the world's stock of charity: 'These fellow-mortals, every one, must be accepted as they are . . . it is these . . . you should tolerate, pity, and love: it is these more or less ugly, stupid, inconsistent people . . . for whom you should cherish all possible hopes, all possible patience.' By recommending an acceptance of the obscure, the imperfect and the commonplace, the narrator also recommends, in fact, her own fictional practice as an antidote to meanness and intolerance. A better world, presumably, would be composed of figures such as Wordsworth's Wanderer or George Eliot's narrators, telling one another endless stories, including all detail within the sphere of significance, and thereby gradually expanding one another's sympathy. We get from facts to values by the process of inclusion, equalization, and acceptance, by that slow-moving narrative method we now call metonymic realism.

Harriet Martineau and George Eliot, then, held similar metaphysical assumptions: meaning is incrusted in the details of everyday reality; the universe is orderly and determined; facts and values are inseparable. And yet, if we are to trust Martineau's account of their 1861 conversation, George Eliot, so suddenly silenced, no longer seemed eager to argue that the artist need only multiply facts to arrive at essences and values. Was she simply exasperated, perhaps tired of shouting responses at an almost completely deaf companion? Or had Martineau hit on a difficulty that George Eliot had herself found increasingly perplexing? As U. C. Knoepflmacher and, more recently, Walter M. Kendrick have shown, George Eliot's latent idealism had always been at odds with her programmatic belief in the objective recording of fact.[6] In 1861, the year of *Silas Marner*, the romance that had interposed itself between the composition of *The Mill on the Floss* and *Romola*, she seemed at the threshold of a new phase – a phase that would lead her to a rejection of the metonymic method to which she had until then adhered.

George Eliot's early novels are metonymic in the simple sense mentioned above: they operate on the assumption that observable appearances bespeak deeper moral essences. We come to know her characters through what they wear, how they use words, furnish rooms, or dress their hair. We arrive at moral essences by accumulating the specific details of appearance that surround these essences. Flaubert expressed the same idea when he advised Guy de Maupassant. 'When you pass a grocer sitting in his doorway . . . [or] a porter smoking his pipe . . . show me that grocer and that porter, their attitude and their whole physical aspect, including, as indicated by the skill of the portrait, their whole moral nature.'[7] This faith, however, only half conceals a correlative doubt. The stress on 'whole' in Flaubert's advice indicates the realist's acknowledgment that signs are not individually very telling. The need to heap sign upon sign thus grows out of a recognition of the insufficiency and ambiguity of signs. Indeed, most realistic novels, *Adam Bede* or *The Mill on the Floss* among them, ironically exploit the incongruity between appearances and essences; they are full of misunderstandings, isolation, the indequacy of conventional signifiers. Realists thus are forced to supplement metonymic representation with other forms of signification. Indeed, if appearances were as self-sufficient as realists sometimes claim, there would probably be no need for novels, certainly no need for omniscient narrators with access to their characters' subjective inner lives, and surely no need for a body of critical explication.

Realistic fiction, then, invariably undermines, in practice, the ideology it purports to exemplify. The discontinuity between facts and values, already apparent in her earlier work, became increasingly obtrusive in George Eliot's fiction during the 1860s. Why did this latent tension manifest itself so much more pronouncedly in her writing during that decade? Miriam Allott, in 'George Eliot in the 1860s', rightly notes that 'ill-health and the emotional depressions of middle age' were quite 'possibly deepened by the scepticism which is usually associated with this decade's movement of ideas'; George Eliot, she stresses, 'was now facing for the first time the more sombre implications of her own doctrines'.[8] Yet Allott does little to connect the artistic impasse that the novelist reached after *Silas Marner* with her changing social and political doctrine, the skepticism about reform and amelioration that now distanced her from thinkers like Harriet Martineau. In the 1860s George Eliot seemed to have become acutely aware of a larger crisis in something that, for want of a better word, is generally called liberalism. This new awareness seems most clearly illustrated in *Felix Holt*, a novel that not only calls in question some of her former social theories but also relentlessly separates facts from values.

George Eliot's earlier notions of realism had been closely tied to liberal ideas of social reform. In chapter 17 of *Adam Bede*, by likening her narrative method to the workings of family love, she seems to lend her support to those liberal humanists who recommended the extension of family feeling as a cure for the conflicts of Victorian society.[9] The idea of a communal family, capable of conferring significance on the least of its members, was at variance with the hierarchical notions of Tory paternalism. It was a metaphor that could be aligned with the other liberal metaphor of the free marketplace; as such, both could be – and were – described through the use of some of George Eliot's favourite adjectives, the same adjectives she applied to her own realism: 'wide', 'inclusive', 'encompassing', 'gradually developing', and 'common-place'. Though hardly a simple-minded free trader, nor even a staunch political liberal, the early George Eliot thus displays, nonetheless, certain affinities with social thinkers of the 1850s, such as John Bright: she is anti-hierarchical in her social and artistic outlook; she insists on equalizing by raising all to the level of significance; and she hopes that inclusion and acceptance will of themselves lead to the production of meaning, order, and universal understanding.

As Joseph Butwin* [has shown] by contrasting *Romola* to the earlier *Scenes of Clerical Life*, the George Eliot of the 1860s became disenchanted with the principle of mere aggregation. She was only one of many liberals to undergo an ideological transformation at a time when working-class reformers and their allies appropriated the earlier rhetoric of market-place accumulation to urge an extension of the franchise and to argue that including more classes in the political process would result in an improvement of that process. By mid-decade, when the agitation for the second Reform Bill was reaching its height, George Eliot had joined Matthew Arnold in the task of redefining the relationship between what is and what ought to be.[10]

That task demanded major rhetorical shifts. The metaphor of the market-place gives way to tropes that imply notions of hierarchy: the public realm now becomes a church or state.[11] Though retained, the metaphor of the family undergoes significant changes: instead of loving inclusiveness, the new stress falls on order and subordination.[12] What is more, the notion of family is now infused with the Burkean idea of a collective inheritance, a large portion of which is called 'culture'. As a repository of values, however, culture becomes an elusive legacy, as Romola or Fedalma sadly discover: by its very nature, culture cannot be possessed, only pursued, and its relationship to daily life is uncertain. Material structures such as the Hall Farm, Dorlcote Mill, or Squire Cass's Red House give way to the transcendent legacies to which a Romola or Fedalma must cling. Unlike the earlier values of charity and fellow feeling, culture does not grow out of commonplace events. Ordinary people do not produce it in their daily lives. By the end of George Eliot's career, in *Daniel Deronda*, Daniel and Mirah become the recipients of a higher destiny that removes them from the aggregated facts of a too provincial English life.

Like *Romola* before it, *Felix Holt* reflects the formal consequences for George Eliot's realism of the new need for a transcendent realm of values and ultimate meanings. Whereas in *Romola* she could retreat to a more epic past, in *Felix Holt* she returns to the Midland landscapes of her earlier

* [Ed.] See Joseph Butwin, 'The Pacification of the Crowd: From "Janet's Repentance" to *Felix Holt*', *Nineteenth-Century Fiction*, 35 (1980), pp. 349–71.

realism to re-examine the problem of facts and values and addresses herself more directly to the sociopolitical crises of the 1860s. With its emphasis on radical politics and on the working class's demands for the franchise, this novel connects the author's skepticism about democracy to her reactivated doubts about facts and values. The formal consequences of this decision are various, and result in certain imbalances and contradictions. The intertwining of individual and family destinies now requires Dickensian intricacies of plot; there are abrupt changes in narrative tone, with a larger number of discursive passages that often resemble self-parodies. The most startling difficulty of the novel, however, results from Felix's opposition to George Eliot's own realistic method of metonymic representation. No longer able to squelch an imaginary idealist opponent, as in *Adam Bede*, the narrator now seems undermined by Felix's own 'cultured' mode of beholding reality.

Felix Holt is full of comments about the nature of signs and portents. The first meeting between Felix and the Reverend Rufus Lyon explicitly introduces the subject of the relationship between outward signs, or facts, and inner essences, or values. Felix and Mr Lyon, the book's two moral arbiters, admit to one another that they scarcely see the conventional physical signs by which their fellows communicate their importance and priorities. Hence, when Felix enters the room, we are told what he does not see. He does not see the wax candle on the table that the dissenting minister feels uneasy about:

> when, after seating himself, at the minister's invitation, near the little table which held the work-basket, he stared at the wax-candle opposite to him, he did so without any wonder or consciousness that the candle was not of tallow. But the minister's sensitiveness gave another interpretation to the gaze which he divined rather than saw; and in alarm lest this inconsistent extravagance should obstruct his usefulness, he hastened to say –
>
> 'You are doubtless amazed to see me with a wax-light, my young friend; but this undue luxury is paid for with the earnings of my daughter, who is so delicately framed that the smell of tallow is loathsome to her.'
>
> 'I heeded not the candle, sir. I thank Heaven I am not a mouse to have a nose that takes note of wax or tallow.'[13]

Mr Lyon, who has not even actually seen Felix's gaze, replies that he is 'equally indifferent'.

The implied 'mouse' who does have a nose for wax or tallow is, of course, the minister's unregenerate daughter, Esther. But we must note that the narrator also falls into this category of 'mouse', and so do all of us who are forced by the narrative method to read an external world through its metonymic signs. Narrator and reader must make meaning out of the low facts that Felix is too cultivated and 'abstracted', as the narrator repeatedly tells us, to notice. It is through wax candles that we come to know Esther, and it is through the detail of Felix's inattention to such details that we come to know him. Our first introduction to Felix, then, reveals the wide discrepancy in this novel between the state of mind explicitly recommended in the 'cultured' person of Felix and the mental practices actually encouraged by the method of inductive realism.

Moreover, we soon learn that Felix's inattention to metonymic signs is not just a casual abstraction but a programmatic denial of the meanings and values conventionally attached to signs. In his person, Felix is more than an escapee from realism (as the Reverend Rufus Lyon is); he represents an attack on conventional reading. This fact becomes clear when he discusses his own metonymic unreadability. Referring to himself, Felix says to Rufus:

> 'You're thinking that you have a roughly-written page before you now.'
>
> That was true. The minister, accustomed to the respectable air of provincial townsmen, and especially to the sleek well-clipped gravity of his own male congregation, felt a slight shock as his glasses made perfectly clear to him the shaggy-headed, large-eyed, strong-limbed person of this questionable young man, without waistcoat or cravat.
>
> (CHAPTER 5)

Faced with this illegible creature, Rufus tries to suspend 'interpretations'. Nevertheless, he inadvertently gives a spiritual reading of Felix's appearance: 'I myself have experienced that when the spirit is much exercised it is difficult to remember neckbands and strings and such small accidents of our vesture, which are nevertheless decent and needful so long as we sojourn in the flesh. And you too, my young friend . . . are undergoing some travail of mind' (chapter 5).

But Rufus has misread these significant absences about Felix's person; they do not betoken the carelessness of an unquiet spirit. Felix is not simply inattentive to all conventional signs of prosperity; he is, rather, actively hostile to some, for he sees them not as arbitrary signs but as material cause of spiritual degeneration. Rufus tries to bring him to a relatively settled Protestant view of the relationship between outward appearance and inward essence, a view that stresses the conventionality of signs: 'The ring and the robe of Joseph were no objects for a good man's ambition, but they were the signs of the credit which he won by his divinely-inspired skill, and which enabled him to act as a saviour to his brethren' (chapter 5). But Felix will have none of this talk about the importance of crediting such appearances. It is his avowed purpose to prove these so-called signs are not signs at all, but actual promoters of inner corruption. He answers Rufus:

> 'O yes, your ringed and scented men of the people! – I won't be one of them. Let a man once throttle himself with a satin stock, and he'll get new wants and new motives. Metamorphosis will have begun at his neck-joint, and it will go on till it has changed his likings first and then his reasoning, which will follow his likings as the feet of a hungry dog follow his nose.'
>
> (CHAPTER 5)

Oddly, Felix, who professes not to be interested in outward appearances, actually believes some of those appearances to be absolutely related to inner states. He reverses the normal causality of metonymy: instead of believing that meanings find expression in signs, he believes that signs cause their meanings. In Felix's image, the sign literally becomes the meaning; the two are indistinguishable.

Felix, therefore, first attributes too little and then too much to the world of appearances. This apparent inconsistency is appropriate in a character who stands for culture, for a realm of values independent of facts but also a realm of values that are absolutely and eternally fixed, where appearances that are recognized are equated with essences.

This second attitude toward material signs is as antithetical to Eliot's inductive realism as was Felix's earlier indifference, for it turns the hero into one of those spokesmen for didacticism whom the narrator scolded in *Adam Bede* and whom she still criticizes in *Felix Holt*. The real world, the narrator of *Felix Holt* assures us, is not one in which good and bad are easy to separate or in which signs always mean the same thing. She criticizes the 'little minister' for wanting a more fixed and obvious relationship between signs and their meanings than an ambiguous world permits: 'He cared intensely for his opinions, and would have liked events to speak for them in a sort of picture-writing that everybody could understand. The enthusiasms of the world are not to be stimulated by a commentary, in small and subtle characters which alone can tell the whole truth' (chapter 37). Still, the narrator seems more lenient towards Felix, who, after all, insists on 'picture-writing', on didactic simplicity, even more strenuously than Rufus does. Felix gets into trouble because he cannot stand to see his cause compromised by the mixed motives of others. Somehow Felix's truth, unlike that of the narrator, can dispense with the testimony of 'small and subtle characters'.

Moreover, Felix is himself a piece of that 'picture-writing' the narrator ostensibly repudiates. In her descriptions of Felix, the narrator gives the same details repeatedly and always makes them stand for the same inner qualities, qualities that can be summed up in the word 'culture':

> Felix Holt's face had the look of the habitual meditative abstraction from objects of mere personal vanity or desire, which is the peculiar stamp of culture, and makes a very roughly-cut face worthy to be called 'the human face divine'. Even lions and dogs know a distinction between men's glances; and doubtless those Duffield men, in the expectation with which they looked up at Felix, were unconsciously influenced by the grandeur of his full yet firm mouth, and the calm clearness of his grey eyes.
>
> (CHAPTER 30)

With his booming voice, his massive frame, his leonine head, and his perfect integrity, Felix has nothing 'small' or 'subtle' about him. His meaning is known 'unconsciously' by those he encounters, and therefore he need not be perceived in detail and deciphered. He completely lacks ambiguity; in his character, appearance and essence seem pure and identical. We do not need to see much of Felix because what we do see is wholly expressive, a 'picture-writing that everybody could understand'.

Felix's characterization, then, is even more incongruous than the presentation of similarly idealized figures in previous novels, *Adam Bede*, say, or *Romola*. It is significant that the narrator should rely on epithets borrowed from other writers (for example, 'the human face divine') when she describes her hero. It is true that George Eliot tries to complicate Felix's presence in the novel when she involves him in a compromising situation: he appears to be guilty of leading a riot and is accused of manslaughter. He is arrested and placed on trial, where the prosecution produces 'picture-writing', the outline of appearances, against him. Indeed, this trial is the context for the narrator's disparaging remarks about oversimplifying the relationship between facts and values. Here at last, it seems, Felix can only be acquitted by a 'commentary in small and subtle characters'. The trial, one expects, will be a triumph of inductive realism in which truth is rendered by filling in the details that completely change the picture.

This expectation, however, is disappointed, for instead of filling in the facts of Felix's case, the defense's most important witness, Esther, simply sweeps them aside: 'His nature is very noble; he is tender-hearted; he could never have had any intention that was not brave and good' (chapter 46). This testimony would hardly seem sufficient to exonerate Felix in the eyes of the law, yet everyone in the courtroom is willing to believe it. Felix's character is not complicated in the least by this episode; no one who has the slightest contact with him ever doubts his innocence. He is finally delivered simply because he is obviously and indisputably good. His 'cultured nature' (chapter 43), as Esther calls it, overwhelms the evidence, the facts, once again emphasizing that the meaning of Felix Holt cannot be reached by multiplying appearances.

Thus Felix and the plot that revolves around him contradict the inductive metonymic assumptions of the rest of the novel. What is explicitly recommended in the exemplary person of Felix Holt is implicitly denied in the book's dominant narrative method. Felix's own discourse is even more didactic than Harriet Martineau's, and his 'habitual meditative abstraction . . . which is the peculiar stamp of culture' bars him from the world of inductive realism in which metonymic signs are produced and exchanged. That is why we see almost nothing in this novel through Felix's eyes. The narrator takes up the perspective of every other major character; Felix, we are repeatedly told, has a 'high' view of things; it is too high, apparently, for the narrator to reach.

The treatment of Felix's character shows George Eliot swinging far beyond Harriet Martineau's position in their 1861 debate. For not only Martineau but George Eliot herself had clearly recognized all along that a mere delineation of appearances, no matter how detailed, could not yield essential truths and values. The political concerns of the 1860s so unsettled the novelist that her accommodation in *Felix Holt* of Martineau's side of the argument may seem as crude and disruptive as the older woman's own didactic parables. But for an author who regarded each of her works as but a distinct 'mental phase', *Felix Holt* must be seen as part of a movement towards more sophisticated and self-conscious narrative forms. That movement was to reach two very different climaxes: the knowing, artful compromise of *Middlemarch*, in which reform and the 1832 Reform Bill become themselves metaphors, and the daring experiment of *Daniel Deronda*, which undoes that compromise. The rejection of inductive realism, moreover, was to be completed by later novelists. Writers such as Henry James, D. H. Lawrence and Virginia Woolf would declare it impossible to reach a character's essence and value by concentrating on the outward facts of his or her 'social being'. *Felix Holt* should be seen as a significant step in the progress towards that understanding.

Notes

1. This story, originally recorded in a letter from Harriet Martineau to Henry Reeve (7 May 1861) is retold by R. K. Webb in *Harriet Martineau: A Radical Victorian* (New York: Columbia University Press; London: Heinemann, 1960), p. 39.
2. Dorothy Van Ghent, 'On *Adam Bede*', *The English Novel: Form and Function* (New York: Rinehart, 1953), p. 1972. For a summary of the debunking criticism

of the 1890s and 1910s, see David Carroll, Introduction, *George Eliot: The Critical Heritage*, ed. David Carroll (London: Routledge; New York: Barnes and Noble, 1971), pp. 41–3; and Elaine Showalter, 'The Greening of Sister George', *Nineteenth-Century Fiction*, 35 (1980), pp. 292–311.

3. *Adam Bede*, ed. Stephen Gill (Harmondsworth: Penguin, 1980), ch. 17.
4. Twentieth-century commentators have softened the outline of Martineau's reputation. Thus, R. K. Webb defends her against charges of hard-heartedness (see *Harriet Martineau, passim*); and Mark Blaug, *Ricardian Economics: A Historical Study*, Yale Studies in Economics, 8 (New Haven: Yale University Press, 1958), pp. 129–39, sees her as an optimistic humanitarian when contrasted to the political economists she popularized.
5. Indeed, MARTINEAU chose to write her *Illustrations of Political Economy* because she regarded political economy to be itself an 'illustration' of providential necessity, a science that showed how 'facts' were generated by divine laws. See Martineau's review of Samuel Bailey's *Essays on the Pursuit of Truth, on the Progress of Knowledge, and on the Fundamental Principle of all Evidence and Expectation*, reprinted in her *Miscellanies*, 2 vols (Boston: Hilliard, Gray, 1836), II, pp. 174–96.
6. KNOEPFLMACHER, *George Eliot's Early Novels: The Limits of Realism* (Berkeley and Los Angeles: University of California Press, 1968), *passim*; Kendrick, 'Balzac and British Realism: Mid-Victorian Theories of the Novel', *Victorian Studies*, 20 (1976), pp. 5–24.
7. GUY DE MAUPASSANT, 'Of "The Novel"', *Pierre and Jean*, trans. Clara Bell (New York: Collier, 1902), p. lxi.
8. 'GEORGE ELIOT in the 1860s', *Victorian Studies*, 5 (1961), p. 97.
9. The 1840s and 1850s saw the adoption of the family–society metaphor by industrialists. See John Foster, *Class Struggle and the Industrial Revolution: Early Industrial Capitalism in Three English Towns* (London: Weidenfeld & Nicolson, 1974), pp. 188 ff.; Sidney Pollard, *The Genesis of Modern Management: A Study of the Industrial Revolution in Great Britain* (Harmondsworth: Penguin, 1968), pp. 189–242; and my own 'British Industrial Narratives, 1830–1855', Dissertation, University of California, Berkeley, 1979, pp. 191–215.
10. GEORGE ELIOT's innate conservatism, evident in 'The Natural History of German Life', *Westminster Review*, 66 (1856), pp. 51–79; reprinted in *Essays of George Eliot*, ed. Thomas Pinney (New York: Columbia University Press, 1963), pp. 266–99, resurfaced in the 1860s, but only with the positive focus on the idea of culture did that conservatism become strong enough to allow her to uncouple facts from values.
11. In *Culture and Anarchy* (1932; reprinted, with corrections, Cambridge: Cambridge University Press, 1935), Matthew Arnold wishes to reintegrate into the 'main current of the national life' those excluded from the Church of England (p. 34). He also bemoans the lack of a strong idea of 'a *State*' in England (p. 81).
12. ARNOLD compares society to an overly permissive and indulgent family; ironically contrasting its disparate treatment of an Irish Fenian and a Hyde Park rioter, he claims that the latter is forgiven because he is of 'our own flesh and blood' (*Culture and Anarchy*, pp. 79–80).

13. *Felix Holt, the Radical* (Harmondsworth: Penguin, 1972), chapter 5. Further citations in the text are from this edition.

10 The End of a Metalanguage: From George Eliot to *Dubliners (Middlemarch* and *Daniel Deronda)**

COLIN MACCABE

Colin MacCabe, in common with several British post-structuralist critics, sees George Eliot's fiction as fundamentally reflective in its mode of realism since, unlike the work of a Modernist like Joyce, it fails to problematize the relation between language and reality. He claims that *Middlemarch* should be categorized as a 'classic realist text', a defining feature of which is that the language of the narrator functions as a metalanguage which is superior to all the other forms of discourse in the text. Thus the narration refuses to acknowledge that writing is a signifying process rather than simply a means of reflecting the world (see Introduction, pp. 5–7).

In order to carry out its task of interpretation, the discourse of literary criticism must always be able to identify what is represented, independently of the form of the representation. This identification is only possible if the discourse of the critic is in a position to transform the text into content, and, to undertake this transformation, the relation between the language of the text and the language of the critic must be that which obtains between an object- and a metalanguage. A metalanguage 'talks about' an object-language and transforms it into content by naming the object-language (accomplished through the use of inverted commas) and thus being able to identify both the object-language and its area of application.† It is from the position of the metalanguage that correspondence between word and world can be established.

A text is made up of many languages, or discourses, and the critic's ability to homogenise these articulations is related to their prior organisation within the text. Joyce's texts refuse the very category of

---

* Reprinted from Colin MacCabe, *James Joyce and the Revolution of the Word* (London: Macmillan Press, 1978), pp. 13–28, 35–6.

† The definition of a metalanguage is taken from Tarski's classic article on the

metalanguage and a critical discourse is thus unable to obtain any purchase on the text. None of the discourses which circulate in *Finnegans Wake* or *Ulysses* can master or make sense of the others and there is, therefore, no possibility of the critic articulating his or her reading as an elaboration of a dominant position within the text. In Joyce's writing, indeed, all positions are constantly threatened with dissolution into the play of language. The critic cannot grasp the content of Joyce's texts, for the texts investigate the very processes which produce both content and form, object-languages and metalanguage.

The absence of a metalanguage in Joyce's work is evident in his refusal, a refusal which dates from his earliest writings, to use what he called 'perverted commas' (letter to Harriet Shaw Weaver, 11 July 1924). While those sections in a work which are contained in inverted commas may offer different ways of regarding and analysing the world, they are negated as real alternatives by the unspoken prose that surrounds and controls them. The narrative prose is the metalanguage that can state all the truths in the object-language(s) (the marks held in inverted commas) and can also explain the relation of the object-language to the world. This relation of dominance allows the metalanguage to understand how the object discourses obscurely figure truths which find clear expression in the meta language. A metalanguage regards its object discourses as material but itself as transparent. And this transparency allows the identity of things to shine through the window of words in the unspoken narrative whereas the spoken discourses which clothe meaning with material are necessarily obscure. At all costs the metalanguage must refuse to admit its own materiality, for in so far as the metalanguage is itself treated as material, it, too, can be reinterpreted; new meanings can be found for it in a further metalanguage. The problem of the infinite regress of metalanguages brings us to the heart of the problem of meaning and interpretation. What the materiality of language constantly insists on, and what is insistently repressed in our society, is the separation between speech (or writing) and consciousness. This separation can be understood as the gap between the act of saying and what is said; a gap which occurs both temporally and spatially. For the

---

semantic conception of truth (Tarski 1949). Throughout this work language (and its compounds) will be used as a synonym for discourse, that is to say as a term to refer to any system of lexical combination which has as effect a distinct subject position. It is thus not synonymous (except where the context demands it) with that everyday use of the word 'language' to refer to different national tongues, nor to Saussure's definition of language (*la langue*) as a system of differences, a definition which ignores any reference to subject position. An everyday use which approaches closely the sense desired can be identified in a phrase like 'They speak a different language', when the speaker is indicating differences of position and attitude amongst speakers of a single national language.

time that it takes to traverse a page or listen to a sentence forbids any instantaneous grasping of meaning. Interpretation is perpetually deferred as each segment of meaning is defined by what follows. And in the space that separates eye from page or ear from mouth, there is a constant possibility of an interference, a misunderstanding, that similarly disrupts the presence of meaning. The problem arises from the fact that meaning is distributed through material and is constantly, therefore, open to further interpretations, even though as we say or write a sentence the meaning seems fixed and evident. This formulation of the problem is itself misleading because it presupposes an original moment when there is strict coincidence between meaning and material. The difficulty is more radical because there is no such original moment. The act of enunciation and what is enounced, the saying and the said, are always separated.

It is to ignore this separation that a text uses inverted commas. The metalanguage within such a text refuses to acknowledge its own status as writing – as marks of material difference distributed through time and space. The text outside the area of inverted commas claims to be the product of no articulation, it claims to be unwritten. This unwritten text can then attempt to staunch the haemorrhage of interpretations threatened by the material of language. Whereas other discourses within the text are considered as materials which are open to reinterpretation, the narrative discourse functions simply as a window on reality. This relationship between discourses can be taken as the defining feature of the *classic realist text*. The normal criterion for realism (whether a discourse is fully adequate to the real) merely accepts the conception of the real which the classic realist text proposes for its own project. Thus a traditional anti-realist position that no discourse can ever be adequate to the multifarious nature of the real assumes the classic realist division of language and reality. The classic realist text should not, however, be understood in terms of some homology to the order of things but as a specific hierarchy of discourses which places the reader in a position of dominance with regard to the stories and characters. However, this position is only achieved at the cost of a certain fixation, a certain subjection. George Eliot's texts provide an example of this discursive organisation.

In the scene in *Middlemarch* where Mr Brooke goes to visit Dagley's farm we are presented with two discourses. One is the educated, well-meaning, but not very intelligent discourse of Mr Brooke and the other is the uneducated, violent and very nearly unintelligible discourse of the drunken Dagley. But the whole dialogue is surrounded by a metalanguage (which being unspoken is also unwritten) which places these discourses in inverted commas and can thereby discuss their relation to truth – a truth illuminatingly revealed in the metalanguage. The metalanguage reduces the object languages into a simple division between form and content and extracts the meaningful content from the useless form. Thus we find the following passage towards the end of the chapter:

> He [Mr Brooke] had never been insulted on his own land before, and had been inclined to regard himself as a general favourite (we are all apt to do so, when we think of our own amiability more than of what other people are likely to want of us). When he had quarrelled with Caleb Garth twelve years before he had thought that the tenants would be pleased at the landlord's taking everything into his own hands.
>
> Some who follow the narrative of his experience may wonder at the midnight darkness of Mr Dagley; but nothing was easier in those times than for an hereditary farmer of his grade to be ignorant, in spite somehow of having a rector in the twin parish who was a gentleman to the backbone, a curate nearer at hand who preached more learnedly than the rector, a landlord who had gone into everything, especially fine art and social improvement, and all the lights of Middlemarch only three miles off.
>
> (George Eliot 1880, vol. 2, p. 188)

In this passage we are given the necessary interpretations for the discourses that we have just read. The words of Dagley and Mr Brooke are revealed as springing from two types of ignorance which the metalanguage can expose and reveal. Thus we have Mr Brooke's attitude to his tenants contrasted with the reality which is available to us through the narrative prose. No discourse, except that charged with the narrative, is allowed to speak for itself, instead each speech must be placed in a context which will reduce it to a simple explicable content. The claim of the narrative prose to grant direct access to a final reality guarantees the claim of the realist novel to represent the invariable features of humanity. To reveal the truth about Mr Brooke permits the generalisations about human nature.

But it is not only the vanity of Mr Brooke that is laid bare; there is also the 'midnight darkness' of drunken Dagley. The metaphor employed contrasts the darkness of Dagley's discourse with the daylight clarity of the prose that surrounds and interprets it. Dagley's darkness has already been indicated through the attempt to render his accent phonetically. The emphasis on the material sounds of Dagley's discourse is directly in proportion to the difficulty in understanding it. The material of language is essentially a material that obscures. It is in so far as the narrative prose is not material that the truths of the world can shine through it.

The irony of the passage, which expresses its mock astonishment at the fact of Mr Dagley's ignorance when surrounded by such illuminating figures (and having 'all the lights of Middlemarch' only three miles away), works through the knowledge that the text has already conveyed and in no way damages the narrative's claim to be representing reality without intermediaries. There is a kind of irony (we will come to it later in our reading of Joyce) which works without any fixed rules for rewriting the ironic passage. This lack of interpretative rules is what makes for the difficulty of reading Joyce's texts. However, in this example from George Eliot we can read an example of classical irony. Classical irony is established in the distance between the original sentence and the sentence as it should be, given the knowledge of reality that the text has already conferred on us. For readers there is no astonishment that such midnight darkness as Mr Dagley's should exist not three miles from Middlemarch because the lights of that town have been exposed as shadows by the greater light of the text itself.

The conviction that the real can be displayed and examined through a perfectly transparent language is evident in George Eliot's Prelude to *Middlemarch*. In that Prelude she talks of those who care 'to know the history of man, and how the mysterious mixture behaves under the varying experiments of Time' and this language of empiricism runs through the text. The view of science as a matter of experiment is of a piece with a view of the immutable quality of human nature. For as language disappears and absents itself from the stage, we can clearly see the two-faced character Janus, the god of communication, one face that of human nature and the other that of the external physical world. To transform language into pure communicative absence is to transform the world into a self-evident reality where, in order to discover truth, we have only to use our eyes. This complete refusal to interrogate the form of the investigation, the belief in language's transparency, is evident on those occasions (frequent enough) when George Eliot reflects on that form. Thus in *Middlemarch* at the beginning of chapter 15:

> A great historian, as he insisted on calling himself, who had the happiness to be dead a hundred and twenty years ago, and so to take his place among the colossi whose huge legs our living pettiness is observed to walk under, glories in his copious remarks and digressions as the least imitable part of his work, and especially in those initial chapters to the successive books of his history, where he seems to bring his armchair to the proscenium and chat with us in all the lusty ease of his fine English. But Fielding lived when the days were longer (for time, like money, is measured by our needs), when summer afternoons were spacious, and the clock ticked slowly in the winter evenings. We belated historians must not linger after his example, and if we did so, it is probable that our chat would be thin and eager, as if delivered from a camp-stool in a parrot-house. I at least have so much to do in unravelling certain human lots, and seeing how they were woven and

> interwoven, that all the light I can command must be concentrated on this particular web, and not dispersed over the tempting range of relevancies called the universe.
>
> (GEORGE ELIOT 1880, vol. 1, pp. 213–14).

Although, at first sight, George Eliot would appear to be questioning her form, the force of the passage is to leave us convinced that we have finally abandoned forms to be treated to the simple unravelling of the real. Fielding's digressions, which, as it were, placed his fictions as fictions, are held to have been due to the 'lusty ease of his fine English'; that is, to a certain style. It should not go unremarked that George Eliot considers pleasure ('lusty ease' in language) as fatal as materiality to the transparency of language. If Fielding insisted on calling himself an historian, the passage demonstrates to us the impossibility of that claim. No author so preoccupied with his own position on the stage, 'the proscenium', can avoid the materiality and pleasure of language. It is only 'we belated historians' who no longer have any style, whose chat 'would be thin and eager', it is only such as these who can unravel the real.

The digression itself is no real digression because, situated in the middle of the narrative, its function is merely to efface itself; to testify to the reality of the story in which it is held. Where in Fielding the digression testifies to the written nature of the work, situating the narrative as construction, in Eliot the digression situates the narrative as pure representation, in which the author could not interfere because the author can no longer speak. In the same way the disclaimer of the 'tempting range of relevancies called the universe' does not affect the narrative's claim to be representing the world as it really is as long as the particular 'web' is fully illuminated. And significantly, once again, we find the metaphor of 'light', which is what the text is going to produce. These disclaimers have the function of ensuring, like the wealth of irrelevant detail which is heaped up in the text, the innocence and absence of a form and a language in which content might be distorted. We are persuaded that language and form have disappeared, allowing light to shine on the previously obscured world. Another example of the same kind of effect can be found in *Daniel Deronda*:

> She spoke with dignity and looked straight at Grandcourt, whose long, narrow, impenetrable eyes met hers, and mysteriously arrested them: mysteriously; for the subtly-varied drama between man and woman is often such as can hardly be rendered in words put together like dominoes, according to obvious fixed marks. The word of all work Love will no more express the myriad modes of mutual attraction, than the word Thought can tell you what is passing through your neighbour's mind. It would be hard to tell on which side –

> Gwendolen's or Grandcourt's – the influence was more mixed. At that moment his strongest wish was to be completely master of this creature – this piquant combination of maidenliness and mischief: that she knew things which had made her start away from him, spurred him to triumph over that repugnance; and he was believing that he should triumph. And she – ah, piteous equality in the need to dominate! – she was overcome like the thirsty one who is drawn towards the seeming water in the desert, overcome by the suffused sense that here in this man's homage to her lay the rescue from helpless subjection to an oppressive lot.
>
> (GEORGE ELIOT, 1880 vol. 2, pp. 38–9)

Once again, the objections against the form of describing reality, 'the obvious fixed marks' of writing are swept away as we get taken beyond that 'word of all work Love' to be presented with the very mystery of the drama. The spectre of words deforming reality is raised only to be dissolved by the rising sun of the prose, a very common strategy in realist novels of the nineteenth century where within the realist, and hence unwritten, text the common example of that which is most unreal is the novel, the written text.

It would be a distortion to consider George Eliot's texts as totally determined by that discursive organisation that I have defined as the classic realist text. Within her novels there are always images which counter the flat and univocal process which is the showing forth of the real. Casaubon's key to all the mythologies, Romola's blind father and, perhaps most powerfully of all, the Hebrew language which rests uninvestigable at the centre of *Daniel Deronda*, question and hold in suspense the project of Eliot's texts. Romola's blind father, who stands in the same relation to the girl as does the author – the relationship of creator – reveals metaphorically within the text the inability of the author to see the world that she is creating. The impossibility of writing an historical novel is thereby admitted at one level of the text while, at another, the meta-discourse tries to deny the distance between itself and the discourses of the fifteenth-century Florentine burghers. Similarly Deronda's discovery of the Jewish language and the poems of Mordecai trouble the metalanguage in so far as the Jewish language constitutes an area outside its control. Deronda hears the news that Mordecai's work is in Hebrew and untranslatable with 'anxiety'. Such a feeling is not surprising when we recognise that the poems constitute a fatal threat to the metalanguage. Confronted with a discourse that it cannot transform into an object (that it cannot name) the metalanguage forfeits control of the novel. This lack of control has caused anxiety amongst the readers as well as the characters of *Daniel Deronda*.

The problems and method of reading a realist text may be usefully compared to the problems an analyst faces in the analysis of a neurotic's discourses and the methods used to disengage significant interpretations from those discourses. Conflicts within the psyche combine and interact to produce dreams, symptoms, slips, etc. These psychic productions are described and explained by the neurotic in discourses which render the dreams coherent, the symptoms rational and the slips insignificant. The analyst is invited to offer the neurotic alternative explanations within these explanatory discourses. The analyst, however, has, as it were, to disengage the symptoms and the dreams from these explanatory discourses. Such a disengagement will demonstrate to the analysand not only how the conflicts have entered into the elaboration of the explanatory discourses but more importantly how the major conflict of neurosis can be located within the relationship between the explanatory discourses and the dreams, symptoms or slips.

Let us take, for example, the analysis of dreams and examine the formal structure of that analysis, remembering that this formal structure is realised in the analytic situation as a complex and dialectical process in which each element of the analysis interacts with the others. The patient relates a dream that sounds coherent. Starting from that element in the dream which lacks the coherence of the rest of the material (this might be an addition or a hesitation), the analyst attempts to disengage the dream from the operations of the secondary revision. The secondary revision renders coherent the material produced by the primary operations of the dream work (*displacement* and *condensation* limited by *considerations of representability*). The secondary revision thus provides the dream's own explanatory discourse. Therefore, when the analyst has stripped away the operations of the secondary revision from the dream, the dream has been transformed and it is this already transformed material which forms the basis for the next stage of the analysis.

In the course of an analysis certain key conflicts will repeat themselves. These conflicts are the result of unconscious desires which are denied access to consciousness. But, if the desires do not appear, their absence does. It is the gaps in the narrative of the dream that make evident the working of a censorship which suppresses those elements of the dream that would carry traces of the unconscious desires into consciousness. But the gaps themselves bear witness to an activity of repression and the existence of unconscious desire and it is in an attempt to refuse even the testimony of silence that the secondary revision recasts the dream in a new, coherent form. Now these unconscious desires will none the less affect the form and content of the secondary revision but, more importantly, it is in the need of the secondary revision to accomplish its work that one can locate the fundamental neurotic conflict. Independently of the content of the particular neurosis, one could aphoristically describe the condition of the neurotic as the refusal to recognise the existence of the unconscious.

This refusal naturally produces two stages within the neurotic's repression of the workings of the unconscious. We have the original repression of the desire because it is unacceptable to consciousness and then we have the further repression of the evidence of the original repression. The analyst, therefore, attempts in one and the same moment to bring the existence of unconscious desire to the attention of the neurotic and to persuade the neurotic to abandon those explanatory discourses which would link all the results of repression to reality. For the neurotic has constant recourse to reality in order to provide a coherent explanation of the troubling symptoms and slips, dreams and parapraxes that compose his or her being.

One can suggest how this comparison can be used to read a realist text by a further brief consideration of one of George Eliot's novels. One can regard the discrete events and dialogues of the story as the original psychic productions and the narrative as the secondary revision which welds these elements into a coherent whole. An analysis of the story of Daniel in *Daniel Deronda* can indicate, if not fully explain, the constitutive relation between the repression of content and the production of form.

Given the importance of the metalanguage within Eliot's text, we could pick on the Hebrew language, which cannot be turned into content, as a moment of weakness within the text's coherence. At the start of the novel Daniel Deronda is under kindly pressure from his guardian, Sir Hugo, to choose a career, but he is strangely reluctant to make a decision. In the course of his deliberations he encounters, and becomes fascinated with, the strange and intense character of Mordecai. He is determined to read Mordecai's poetry but Mordecai informs him that it is written in Hebrew and is untranslatable. Daniel, however, learns the language and late in the book, when he meets his mother and learns that he is a Jew, this strange interest in Hebrew is validated. At this point he can justifiably refuse his guardian's request to choose a profession, and he leaves England for Palestine to find a new life and a new state.

Ignoring the rationality of the narrative, we can understand the Hebrew language as significant not because Deronda *really* is a Jew but because it offers, as imaginary mother-tongue, the undifferentiated plenitude which is an escape from the law of the father. The law of the father attempts to impose difference and loss on the son, but, in this case, it can be ignored by Daniel because Sir Hugo is not *really* his father. Within English and England, Deronda must choose a career. Such a choice means defining himself in terms of difference. The mother, however, holds out the promise of a future without loss, for, in Israel, his full being will flower. This escape from the domination of the father (the law of difference signalled by the possession or non-possession of the phallus) is also the crucial articulation in the story of Gwendolen's conflict with Grandcourt, that Victorian struggle between the sexes. For what is Grandcourt's ambition but to define Gwendolen and what is Gwendolen's response but to kill Grandcourt (of course, she does not *really* kill him)?

In the text of *Daniel Deronda*, we can read the desire to transgress the law of the father but, at the same time, the constant disavowal of that desire through an appeal to reality. This appeal is guaranteed by the privileged status of the language charged with the narrative. Narrative *works*, but its workings are repressed by the text's internal discursive relations. Only one language is absolved from any connection with the material of sound or the pleasure of style and it is that language which tells us what is *really* happening. This appeal to the real and the belief in the transparency of language weave the very text of neurosis ensuring the repression of desire. The neurotic refuses to accept that meanings, both sexual and linguistic, are constituted by difference, and, instead, demands constant identities uncontaminated by the world of absence and loss. It is the same refusal and the same demand that dictate the metalanguage of realism.

The existence of a metalanguage within the text allows the reader (and critic) to read from a position of dominance. It is not necessary for the reader to accept the identifications of the metalanguage as long as he or she accepts its position. It is the position that is essential to this textual organisation and not the particular content that is given to reality. It is possible, however, as has already been suggested, to read against the position of the metalanguage. To undertake such a challenge is to read against the alibi of reality and to enter into the world of fantasy where language figures and re-figures desire; where the letter is inscribed in the sex and the sex in the letter. It is such a reading that Joyce's texts invite.

Before turning to Joyce, however, it is necessary to emphasise the partial nature of the reading of *Daniel Deronda*. If we take the model of the analyst and the neurotic seriously then it is obvious that it will be necessary to return again and again to the original text (as the analyst returns to the original dream) in order to seek fresh gaps in the narrative with which the text can be re-read. On each occasion the interpretation will be determined by whether the desire uncovered can be located in many parts of the text, not least within the narrative itself. For if such an analysis starts by ignoring the rationality of the narrative, it will finally need to give an account of it.

These considerations raise a final theoretical problem which must be faced before addressing Joyce's texts. Signifying systems of any complexity generate texts which are susceptible to a practical infinity of readings. Psychoanalysis locates the limit on interpretations not in any feature of the dream but in the progress of the analysis. The correctness of an interpretation is not in terms of an ideal homology but in the process of the cure. It is the extent to which an interpretation provokes new material that it will validate itself. But, given this process of validation, it is clear that psychoanalysis's use of the term 'interpretation' bears little relation to classical uses of the same term. Further, it leaves us with the problem of how, outside the process of the cure, we can determine the limits on readings of literature.

The obvious answer, which would grant some ontological status to the text over and above its physical existence, has the unfortunate effect of granting to a text just that identity on which literary criticism depends. On the other hand, to dissolve the text into its readings would seem to leave the way open for voluntaristic appropriations of the most paranoid kind. The way out of this dilemma is to recognise the institutional *weight* of certain readings. George Eliot's texts can be read as classic realism not only because they allow that possibility but because they have been formed institutionally not only in the universities but also, more generally, in those multitudes of contemporary practices which reproduce and sustain an ideology of realism. In analysing literature one is engaged in a battle of readings, not chosen voluntaristically but determined institutionally. The validity of the interpretation is determined in the present in the political struggle over literature. Benjamin recognised this relation between present and past when he wrote, over forty years ago:

> To articulate the past historically does not mean to recognise it 'the way it really was' (Ranke). It means to seize hold of a memory as it flashes up at a moment of danger. Historical materialism wishes to retain that image of the past which unexpectedly appears to man singled out by history at a moment of danger. The danger affects both the content of the tradition and its receivers. The same threat hangs over both: that of becoming a tool of the ruling classes. In every era, the attempt must be made anew to wrest tradition away from a conformism that is about to overpower it.
>
> (BENJAMIN 1973, p. 257)

Benjamin's understanding of the determination of the present on the past should not be read as a call for political reductionism. In each practice there will be specific features independently of any political determination and each practice will enter into specific relations *both* with other practices *and* with its political determinations. Above all it must be remembered that the content of politics is not given in terms of any specific representations, let alone those which predominate within capitalist society. A political reading of literature (and all readings are political) will not only involve questions about the place of the text within the ideological struggles of the day but will also involve questions about the nature of that ideological struggle. When we talk of literature, we talk not only of the politics of form but also of the form of politics.

What Benjamin alerts us to are the dangers of a history determined by chronology and the necessity to refuse any linear representations of the past. To support the assertion that Joyce's texts break with classic realism, I will advance arguments that may seem historically misplaced. Would it not be possible to read that break in Conrad, in Hardy, in Dickens? – one could continue the list in a vertiginous search for a moment of origin. Classic realism, however, exists in the present. To break with it is a contemporary struggle in which we must attend to those images from the past which are summoned in response to the dangers of conformism. That Joyce is the most necessary of those images is the thesis of this book.

Classic realism can never be absolute; the materiality of language ensures there will always be fissures which will disturb the even surface of the text. It is in terms of the multiplicity of such fissures that one might approach the question of the value of an individual text. It is in so far as the text bears witness to its own activity of repression – in so far as the repressed makes a return – that evaluation within classic realism is possible (see Barthes 1970). But whereas we have to read against the metalanguage in a realist text, Joyce's texts, without inverted commas, lack any final and privileged discourse within them which dominates the others through its claim of access to the real. If we continue briefly the use of psychoanalytic theory as a model we could say that whereas the realist text is a neurotic discourse, Joyce's texts might be considered as psychotic discourses. For the neurotic attempts to repress certain desires and ignores the compromise formations which find their way into consciousness through an appeal to 'reality', whereas, in the psychotic, the desires dominate the ego and the ego therefore produces discourses which ignore reality (delusions). . . .

. . . Where in Joyce's texts the division between signifier and signified becomes an area in which the reader is in (and at) play-producing meaning through his or her own activity, in George Eliot's texts this division is elided at the level of the metalanguage. The metalanguage attempts to suppress its own activity of signifying (the distribution of signifiers) and to leave a predetermined signified in place. This signified is the evident reality of things, a reality which denies any effectivity to fantasy and language. Because there is an elision of the act of writing and what is written, so, similarly, there is an elision of the act of reading and what is read. Deprived of any experience of language, the reader becomes an observer and can ignore the productive effects of his or her discourses.

In our brief analysis of George Eliot's texts, it was argued that the form and content of her novels reproduced the very structure of neurosis. In the search for plenitude undertaken both by Deronda and the metalanguage, we can locate the neurotic negation of desire. For desire depends entirely on difference; on the establishment of an object that can be desired in so far as it does not appertain to the subject, in so far as it is radically other. The experience of language as signifier is the condition of existence of desire. For as a word only finds a meaning through the differential relations it enters into, so the object as it is produced by language is always contaminated by absence – by what it is not. It is only with the establishment of absence that desire can function. George Eliot's texts are devoted to repressing the operations of the signifier by positing a metalanguage which exists outside of materiality and production. The multitude of objects which appear in her texts do not bear witness to the activity of signification, to the constitutive reality of absence, but rather, in their massive identity, they deny the existence of such activity. And denying this activity, they deny the reality of absence. It is such a denial that constitutes the repression of desire.

References

BARTHES, ROLAND (1970), *S/Z*. Paris.

BENJAMIN, WALTER (1973), *Illuminations*, ed. and with an introduction by Hannah Arendt. London.

ELIOT, GEORGE (1880), *The Works of George Eliot* (Cabinet Edition), 20 vols. Edinburgh, 1878–80.

TARSKI, ALFRED (1949), 'The Semantic Conception of Truth', in *Readings in Philosophical Analysis*, ed. H. Feigl and W. Sellars. New York, pp. 52–84.

11 *Middlemarch* and the Idea of the Classic Realist Text*

DAVID LODGE

David Lodge's essay is a critique of Colin MacCabe's contention that *Middlemarch* is a 'classic realist text'. Lodge's criticism reflects the influence of Anglo-American techniques of close analysis, structuralism – particularly the work of Roman Jakobson – and Bakhtinian dialogic criticism, and he employs all of these to argue that the narration of *Middlemarch* cannot be seen as a metalanguage in any simple sense since, for example, the extensive use of free indirect speech gives a 'polyphonic' quality to the narrator's discourse (see Introduction, pp. 7–8).

Middlemarch has achieved a unique status as both paradigm and paragon in discussion of the novel as a literary form. If a teacher or critic wishes to cite a representative example of the nineteenth-century English novel at its best, the chances are that it will be *Middlemarch*. Indeed it is scarcely an exaggeration to say that, for many critics, *Middlemarch* is the *only* truly representative, truly great Victorian novel – all other candidates, including the rest of George Eliot's fiction, being either too idiosyncratic or too flawed. Barbara Hardy was surely right when she said in her introduction to *Middlemarch: critical approaches to the novel* (1967) that 'if a poll were held for the greatest English novel there would probably be more votes for *Middlemarch* than for any other work';[1] while one of her contributors, Hilda Hulme, quoted a judgement that 'every novel would be *Middlemarch* if it could'.[2]

That symposium edited by Barbara Hardy probably registered the high water mark of *Middlemarch*'s modern reputation. More recently criticism has begun to express a more reserved admiration for George Eliot's masterpiece, echoing and amplifying Henry James's suave judgement on reviewing *Middlemarch*: 'It sets a limit, we think, to the

* Reprinted from *The Nineteenth-Century Novel: Critical Essays and Documents*, ed. Arnold Kettle, (London: Heinemann, 1981), pp. 218–38.

development of the old-fashioned English novel.'[3] George Eliot's realism is now regarded not as a kind of timeless truthfulness to human experience (as implied by the tribute, every novel would be *Middlemarch* if it could), but as an historically conditioned, ideologically motivated construction of 'the real'. J. Hillis Miller, for instance, while acknowledging that *Middlemarch* is 'perhaps the masterwork of Victorian realism',[4] is concerned to expose the rhetorical devices by which George Eliot achieves her 'totalizing' effect, and to reveal, beneath her apparently serene mastery of her fictional world, a gnawing epistemological doubt. A still more radical critique of George Eliot's realism, especially as displayed in *Middlemarch*, is to be found in a recent book by Colin MacCabe, *James Joyce and the Revolution of the Word* (1979), which I propose to use as my real starting point for this essay.

Colin MacCabe's book is an important and valuable study of Joyce, but gets some of its impetus from what seems to me a tendentious account of the nineteenth-century novel (the so-called 'classic realist text'), which is in its own way as misleading as the naïve assumption that realistic fiction simply reflects a pre-existing reality more or less truthfully, and which should perhaps be challenged before it becomes a new orthodoxy.

Colin MacCabe is a British disciple (and an exceptionally lucid and articulate one) of that school of Parisian criticism to which I would give the general name of post-structuralism: in which the purely formal, semiological analysis of literary texts and genres, with which structuralist criticism was originally concerned, has been polemicized by the infusion of Roland Barthes's literary historicism, Jacques Lacan's reading of Freud, Louis Althusser's reading of Marx, and Jacques Derrida's deconstruction of the metaphysical basis of Western philosophy.[5] In this school of thought, the purely methodological separation made by Saussure between the signifier and the signified in the sign is given ontological status and importance. There is never a perfect fit between language and the world. It is impossible absolutely to say what we mean or mean what we say, since the subject who completes an utterance is no longer exactly the same as the subject who originated it, and the language used by the subject has its own materiality capable of signifying beyond the subject's intention or control. The subject (what George Eliot would have called the individual man or woman) is not a concrete, substantial identity situated outside language, but is produced and continually modified by the entry into language. It is the ideas of language as a kind of 'material' and of consciousness and social relations as a kind of 'production' which perhaps enable proponents of this school of thought to reconcile their rather bleakly anti-humanist semiology with their commitment to revolutionary politics. Certainly they seem closer in spirit to Nietzsche than to Marx, and at times to come perilously near a kind of epistemological abyss of infinitely recessive interpretations of interpretations, rendering all human intellectual effort essentially futile. The underlying message seems to be that, however bleak and frightening this view of man and consciousness may be, it is true; and to deny it can only have the ill effects of all repression – whether in society, the psyche, or literature.

Colin MacCabe claims that Joyce's importance resides in the fact that he puts his readers to school in precisely this way, though his critics have misunderstood the lesson and obstinately persisted in trying to explain (or 'recuperate') his works, making them conform to a notion of stable 'meaning' such as it was precisely his intention to undermine. In his mature work, Joyce was concerned 'not with representing experience through language, but with experiencing language through a destruction of representation'.[6] To throw into relief Joyce's liberation of language, and destruction of representation, Colin MacCabe contrasts his fiction with 'the classic realist text', as represented by *Middlemarch*, 'which purports to represent experience through language'.

The 'classic realist text' is a term that derives from the criticism of Roland Barthes, especially *S/Z* (1970), and MacCabe is certainly indebted to Barthes in some ways. But his definition of the classic text is simpler, and I think less subtle, than Barthes'. According to MacCabe, a novel is a tissue of discourses – the discourses of the characters, as rendered in their speech, and the discourse of the narrator; and it is characteristic of the classic realist text that in it the narrative discourse acts as a 'metalanguage',[7] controlling, interpreting, and judging the other discourses, and thus putting the reader in a position of dominance over the characters and their stories. Joyce, in contrast, refuses to privilege one discourse over another in his writing, or to privilege the reader's position *vis-à-vis* the text. Even in his early work, such as the stories of *Dubliners*, superficially consistent with the techniques of classic realism, the narrator's discourse proves ambiguous and enigmatic on close examination; while in, for instance, the Cyclops episode of *Ulysses*, a characteristic specimen of his mature work, the conflicting discourses of the anonymous patron of Barney Kiernan's pub who narrates the main action, the Citizen, Bloom, and all the other characters in the bar, are interrupted not by the metalanguage of a reliable authorial narrator but by passages of parodic inflation and hyperbole (sanctioned purely aesthetically by the 'gigantism' theme of the episode) – a counter-text, MacCabe calls it which 'far from setting up a position of judgement for the reader, merely proliferates the languages available'.[8] Thus the reader of *Ulysses* is never allowed to sink into the comfortable assurance of an interpretation guaranteed by the narrator, but must himself produce the meaning of the text by opening himself fully to the play of its diverse and contradictory discourses.

One symptom of Joyce's rejection of the conventions of reading and representation employed in the classic realist text, which MacCabe seizes on with understandable enthusiasm, is Joyce's refusal, from his earliest days as a writer, to employ what he called 'perverted commas' in rendering direct speech – using an introductory dash instead. It is the typographical marking off of direct speech from narrative by quotation marks that enforces the authority of the narrator's metalanguage, in MacCabe's view. 'The narrative prose is the metalanguage that can state all the truths in the object-language(s) (the marks held in inverted commas) and can also explain the relation of the object-language to the world.'[9]

MacCabe uses George Eliot as a foil to show up certain features of Joyce's work, and an element of exaggeration and caricature is always apt to creep into such manoeuvres. Let us acknowledge that there is a real difference between the art of George Eliot and the art of James Joyce which MacCabe helps to define. Let us note also that MacCabe himself admits that classic realism is never absolute, and that within George Eliot's novels 'there are always images which counter the flat and univocal process which is the showing forth of the real'.[10] Nevertheless it seems to me that the distortion of George Eliot's practice implied by MacCabe's model of the classic realist text is sufficiently great to be worth contesting, and that this might be a way of extending our understanding of classic realism generally, and of George Eliot's art in particular.

What MacCabe calls a metalanguage (a term borrowed from linguistics and philosophy) will be better known to students of George Eliot as the convention of the omniscient and intrusive narrator, which has a venerable history as a subject of contention in criticism of her work. In the period of her relative eclipse, in the 1920s, 30s and 40s, when the Jamesian aesthetic of 'showing' rather than 'telling' was dominant in novel criticism, this feature of her work counted heavily against her. In the 1950s and 1960s several critics such as Wayne Booth, W. J. Harvey and Barbara Hardy instituted a successful defence of the convention and George Eliot's exploitation of it, thus complementing on the aesthetic plane the reinstatement of George Eliot as a great novelist which F. R. Leavis had achieved on the ethical plane.

As Gérard Genette has observed, in his excellent study *Narrative Discourse*, the James–Lubbock distinction between 'showing' and 'telling', and the corresponding pair of terms, 'scene' and 'summary', derive from the distinction drawn between mimesis and diegesis in the third book of Plato's *Republic*; and MacCabe's discussion of the matter seems particularly close to Plato's (though it reverses Plato's preferences) because of the importance he gives to the marking off of speech from narration in the classic realist text. Plato illustrates the distinction between mimesis and diegesis by reference to the opening scene of the *Iliad* in which Chryses appeals to the Achaeans to let him ransom his daughter.

> You know that as far as the lines
>
> *He prayed the Achaeans all,*
> *But chiefly the two rulers of the people,*
> *Both sons of Atreus*
>
> the poet himself speaks, he never tries to turn our thoughts from himself or to suggest that anyone else is speaking; but after this he speaks as if he was himself Chryses, and tries his best to make us think that the priest, an old man, is speaking and not Homer.[11]

Mimesis, then, is narrating by imitating another's speech. Diegesis is narrating in one's own voice. To make his distinction clearer, Plato, through his mouthpiece Socrates, rewrites the scene from Homer in unbroken diegesis, in which Chryses' actual words are summarized in indirect form, *oratio obliqua*, and assimilated to the linguistic register of the narrator, Homer himself. A typology of literary modes (later to evolve into a typology of literary genres)[12] thus emerges: pure diegesis, as exemplified by dithyramb (a kind of hymn), in which the poet speaks exclusively in his own voice; pure mimesis, as exemplified by tragedy and comedy, in which the poet speaks exclusively in imitated voices; and the mixed form of the epic, which combines both modes. Needless to say, Plato greatly distrusted the most mimetic kind of writing, since it is ethically undiscriminating; and he will admit into the Republic only the most austere kind of writing – the purely diegetic, or that which combines diegesis with a little mimesis, but of good personages only.

Plato's discussion is more relevant to the comparison of George Eliot and James Joyce than might at first appear. Realism as a literary quality, or effect, of verisimilitude, is something we think of as very close to, if not quite synonymous with, the classical notion of mimesis or imitation, and we often describe the novel casually as a 'mimetic' literary form. In fact, of course, only drama is a strictly mimetic form, in which only words are imitated *in* words, and what is non-verbal – spectacle, gesture, etc. – is imitated non-verbally. Anything that is not dialogue in a novel, if only *he said* and *she said*, is diegesis, the report of a narrator, 'the poet himself' however impersonal. The only way of getting round this rule is to put the narrating entirely into the hands (or mouths) of a character or characters, as in the pseudo-autobiographical novel or the epistolary novel: then the narrative becomes mimetic of diegesis. But as Genette concludes, 'the truth is that mimesis in words can only be mimesis of words. Other than that, all we have and can have is degrees of diegeses.'[13]

There is no *necessary* connection between mimesis and realism: some novels that consist largely of dialogue (Ronald Firbank, Henry Green, Ivy

Compton-Burnett) are highly artificial; and some of the most realistic (i.e. convincing, lifelike, compelling) passages in *Middlemarch* are diegetic (for example the account of Lydgate's unpremeditated declaration to Rosamond in chapter 31). But it is true that mimesis is inherently better adapted to realistic effect than diegesis, simply because it uses words to imitate words. The classic realist novel of the nineteenth century maintained a fairly even balance between mimesis and diegesis, showing and telling, scene and summary, and it did so at the expense of some degree of realistic illusion, in the interests of ethical control of the story and the reader's response.

The eighteenth-century novel began with the discovery of new mimetic possibilities in prose fiction – the pseudo-confessions of Defoe, the pseudo-correspondences of Richardson. But these achievements, remarkable as they were, tended to confirm Plato's fears about the morally debilitating effects of skilful mimesis of imperfect personages without diegetic guidance from the author. However high-minded the intentions of Defoe (which is doubtful) or of Richardson (which is not), there is no way in which the reader can be prevented from delighting in and even identifying with the vitality, energy and resourcefulness of Moll Flanders or Lovelace, even in their wicked actions. Fielding, his mind trained in a classical school, restored the diegetic element in his 'comic-epic poem in prose' – though paradoxically in the interests of a more liberal morality than Richardson's or Defoe's. And it was Fielding's narrative method (though not his morality) which provided the model for the nineteenth-century novelists from Scott to George Eliot. In the classic Victorian novel, not only is there a great deal of narrative in proportion to speech, summary in proportion to scene, but the writers exploit the diegetic possibilities of the mixed form to speak very much 'in their own voice' – not merely reporting events, but delivering judgements, opinions, and evaluations about the story and about life in general. Even when characters act as narrators (e.g. in *Jane Eyre, Great Expectations*), they behave more like novelists, shaping and improving their own stories, than do the naïve memoir-writers of Defoe, or the pressured correspondents of Richardson.

With the advent of the modern novel, the pendulum swings back towards mimesis, in more subtle and sophisticated forms. Flaubert begins the process: in *Madame Bovary* the narrator is omnipresent, but it is impossible to discover what he thinks about the story he is telling. In James, the narrator is either a created character of doubtful reliability (e.g. the governess in *The Turn of the Screw*) or an authorial narrator who deliberately restricts himself to the limited perspective of a character (such as Lambert Strether in *The Ambassadors*) entangled in circumstances he does not fully understand. In Joyce, the author is progressively 'refined out of existence, indifferent, paring his fingernails'. The impersonal, but reliable and tonally consistent narrator of the early episodes of *Ulysses*, who tells us, for instance, that 'Stately, plump Buck Mulligan came from the stairhead, bearing a bowl of lather on which a mirror and a razor lay crossed', or that 'Mr Leopold Bloom ate with relish the inner organs of beasts and fowls', gradually disappears under a welter of different discourses, parodies and pastiches of journalese, officialese, obsolete literary styles, pub talk, women's magazine language, scientific description, and is finally displaced by the supreme example of mimesis in English narrative literature, the interior monologue of Molly Bloom.

I think there is some advantage to be gained from substituting the Platonic distinction between mimesis and diegesis for MacCabe's distinction between language and metalanguage. Instead of seeing a total break of continuity between the classic realist text and the modern text, we see rather a swing of the pendulum from one end of a continuum of possibilities to the other, a pendulum that has been swinging throughout literary history. Mimesis and diegesis, like metaphor and metonymy, are fundamental, and, on a certain level, all-inclusive categories of representation, and a typology of texts can be established by assessing the dominance of one over the other. We are also better placed to show how MacCabe misrepresents the art of George Eliot. Two main points have to be made: (1) the distinction between mimesis and diegesis in George Eliot is by no means as clear-cut as MacCabe implies; and (2) the diegetic element is much more problematic than he allows.

When Plato refers to the epic as a mixed form, he means that it combines, or alternates between, mimesis and diegesis, the voice of the poet and the voices of the characters he imitates in dialogue. But the classic realist novel 'mixes' the two discourses in a more fundamental sense: it fuses them together, often indistinguishably and inextricably, through the device of free indirect speech by means of which the narrator, without absenting himself entirely from the text, communicates the narrative to us coloured by the thoughts and feelings of a character. The reference to this character in the third person pronoun, and the use of the past tense, or 'epic preterite', still imply the existence of the author as the source of the narrative; but by deleting the tags which affirm that existence, such as *he said, she wondered, she thought to herself*, etc., and by using the kind of diction appropriate to the character rather than to the authorial narrator, the latter can allow the sensibility of the character to dominate the discourse, and correspondingly subdue his own voice, his own opinions and evaluations. It was Jane Austen who first perfected the use of free indirect speech in English fiction, and thus showed succeeding novelists, including George Eliot, how the novel might combine Fielding's firm diegetic control with Richardson's subtle mimesis of character. The device is an extremely flexible one, which allows the narrator to move very freely and fluently between the poles of mimesis and diegesis within a single paragraph, or even a single sentence; and its effect is always to make the reader's task of interpretation more active and problematic. If we are looking for a single formal feature which characterizes the realist novel of the nineteenth century, it is surely not the domination of the characters' discourses by the narrator's discourse (something in fact more characteristic of earlier narrative literature) but the extensive use of free indirect speech, which obscures and complicates the distinction between the two types of discourse.

The work of the Russian literary theorists Mikhail Bakhtin and Valentin Volosinov, which goes back to the 1920s, but has only recently been translated into English, is very relevant here. They (or he – for they may be one and the same person) have suggested that it is precisely the dissolution of the boundaries between reported speech and reporting context (i.e., the author's speech) that characterizes the novel as discourse and distinguishes it from earlier types of narrative prose and from lyric verse. Bakhtin characterized novel discourse as 'polyphonic' or 'polyglottal', and maintained that 'One of the essential peculiarities of prose fiction is the possibility it allows of using different types of discourse, with their distinct expressiveness intact, on the plane of a single work, without reduction to a single common denominator'.[14] Different types of discourse can be represented in fiction, of course, as the direct speech of characters, without serious disturbance to the authority of the narrator, as in the novels of Fielding or Scott. But once these discourses enter into the narrative discourse itself, in various forms of reported speech, or thought, the interpretative control of the author's voice is inevitably weakened to some degree, and the reader's work increased.

Derek Oldfield, in an essay entitled 'The Character of Dorothea', contributed to that symposium on *Middlemarch* edited by Barbara Hardy to which I have already referred, pointed out how George Eliot's narrative method is complicated by this alternation of narrator's and characters' voices, compelling to the reader to, in his words, 'zig-zag' his way through the discourse, rather than following a straight, well-marked path.[15] One of the examples he gives describes Dorothea's naïve ideas about marriage at the beginning of the story. I shall cite the same passage, hoping to add a few points to his excellent commentary:

> She was open, ardent, and not in the least self-admiring; indeed, it was pretty to see how her imagination adorned her sister Celia with attractions altogether superior to her own, and if any gentleman appeared to come to the Grange from some other motive than that of seeing Mr Brooke, she concluded that he must be in love with Celia: Sir James Chettham, for example, whom she constantly considered from

> Celia's point of view, inwardly debating whether it would be good for Celia to accept him. That he should be regarded as a suitor to herself would have seemed to her a ridiculous irrelevance. Dorothea, with all her eagerness to know the truths of life, retained very childlike ideas about marriage.[16]

So far, this is diegetic: the narrator describes Dorothea's character authoritatively, in words that Dorothea could not use about herself without contradiction. (She cannot say or think about herself that she is not self-admiring, for that would be to admire herself. Nor can she acknowledge that her ideas about marriage are childlike without ceasing to hold them.) It is the justification of the diegetic method that it can give us such information, lucidly, concisely, and judiciously. In the rest of the passage, however, the narrator's discourse becomes permeated with Dorothea's discourse, but without wholly succumbing to it.

> She felt sure that she would have accepted the judicious Hooker, if she had been born in time to save him from that wretched mistake he made in matrimony: or John Milton when his blindness had come on; or any of the other great men whose odd habits it would have been glorious piety to endure; but an amiable handsome baronet, who said 'Exactly' to her remarks even when she expressed uncertainty – how could he affect her as a lover? The really delightful marriage must be that where your husband was a sort of father, and could teach you even Hebrew, if you wished it.[17]

As Oldfield observes, the tag, 'she felt' is an ambiguous signal to the reader, since it can introduce either objective report or subjective reflection. Such colloquial phrases in the sequel as 'that wretched mistake' and 'when his blindness had come on', seem to be the words in which Dorothea herself would have articulated these ideas, though the equally colloquial 'odd habits' does not. Why does it not? Because, in unexpected collocation with 'great men' it seems too literary an irony for Dorothea, and so we ascribe it to the narrator. But that is not to imply that Dorothea is incapable of irony. '[W]ho said "Exactly" to her remarks even when she expressed uncertainty' – do we not infer that Sir James' illogicality has been noted by Dorothea herself in just that crisp, dismissive way? Then what about the immediately succeeding phrase, ' – how could he affect her as a lover?' This is a really interesting challenge to analysis. If the immediately preceding phrase is attributed to Dorothea, as I suggest, then it would be natural to ascribe this one to her also; and the immediately following sentence is certainly Dorothea's own thought, communicated in free indirect speech: 'The really delightful marriage must be that where your husband was a sort of father, and could teach you even Hebrew, if you wished it.' But a problem of contradiction arises if we attribute the rhetorical question to Dorothea. For if Dorothea can formulate the question, 'How can Sir James affect me as a lover?' her alleged unconsciousness of her own attractions to visiting gentlemen is compromised. Is the question, then, put by the narrator, appealing directly to the reader, over Dorothea's head, to acknowledge the plausibility of her behaviour, meaning: 'You do see, gentle reader, why it never crossed Dorothea's mind that Sir James Chettham was a possible match for her.' There is such an implication, but the reason given – that Sir James says 'Exactly' when Dorothea expresses uncertainty – seems too trivial for the narrator to draw the conclusion, 'How could he affect her as a lover?' We can perhaps naturalize the utterance by interpreting it as Dorothea's likely response to a hypothetical question – 'Do you think you could fall in love with Sir James Chettham?' But the fact is that mimesis and diegesis are fused together inextricably here, and for a good purpose. For there is a sense in which Dorothea knows what the narrator knows – namely, that Sir James is sexually attracted to her – but is repressing the thought, on account of her determination to marry an intellectual father-figure. When Celia finally compels Dorothea to face the fact that not only Sir James, but even the servants, assume that he is courting Dorothea, the narrator tells us that she was 'not less angry because details asleep in her memory were now awakened to confirm the unwelcome revelation'. One of those details was surely that very habit of Sir James's of saying 'Exactly' when she expressed uncertainty – a sign, surely, of his admiration, deference, and anxiety to please.

I am not claiming a Flaubertian *impassibilité* for the narrator of *Middlemarch*. The first part of the passage under discussion establishes very clearly the ethical terms in which Dorothea is to be judged: selflessness on the one hand, self-deception on the other. But as the writing proceeds to flesh out this diegetic assessment more mimetically, the reader is progressively more taxed to negotiate the nuances of irony and to resolve the ambiguities of diexis. Exactly how far Dorothea misconceives the nature of the great intellectual figures of the past; whether she is right or wrong in her assessment of Sir James Chettham's intelligence; whether she emerges from the whole passage with more credit than discredit, are questions which the reader must finally decide for himself. I think it will be granted that there are many other such passages in *Middlemarch*.

It is not, however, only because mimesis often contaminates diegesis in this way that MacCabe's account of the narrator's voice in George Eliot's fiction seems inaccurate.

> The metalanguage within such a text refuses to acknowledge its own status as writing. The text outside the area of inverted commas claims

> to be the product of no articulation, it claims to be unwritten. This unwritten text can then attempt to staunch the haemorrhage of interpretations threatened by the material of language. Whereas other discourses within the text are considered as materials which are open to reinterpretation, the narrative discourse functions simply as a window on reality. This relationship between discourses can be taken as the defining feature of the classic realist text.[18]

The assertion that the narrator's discourse claims to be 'unwritten' may be puzzling unless one traces it back to Derrida's argument that Western culture has always privileged the spoken word over the written, because the spoken word appears to guarantee the 'metaphysics of presence' on which our philosophical tradition is predicated. Speech implies the presence of a speaker, and by inference of an authentic, autonomous self who is the arbiter of his own meanings and able to pass them intact to another. But Derrida argues that this is a fallacy and an illusion. It is the absence of the addresser from the message which allows the materiality of language to generate its own semantic possibilities among which the addressee may romp at will. Writing, in which such absence is obvious, is thus a more reliable model of how language works than speech; and writing which claims truthfulness by trying to disguise itself as speech, as the discourse of a man speaking to men, is in bad faith, or at least deluded.

Now it is true that the narrator's discourse in George Eliot's fiction is modelled on the I–thou speech situation, and certain that she would have endorsed Wordsworth's description of the writer as a man speaking to men. But in obvious ways, whether consciously or unconsciously, she reminds us that her narration is in fact written. This is particularly true of the more ostentatiously diegetic passages, when she suspends the story to deliver herself of opinions, generalizations, judgements. To call these passages transparent windows on reality, as MacCabe does, seems quite inappropriate. They are in fact often quite obscure, or at least very complicated, and have to be scrutinized several times before we can confidently construe their meaning – a process that is peculiar to reading, and cannot be applied to the spoken word. Consider, for example, this comment on Mr Farebrother, shortly after Lydgate has voted against him in the selection of the hospital chaplaincy.

> But Mr Farebrother met him with the same friendliness as before. The character of the publican and sinner is not always practically incompatible with that of the modern Pharisee, for the majority of us scarcely see more distinctly the faultiness of our own conduct than the faultiness of our own arguments, or the dullness of our own jokes. But the Vicar of St Botolph's had certainly escaped the slightest tincture of

> the Pharisee, and by dint of admitting to himself that he was too much as other men were, he had become remarkably unlike them in this – that he could excuse others for thinking slightly of him, and could judge impartially of their conduct even when it told against him.[19]

I would defy anyone to take in the exact sense of this passage through the ear alone. There are too many distinctions being juggled, and too many swerves and loops in the movement of the argument: first, we encounter the idea (stated in a double negative, and thus made more difficult to assimilate) that the modern publican and sinner may be combined with the modern Pharisee in the same person, unlike their Biblical prototypes. Is Mr Farebrother, who has just been mentioned, such a person, we may wonder, as we begin to negotiate this passage? This would be inconsistent with the previous presentation of his character, but we have to wait for some time to be reassured that this is *not* what the narrator means. Before we come to that point, we have to wrestle with another distinction – between faults of manners (arguments and jokes) and faults of morals (conduct) – a distinction which doesn't correspond exactly to the one between publicans and sinners and Pharisees. The exculpation of Farebrother is highly paradoxical: by admitting that he is too much like other men, he becomes remarkably unlike them: which is to say, that by admitting he is a publican and a sinner, he avoids being a Pharisee as well. So why has the narrator introduced the concept of Pharisee at all? It seems to be floating free, and we puzzle our way through the paragraph, waiting to see to whom it applies. We may be disconcerted to realize that it is applied, explicitly, only to 'the majority of us' ourselves. Perhaps it is also applied implicitly to Lydgate, whose conduct over the election, as he himself is well aware, was not entirely disinterested. On reflection we may decide that the negative comparison between Farebrother and Pharisee is justified by the fact that the Pharisees were a Jewish religious sect and that Phariseeism is an occupational failing of men of religion, but this explanation scarcely leaps off the page.

Mr Farebrother seems to emerge from these complex comparisons with credit. But only a few lines later, after a speech from Mr Farebrother in direct (i.e. mimetic) form –

> 'The world has been too strong for *me*, I know', he said one day to Lydgate. 'But then I am not a mighty man – I shall never be a man of renown. The choice of Hercules is a pretty fable; but Prodicus makes it easy work for the hero, as if the first resolves were enough. Another story says that he came to hold the distaff, and at last wore the Nessus shirt. I suppose one good resolve might keep a man right if everybody else's resolve helped him.'[20]

– we encounter this diegetic comment:

> The Vicar's talk was not always inspiriting: he had escaped being a Pharisee, but he had not escaped that low estimate of possibilities which we rather hastily arrive at as an inference from our own failure.[21]

This seems to check any inclination on the reader's part to overestimate Mr Farebrother's moral stature; and if, in reading the preceding diegetic passage, we mentally defend ourselves against the accusation of Phariseeism by identifying ourselves with Farebrother's candid admission of his faults, we now find ourselves implicated with him in another kind of failing – complacency about one's faults. But if we make *another* adjustment, and take this as a cue to condemn Farebrother, we may be surprised and disconcerted once more, to find ourselves identified with Lydgate – for the passage immediately continues, and ends (as does the whole chapter) with this sentence: 'Lydgate felt that there was a pitiable lack of will in Mr Farebrother.' Since Lydgate has just been portrayed as subordinating his own will to expendiency in the matter of the chaplaincy election, he is hardly in a position to throw stones at this particular moral glasshouse, and the sequel will show even greater 'infirmity of will' on his part in the matter of Rosamond.[22] To sum up, the authorial commentary, so far from telling the reader what to think, or putting him in a position of dominance in relation to the discourse of the characters, constantly forces him to think for himself, and constantly implicates him in the moral judgements being formulated.

I like to call this kind of literary effect, the 'Fish effect', because the American critic Stanley Fish has made the study of it so much his own in a series of books and articles published over the last fifteen years – primarily on seventeenth-century poetry and prose, but more lately with a wider range of reference.[23] Basically, his argument is that as we read, lineally, word group by word group, we form hypotheses and expectations about the meaning that is going to be delivered at the end of the sentence, or paragraph, or text; but, as Fish shows by skilful analyses of particular passages – action-replays of reading in slow motion – very often our expectations are disconfirmed, a different and perhaps entirely opposite meaning from that which we expected is formulated, yet without entirely abolishing the mistakenly projected meaning. In his early work Fish suggested that this effect was contrived by writers who had didactic, usually religious, designs upon their readers, using it to defamiliarize familiar truths; thus Milton reminds us that we are fallen creatures not merely by the fable of *Paradise Lost* but by constantly tripping us up with his syntax. More recently, Fish has argued that the effect is inherent in all discourse, but especially literary discourse, because the meaning of an utterance is determined entirely by its context and the interpretative assumptions that are brought to it – which, in the case of literary utterances, are never simple or fixed. I think both arguments are valid, and both apply to George Eliot's diegetic style, although such deviousness might, superficially, seem incompatible with her chosen stance as narrator: the privileged historian of the moral lives of characters who, it suits her purpose to pretend, are real people in real situations. The opening paragraph of chapter 15 is *à propos*:

> A great historian, as he insisted on calling himself, who had the happiness to be dead a hundred and twenty years ago, and so to take his place among the colossi whose huge legs our living pettiness is observed to walk under, glories in his copious remarks and digressions as the least imitable part of his work, and especially in those initial chapters to the successive books of his history, where he seems to bring his arm-chair to the proscenium and chat with us in all the lusty ease of his fine English. But Fielding lived when the days were longer (for time, like money, is measured by our needs), when summer afternoons were spacious, and the clock ticked slowly in the winter evenings. We belated historians must not linger after his example; and if we did so, it is probable that our chat would be thin and eager, as if delivered from a camp-stool in a parrot-house. I at least have so much to do in unravelling certain human lots, and seeing how they were woven and interwoven, that all the light I can command must be concentrated on this particular web, and not dispersed over that tempting range of relevancies called the universe.[24]

Colin MacCabe's comment on this paragraph is that 'Although at first sight, George Eliot would appear to be questioning her form, the force of the passage is to leave us convinced that we have finally abandoned form to be treated to the simple unravelling of the real'.[25] But this seems a very stubborn refusal to credit George Eliot with ironic self-consciousness. It is patently obvious by chapter 15 that the narrator of *Middlemarch* is ranging over the tempting range of relevancies called the universe, especially through her famous scientific analogies. And by comparing her own writing of Fielding's, she is implicitly placing it in a tradition of literary fiction, even if this admission is neatly disguised by invoking Fielding's description of himself as a historian. The Fish effect is immediately apparent in the opening of this passage: 'A great historian, as he insisted on calling himself. . . . ' We don't know, yet, of course, who this historian is, and it is quite a time before we discover his identity, and that he is not a historian at all, but a novelist. '[A]s he insisted on calling himself . . . ' might give us a clue that he wasn't a proper historian, but it might equally well be construed as meaning he was a proper historian who insisted on calling himself great. '[W]ho had the happiness to be dead a hundred and twenty years ago . . .' 'Dead' is surely a surprising word in the context. 'Who had the happiness to be alive' would be the more predictable formula, expressing that nostalgia for the good old days which George Eliot so often invokes in her fiction, though in fact seldom quite straightforwardly. The paradox is resolved when we read, 'and so to take his place among the colossi whose huge legs our living pettiness is observed to walk under. . . .' Fielding was lucky to have died a hundred and twenty years ago, then, in the sense that he thus became a literary classic – though if he is dead it is hard to see how this brings him any happiness, and the reverence accorded to a classic seems somewhat undercut by the allusion to Shakespeare's Cassius. The narrator, at any rate, takes no responsibility for the analogy. 'Whose huge legs our living pettiness is observed to walk under. . . .' Observed by whom? By the makers of such extravagant analogies? '[G]lories in his copious remarks and digressions as the least imitable part of his work.' Was Fielding right in thinking them inimitable, or has George Eliot improved upon them? Of course, she disowns any attempt to compete with him, but then the whole passage is a digression disowning the intention to digress.

Several critics have recently pointed out the presence of paradox and contradiction in George Eliot's superficially smooth, unproblematic narrative style. J. Hillis Miller, for instance, in his article 'Optic and Semiotic in *Middlemarch*', identifies three groups of totalizing metaphors or families of metaphors, and comments, 'Each group of metaphors is related to the others, fulfilling them, but at the same time contradicting them, cancelling them out, or undermining their validity.'[26] Thus, for instance, the recurring image of the lives of the characters as a flowing web, an unrolling fabric, objectively there, to which the narrator brings a truth-telling light, is contaminated by other images of the subjectivity of interpretation, the inevitable distortions of perspective. The famous analogy of the candle-flame which confers pattern on the random scratches of the pier-glass, as Miller points out (and Leslie Stephen pointed out before him) applies as well to the narrator's perspective as to that of any character's. Steven Marcus, in an interesting, if quirky article entitled 'Human Nature, Social Orders and Nineteenth-Century Systems of Explanation: starting in with George Eliot' interprets her fondness for setting her novels back in the historical past (a feature of the classic Victorian novel in general) as a defence mechanism designed to control themes that she was both fascinated by and yet feared: sexual passion, class conflict and epistemological scepticism. He notes in her treatment of the past, as early as 'Amos Barton', the first piece of fiction she wrote, the Fish effect, moments when the irony of the narrator's discourse, with which the reader has been feeling a comfortable complicity, suddenly rebounds upon him:

> It is the reader himself who now suddenly discovers that he is being gently but firmly prodded in the ribs, although it is not altogether clear

> why he should all at once find himself on the wrong end of the stick. . . . The effect, however, is momentarily to loosen the reader's grip on the sequence of statements through which he has just worked his way and to cause him to look back, if only for a fraction of an instant, to see if he can ascertain the logical and syntactical course which led him to this uncertainly dislocated and suspended position.[27]

Very recently, Graham Martin, responding directly to Colin MacCabe's book, has argued that 'we learn as much about *The Mill on the Floss* by looking at discontinuities between the authorial metalanguage and the narrated fiction, as by remarking on their fusion'.[28] All these critics tend to regard the fractures they discern in the smooth surface of George Eliot's narrative method as signs or symptoms of the tremendous stresses and strains she experienced in trying to deal truthfully and yet positively with an increasingly alienated and alienating social reality. But it is not necessary to see them as aesthetic flaws. On the contrary, it is precisely because the narrator's discourse is never entirely unambiguous, predictable, and in total interpretative control of the other discourses in *Middlemarch* that the novel survives, to be read and re-read, without ever being finally closed or exhausted. And this, paradoxically, follows inevitably from the post-Saussurian theories about language and discourse to which Colin MacCabe, and other critics of the same persuasion, subscribe. If it is true that language is a system of differences with no positive terms, that the subject is inevitably split in discourse between the 'I' who speaks and the 'I' who is spoken of, that the relationship between words and things is not natural but cultural, not given but produced, then George Eliot could not write fiction that was a 'transparent window on reality' even if she wanted to. The question, therefore, is whether in trying – or pretending – to do so, she was betrayed into false consciousness and bad art. It has been my purpose to suggest that she was well aware of the indeterminacy that lurks in all efforts at human communication, and frequently reminded her readers of this fact in the very act of apparently denying it through the use of an intrusive 'omniscient' authorial voice.

Notes

[Books cited were published in London unless otherwise indicated.]

1. Barbara Hardy (ed.), *Middlemarch: Critical Approaches to the Novel* (1967 Athlone Press), p. 3.
2. Ibid., pp. 94–5.

3. Henry James, *The House of Fiction*, ed. Leon Edel (1962 Rupert Hart-Davis), p. 267.

4. J. Hillis Miller, 'Optic and Semiotic in *Middlemarch*', in *The Worlds of Victorian Fiction*, ed. Jerome Buckley (1975 Cambridge, Mass. Harvard University Press, 1975), p. 127.

5. This catalogue of exotic names may be baffling and irritating to the uninitiated, but limitations of space preclude a detailed explanation of the ideas and theories involved. In fact, it is not necessary to be acquainted with the intellectual history behind the post-structuralist position to understand the argument between myself and MacCabe. Readers seeking further light on these matters, however, might consult the following sources, listed in an order corresponding roughly to a progressive shift of focus from structuralism to post-structuralism: Robert Scholes, *Structuralism in Literature* (1974 New Haven: Yale University Press); Terence Hawkes, *Structuralism and Semiotics* (1977 Methuen, Oxford:); Jonathan Culler, *Structuralist Poetics* (1974 Routledge and Kegan Paul); *Structuralism and Since*, ed. John Sturrock Methuen; and Catherine Belsey, *Critical Practice* (1980 Oxford University Press). The last of these is closest to Colin MacCabe's position, the theoretical bases of which are also expounded in his own book.

6. Colin MacCabe, *James Joyce and the Revolution of the Word* (1979 Macmillan), p. 4.

7. 'Metalanguage: a language or system of symbols used to discuss another language or system', *Collins New English Dictionary*.

8. MacCabe, *op. cit.* p. 100.

9. Ibid., p. 14.

10. Ibid., p. 27.

11. *Great Dialogues of Plato*, trans. W. H. Rouse (New York, New American Library, 1956), p. 190.

12. Gérard Genette has traced this process from Plato and Aristotle to the present day in his monograph, *Introduction à l'architexte* (Paris 1979), arguing that in developing Plato's distinction between three modes of poetic utterance into a theory of three basic genres (lyric, drama, epic), later poeticians not only misrepresented the classical authors, but created a good deal of confusion in poetics. For a short account in English of this work, see James Kearns, 'Gérard Genette: a Different Genre', *The Literary Review* No. 33, Jan. 1981, pp. 21–3.

13. Gérard Genette, *Narrative Discourse*, Trans. Jane E. Lewin, (Oxford, Blackwell 1980) p. 164.

14. Mikhail Bakhtin, 'Discourse Typology in Prose' [an extract from *Problems in Dostoevsky's Poetics* (Leningrad, 1929)] in *Readings in Russian Poetics*, ed. Ladislav Matejka and Krystyna Pomorska (Ann Arbor, University of Michigan 1978), p. 193. This anthology also contains an extract, entitled 'Reported Speech', from Volosinov's *Marxism and the Philosophy of Language* (Leningrad, 1930). For a survey of Bakhtin's work, and a discussion of the vexed question of his relationship to Volosinov, see Ann Shukman, 'Between Marxism and Formalism: the stylistics of Mikhail Bakhtin', *Comparative Criticism: a Yearbook*,

ed. E. S. Shaffer, Vol. II (Cambridge, Cambridge University Press, 1980) pp. 221–34.

15. Barbara Hardy, (Ed.), op. cit., pp. 67–9.
16. George Eliot, *Middlemarch* (Harmondsworth, Penguin Books, 1965), p. 32.
17. Ibid.
18. MacCabe, op. cit., p. 15.
19. *Middlemarch*, p. 217.
20. Ibid., p. 217.
21. Ibid., pp. 217–18.
22. Farebrother's allusions to the various versions of the Hercules myth are indeed full of proleptic irony in application to Lydgate, whose 'resolve' to make a contribution to medical science will be sacrificed to Rosamond's feminine and domestic desires (equivalent to 'holding the distaff'), and who will eventually wear the Nessus shirt of failure and disillusionment in his professional and emotional life.
23. See particularly *Surprised by Sin, The Reader in Paradise Lost* (1967, Macmillan); *Self-Consuming Artefacts: the Experience of Seventeenth-Century Literature* (Berkeley & Los Angeles, University of California Press, 1972); and *Is There a Text in this Class? The Authority of Interpretative Communities* (1981, Cambridge Mass.: Harvard University Press).
24. *Middlemarch*, p. 170.
25. Colin MacCabe, op. cit., p. 19.
26. J. Hillis Miller, Buckley, (Ed.) op. cit., p. 128.
27. Steven Marcus, 'Human Nature, Social Orders, and Nineteenth-Century Systems of Explanation: Starting in with George Eliot', *Salmagundi*, 28 (1975), p. 21.
28. Graham Martin, '*The Mill on the Floss* and the Unreliable Narrator,' Anne Smith, (Ed.), *George Eliot: Centenary Essays and an Unpublished Fragment* (1980, Vision Press), p. 38.

12 George Eliot: 'The Wisdom of Balancing Claims' (*Middlemarch*)*

D. A. MILLER

D. A. Miller is a critic who brings together the Anglo-American tradition of close analysis of an individual text with an awareness of developments in contemporary criticism and theory. He goes part of the way with a critic like Hillis Miller who sees *Middlemarch* as destabilizing realist conventions and assumptions but he argues that this 'deconstructive' aspect of the novel exists in tension with the narrative's drive towards transcendence and closure in the manner of the 'classic realist text'. He finds this 'double valency' of the text characteristic of the major works of nineteenth-century fiction (see Introduction, pp. 14–15).

It was characteristic of Henry James's acuteness to see that *Middlemarch* 'sets a limit to the development of the old-fashioned English novel'.[1] It was equally characteristic of his tact that he never went on to specify what sort of limit it set, or even on which side of the limit the novel ultimately came down: whether the limit was set by remaining – just barely – within the assumptions of traditional form, or by going beyond them to a point where their validity would seem challenged. James's remark suggests *Middlemarch* as an inevitable reference in our study of traditional form in the nineteenth-century novel. Even the ambiguity of his comment offers a useful preliminary formulation of the doubleness that shapes George Eliot's novel itself.

Middlemarch indeed oscillates in a curious and exemplary way: between a confident re-enactment of traditional form, in the magisterial manner of a *summa*, and an uneasy subversion of its habitually assumed validity, as though under the less magisterial pressure of a doubt. If we insist on the extent to which the novel retreads the itinerary of, say, *Emma*, we find

---

* Reprinted from D. A. Miller, *Narrative and Its Discontents: Problems of Closure in the Traditional Novel* (Princeton: Princeton University Press, 1981), pp. 107–10, 169–80, 188–9 (footnotes renumbered from the original).

ourselves embarrassed by those aspects of the text that put a question mark before its own traditional form.[2] Yet if we turn about and stress the novel's 'self-deconstructive' dimension. we are hard put to explain why its deconstructive insights – far from issuing in a novelistic form more fully commensurate with them – impede neither the rhetorical power with which traditional form is able to impose itself nor the earnest moral apology that is made for traditional–formal usages.[3] Moreover, if we allow its full ambiguity to the presence of both a traditional ground and a deconstructive abyss beyond its limits, we seem carried into further ambiguity over the possible meaning of their cofunctioning. Does the novel intend to subject this traditional ground to a covert erosion, slyly destining it for the abyss below, or does the novel mean to use the abyss in a cautionary way, offering its sublime, vertiginous prospect only to frighten us back from it – back to safer, beaten ground whose value is proportionately enhanced by the danger of having strayed?

Like one of those optical drawings that won't resolve once for all into five cubes or six, a vase or two human profiles, *Middlemarch* seems to be traditional and to be beyond its limit, to subvert and to reconfirm the value of its traditional status. We shall explore the double valency of such a text as what matters most about it: not necessarily in the hope of giving its terms their proper balance (as though this were possible), far less of being able to favor one of them over the other, but with the suspicion that their full contradictory value may best define the novel's peculiar relationship to traditional form.

I have already charted what I think are the two basic requirements of traditional novelistic form: a moment of suspense and instability, and a moment of closure and resolved meaning. The first institutes the narratable disequilibrium, which the second converts back to a state of non-narratable quiescence. We might ask again our fundamental question: with what representations of content and value does *Middlemarch* motivate its constructional categories (non-narratability, narratability, closure)? In answer, however, the novel presents nor merely a variety of different determinations, but what are actually different *systems* of determination. How the constructional categories are motivated depends on the level at which the story is being told. Three main levels of motivation easily stand out. The novelistic community (Hegel's world of 'maintaining individuals') views the story according to one scheme of reference and value; the protagonists (that world's 'historical individuals') perceive it according to another; and the narrator (would he be the providential *Geist*?) collaborates with his invented reader to tell it according to still another. The text pluralizes the perspective from which traditional form is commonly perceived and delimited, offering not a single, univocal movement from the narratable to closure, but in effect three such movements. One recalls the virtual unanimity that obtained among levels of telling the story at the end of a Jane Austen novel: Emma finally came to share the narrator's view of her errancy, and even Mary Crawford ended up recognizing 'the better taste acquired at Mansfield'. In *Middlemarch*, the different ways of perceiving and delimiting the story all conspire to identify what is, in terms of its main actions, *the same story*. Yet if they are narratologically identical, they remain to the end hermeneutically distinct. Each system of delimitation accounts for more or less the same events, but each system derives meaning from different sources and puts its stresses and values in different places.

This pluralism of perspectives that are coterminous but not covalent opens up some interesting possibilities. If one perspective (such as the narrator's) includes a consciousness of others, it may need to subvert or parody them, in order to maintain its difference by an effect of transcendence. Yet if despite its difference it shares a common structure with its rivals, it may be running the risk of self-subversion or self-parody in the very attempt to undercut them. The need to protect against this risk may even give rise to certain deflections or hesitations of aim. The main force of the pluralism in *Middlemarch*, however, is surely to make us aware of perspective itself. What traditional form shows us is no longer exhibited in a spirit of naïve realism, as simply what is there to be seen. Instead it must now be taken as a function of a perceiving system with its own desire, disguises, deletions, and disinterests, *which might have been organized otherwise*. . . .

. . . If the novel too is a text – often insistently so – then it too is deprived of a final or fully present meaning, and our provisional, erroneous interpretations can never make good the lack. Yet one shouldn't underestimate the novel's need to get out from under the sway of textuality. What *Middlemarch* explicitly wants to diffuse is not its own narrative or textual dynamic, but the urgent moral ideology menaced by that dynamic. Only by collapsing the polarities responsible for its own existence (self versus other, sign versus meaning), can the novel convincingly argue for the practical validity of its religion of humanity. A closure, then, must take place, and it must take the form of a transcendent experience of fellowship whose transparent signs no longer require interpretation.

This is the dominant function of the four 'great scenes' at the end of the novel ('Look up, Nicholas', Dorothea at the window, Dorothea and Rosamond, Dorothea and Will). Each of them stages an abreaction in which the 'broken intercourse' of egos and texts is overcome in fellow feeling and a wholly present word. They are examples of what Brooks has placed at the heart of melodrama: scenes where the moral imagination finds its voice, naming and enacting its imperatives in a full recognition of 'the sign of virtue'.[4] Not by accident do they come at the end of a narrative whose ongoing production depends on withholding full expression and deferring final meaning. Perhaps the most fundamental moral value of these scenes (far more basic than the values they are 'about') consists in the sheer pressure they put on narrative language to *mean something*, to end its teasing, frustrating suspensiveness. In this sense, their real sign of virtue would be their virtue of no longer merely being a sign.

Yet even with its primary evidence of transcendence, the *Middlemarch* text equivocates. One recalls the radically anti-melodramatic stance of Valéry's M. Teste: 'Je ne suis pas fait pour les romans ni pour les drames. Leurs grandes scènes, colères, passions, moments tragiques, loin de m'exalter me parviennent comme de misérables éclats, des états rudimentaires où toutes les bêtises se lâchent, où l'être se simplifie jusqu'à la sottise.'[5] 'Being simplifies itself to the point of foolishness'. George Eliot assuredly *is* made for novels and plays, and she would hardly share Teste's cerebral haughtiness. However, if 'foolishness' is the wrong term for the powerful scenes that carry the novelist's most precious values, 'simplification' may not be. The frustrations of the novelistic world – in the last analysis, the frictions of the narrative text itself – are not made to vanish in these scenes, but only vanish from view. Without exception, the transcendence of such moments is shown to depend on *not seeing* all that is taking place in them. In the full ambiguity of the phrase, the closures of *Middlemarch* 'make-believe'. Apparently meant to demonstrate once and for all the reality of transcendence, they undermine the reality of their demonstration by basing it on an act of faith. Of course, the transcendence can seem enhanced by the irony: 'Blessed are they that have not seen, and yet have believed.' But it can also seem impeached by it: for what is the nature of the blessing that falls on those who do not see *so that* they may believe? Once again the text will insist on its double legibility.

'Look up, Nicholas'

Harriet Bulstrode is a character whose stability has meant ignoring the tissue of contradiction and division out of which it is woven. 'Knowing very little of [her] own motives' (p. 328),[6] she has never perceived the oxymoronic implications of her 'imitative piety' or her 'native worldliness' (p. 662). Her differences never seem discontinuities ('various little points of superiority' over Mrs Pymdale 'served to give colour to their conversation without dividing them', p. 328); and her limited curiosity is never faced as an active system of suppression. Although she enjoys a 'habitual consciousness that her husband's earlier connections were not quite on a level with her own', it is 'not that she knew much about them' or even tried much to find out. A bare, blanked outline of his past is 'almost as much as she had cared to learn' (p. 661). 'She so much wished to ignore towards others that her husband had ever been a London Dissenter, that she liked to keep it out of sight even in talking to him' (p. 662). In short, the presumptive unity of her character has been 'an odd patchwork', stitching discrepancies together into a mere semblance of consistency (p. 807).

With the news of the Raffles scandal, that patchwork starts to come undone.

> 'God help you, Harriet! you know all.'
>
> That moment was perhaps worse than any which came after. It contained that concentrated experience which in great crises of emotion reveals the bias of a nature, and is prophetic of the ultimate act which ends an intermediate struggle.
>
> (p. 805)

In a sense, the 'intermediate struggle' is a struggle against the fact of intermediacy itself. Something has *come between* her and her husband: a secret – learned only 'from others' (p. 807) – and a silence. ('Leave me in quiet', she begs as she goes to her room; and Bulstrode, alone in his room, finds that 'if he turned to God there seemed to be no answer but the pressure of retribution', pp. 806, 807). Simultaneously, something has also come between her and the entire world. All the social mediations that once seemed to assure her identity now throw it into crisis: into a search for a 'piety' that would no longer be 'imitative', and for a 'native' mode of relating to the world that would no longer depend on 'worldliness'.

Much as trauma calls out for abreaction, or tension for catharsis, the sheer concentration of the struggle demands an ultimate act to end it. The silence, the secrecy, the 'intermediate' barriers between husband and wife – these must be overcome. It thus becomes crucial to appreciate the cognitive ambition underlying Harriet's pledge of loyalty. To an important extent, she offers her sympathy in order to *know what she is offering it for*. Whatever else it might be, her gesture of support is an attempt to elicit her husband's admission of guilt. For her forgiveness will not bear the weight of meaning undertaken by it until she knows (and he knows that she knows) what there is to be forgiven. If their confrontation is to disarm the force of intermediacy, then it must issue in far more than a mere emotional release: it must produce nothing less than a moment of truth, compassionated and confessed.

> 'Look up, Nicholas.'
>
> He raised his eyes with a little start and looked at her half amazed for a moment: her pale face, her changed, mourning dress, the trembling about her mouth, all said, 'I know' and her hands and eyes rested gently on him. He burst out crying and they cried together, she

> sitting at his side. They could not yet speak to each other of the shame which she was bearing with him, or of the acts which had brought it down on them. His confession was silent, and her promise of faithfulness was silent. Open-minded as she was, she nevertheless shrank from the words which would have expressed their mutual consciousness as she would have shrunk from flakes of fire. She could not say, 'How much is only slander and false suspicion?' and he did not say, 'I am innocent'.
>
> (p. 808)

Has a full reconciliation taken place or not? One might first notice the ambiguous status of non-verbal discourse in the scene. On the one hand, the gestures are telling and the weeping fully expressive. 'His confession was silent, and her promise of faithfulness was silent.' It is as though their communication passed over the clumsy paraphrases of language, and its meaning were all the more unimpeachable for transcending them. On the other hand, there is evidence to locate this mute discourse not somewhere beyond speech, but well on this side of it: 'They could not yet speak to each other . . . she shrank from the words . . . she could not say . . . he did not say.' Does the speechlessness depend on an intuition that mere words could never be adequate to express the fullness of the present moment? Perhaps, but there is some question whether the moment is really full without them. 'They could not *yet* speak' implies that at least part of the moment has already been postponed to a later date. All Harriet's gestures may say 'I know', but it is clear at the end of the passage that she does not know and still wants to. 'She could not say, "How much is only slander and false suspicion?" and he did not say, "I am innocent".' That she should desire to put such a question, and hope for such an answer, suggests that she has entertained an incomplete conception of her husband's misdeeds. Implicitly, the validity of her pardon is based on an error about what it actually encompasses.

It is never known how she might face the truth, because she is never enlightened. The revelations here waived until later are later deferred indefinitely:

> The acts which he had washed and diluted with inward argument and motive, and for which it seemed comparatively easy to win invisible pardon – what name would she call them by? That she should ever silently call his acts Murder was what he could not bear. He felt shrouded by her doubt: he got strength to face her from the sense that she could not yet feel warranted in pronouncing that worst condemnation on him. Some time, perhaps – when he was dying – he would tell her all: in the deep shadow of that time, when she held his hand in the gathering darkness, she might listen without recoiling

> from his touch. Perhaps: but concealment had been the habit of his life, and the impulse to confession had no power against the dread of a deeper humiliation.
>
> (p. 882)

The vicious circle is obvious: because he fears that Harriet will withdraw her forgiveness, Bulstrode never confesses; because he never confesses, the benefits of that forgiveness are already withdrawn. By this point, the closural reconciliation has been largely retracted: dissolved back into the narratable polarities and protractions that it wanted to overcome. The Bulstrodes' story is brought to term, but the term seems only a permanent state of suspensiveness. The actual meaning of their scene together remains in the air: blindness matching up with concealment? or both transcending themselves? It is not, of course, that the novel underrates Harriet's impressive gesture, however unseeing and incomplete it is ultimately shown to be. Her character reveals its bias, and she enters into the camp of those whose integrity is made secure through 'direct fellow-feeling'. Yet such purely individual salvation is precisely what the doctrine of sympathy has aspired to go beyond. In this case, at any rate, the 'sign of virtue' is still detached from its meaning.

Dorothea at the window

Not unlike Harriet Bulstrode's, Dorothea's spiritual crisis contains the concentrated experience of what being in a narrative means in *Middlemarch*. 'The limit of resistance was reached, and she had sunk back helpless within the clutch of inescapable anguish' (p. 844). Will's presumed defection to Rosamond has been a betrayal of 'the vibrating bond of mutual speech' (p. 844), and Dorothea's own utterances can barely get further than 'loud-whispered cries and moans' and 'helpless sobs' (p. 845). The 'detected illusion' of Will's 'lip-born words' closes every prospect but that of an endless, pointless narrative (p. 845). In a sense, Will's loyalty to her stood as a bulwark against the dispersive influences of time and change: it offered a 'sweet dim perspective of hope, that along some pathway they should meet with unchanged recognition and take up the backward years as a yesterday' (p. 844). With that hope gone, Dorothea's life threatens to be kept forever in a state of unresolved, unresolvable transition.

Her response to this threat – the narrative threat *par excellence* – comes with violent, all but masochistic intensity. She locks herself in her 'vacant room', as though to underscore the void of her solitude; she presses 'her hands hard on top of her head', as though delivering again the psychic wound inflicted by Will; she lies 'on the bare floor and let[s] the night grow cold around her', as though this were the only appropriate metaphor for her state of mind (p. 844). One might argue that her dramatic gestures are already part of an effort to master the anxiety they repeat. For they stress her despair in a double sense: they emphasize it, *and* they put pressure on it to give way. Dorothea's acting out – what the narrator calls her 'paroxysm' (p. 845) – seems unconsciously organized by the expectation that, if she can only intensify her concentrated experience even further, she may finally provoke 'the ultimate act which ends an intermediate struggle'. To raise the fever might be to break it in the end; to cultivate nightmares might be at last to wake up from them. Compared by the narrator to 'a despairing child', Dorothea unwittingly pursues the logic of tantrum, inflating itself in order to subside.

Her impatience, so to speak, is rewarded: 'She had waked to a new condition: she felt as if her soul had been liberated from its terrible conflict; she was no longer wrestling with her grief, but could sit down with it as a lasting companion and make it a sharer in her thoughts' (p. 845). Once more Dorothea struggles to assert a vision in which 'everyday-things mean the greatest things', though this time with a crucial difference. In the past, we noticed, Dorothea's commitment to the signified took place at the expense of an attention to the signifier. Vehicles were overlooked or dismissed altogether by a peremptory tenor, which then found nothing to carry it. Suggestively, Dorothea's grief can now yield to a less disabling vision precisely through a new interest in detail *together with* a speculation about meanings. 'She began now to live through that yesterday morning again, forcing herself to dwell on every detail and its possible meaning.' What is generally identified as Dorothea's emancipation from ego involves, specifically, a dual challenge: to inspect the details overlooked by a repressively selective selfhood, and to consider the meanings these might have for *others*. In the light of the polycentric perspective Dorothea tries to achieve ('Was she alone in that scene? Was it her event only?'), the range of the world's details and the range of meanings that can be made available to them need no longer restrict one another. If one meaning only reductively grasps a scene, then another meaning – or a whole range of other meanings – may be more adequate to the task. And yet, if meaning may be finally adequate to scene, is scene adequate to meaning? Can scenes fully incarnate the meanings that grasp them? The view from the window would seem decisive in its affirmation:

> She opened her curtains, and looked out towards the bit of road that lay in view, with fields beyond, outside the entrance-gates. On the road there was a man with a bundle on his back and a woman carrying her baby; in the field she could see figures moving – perhaps the shepherd with his dog. Far off in the bending sky was the pearly light; and she

> felt the largeness of the world and the manifold wakings of men to labour and endurance. She was a part of that involuntary, palpitating life, and could neither look out on it from her luxurious shelter as a mere spectator, nor hide her eyes in selfish complaining.
>
> (p. 846)

Meaningfulness and life are in this moment reconciled, immanently charged with one another. As Martin Price has seen, 'the sublimity [Dorothea] has sought in heroic exertions of the ego gives way to a sublimity she finds at a new level of her own being as well as of the world's'.[7] Under the pressure of Dorothea's insight, this tiny diorama of the everyday emblematically extends and insinuates itself beyond its borders so that it comes to implicate, virtually, the entire world. And the world, which before had been seen as irrelevantly petty, now encompasses all that there is to live for. Together with the vision that sees it so, it can sustain the largest and most ambitious meanings available to it.

Yet – one says it almost with regret – even this scene invites us to question its adequacy to the meanings it is supposed to be at last fully representing. What Dorothea sees from the window is inevitably qualified by the text's showing of what she doesn't see. I don't simply mean the fact that the tentativeness of certain details ('*perhaps* the shepherd with his dog') implicitly refers us to her notorious shortsightedness (p. 53), although this does suggest that her capacity to *feel* 'the largeness of the world' depends partly on a physiological inability to *see* it. Her more telling lapse of vision involves passing over the social dimension of the landscape, along with the social conditions of her own observation. Dorothea is the owner of an estate: her view opens out from a window on it and passes directly through its 'entrance-gates'. The fields beyond may well be part of the property. Significantly, Dorothea never sees anyone she knows in this landscape; she never even sees anyone she could know. No male protagonist of *Middlemarch* would ever be seen laboring in the fields, nor would Celia or Rosamond ever appear on the road carrying her baby. The horizontal view across the landscape masks the vertical view downward to a different class. At the moment of Dorothea's greatest participation in 'that involuntary, palpitating life', she is removed from it by obvious social divisions. During her most democratic vision, she is *looking down*, both literally and in terms of social hierarchy. In a sense, the same oversight that permits her to identify with those she sees ironically brings the validity of identification into question.

Moreover, if Dorothea unwittingly censors the scene by not reading its social codes, the resulting picture of the human condition in turn censors her problems by not admitting them into its space. For life seen from the window is stripped to its most essential imperatives: survival (hence work) and procreation (hence 'child-bearing'). The synecdoche whereby Dorothea makes these imperatives stand for her own less elementary dilemmas has its obvious therapeutic uses, but it also leaves out a lot. To the figures in the landscape, of course, physical labor and child-bearing have an immediate and unquestioned relevance. Dorothea's situation, however, is precisely one in which work and womanhood have become *problems*. Both her income and her good faith have made it possible to embark on a quest determined neither by economic necessity nor by traditional social arrangements. In this light, the symbolic equations of the vision ('burden' equals production equals 'man', 'baby' equals reproduction equals 'woman') either make that quest irrelevant or are made irrelevant by it. Once again, the solution seems below the level of the problem, and the answer comes to a question we thought was very different.

Furthermore, the answer isn't all there. Much as in the Bulstrodes' reconciliation, its plenitude is both promised and postponed. The scene has only given voice to 'an approaching murmur that would soon gather distinctness' (p. 847): its full truth will come later. The deferment inevitably detotalizes the scene's glimpse of transcendence, as though it were always a receding vision needing to be filled in, even when it was taking place. Paradoxically, the seemingly all-inclusive moment *lacks something*: its meaning can have the status of an ultimate truth only if it is carried through, supplemented, translated. In other words, the scene commits its closural status to the very processes that define the narratable. The vision thus risks being lost in the effort to find itself. Even before considering the first consequence of that effort (Dorothea's 'second attempt to see and save Rosamond'), one should recognize the insistent disjunction between this scene and that. How is Dorothea to transfer the basic and grand values announced in the view from the window to the sophisticated and petty issue of Rosamond's adulterous temptation? The largeness of Dorothea's vision seems already impugned by the smallness – or simply the otherness – of the first opportunity to carry it through. Since the vision has deferred its meaning until more explicit and specific revelations to follow, much might ride on the visit to Rosamond: no less than the possibility of answering the question, Has Dorothea's vision taken place? . .

In every case, then, what the great scenes of *Middlemarch* aspire to signify is exceeded by their signifiers, which just as easily point to blindness, misunderstanding, egocentric tautology, and textuality, as they do to insight, recognition, fellowship, and transparency. It is as if the novelist could not help seeing the persistence of the narratable even in its closure. As a consequence, closure appears to take place only through a strategic misreading of the data – a misreading that is at once shown to be expedient (expressing a moral command), efficacious (settling the final living arrangements of characters), and erroneous (deconstructed as a repetition of what it is supposed to overcome). The resulting ambiguity, of course, is bound to make conclusion less conclusive. George Eliot herself recognized that 'conclusions are the weak point of most authors, but some of the fault lies in the very nature of a conclusion, which is at best a negation'.[8] Or as we might say: the suspensive and dispersive logic of narrative is such that an effective closure – no matter how naturally or organically it emerges from the story – always stands in a discontinuous (or negative) relation to it.

Notes

1. Henry James, unsigned review, *Galaxy 15* (March 1873), reprinted David Carroll (ed.), *George Eliot: The Critical Heritage* (London: Routledge and Kegan Paul, 1971), p. 359.
2. A perfect instance would be Arnold Kettle, *An Introduction to the English Novel: Defoe to the Present* (New York: Harper and Row, 1968). Kettle begins his chapter on *Middlemarch* by claiming that the novel 'is the same *kind* of novel as *Emma* . . . George Eliot extends the method of Jane Austen, but does not substantially alter it' (p. 160). This perspective governs and simplifies his entire reading of the novel.
3. This seems to me the failing of J. Hillis Miller's two articles, 'Narrative and History', and 'Optic and Semiotic in *Middlemarch*'. Despite it, the articles remain our most sophisticated treatment of the novel's own sophistication, and I shall later, by a long and qualifying detour, want to rejoin some of their conclusions.
4. Peter Brooks, *The Melodramatic Imagination* (New Haven: Yale University Press, 1976), especially in the chapter 'An Aesthetic of Astonishment'.
5. Paul Valéry, *Monsieur Teste* (Paris: Gallimard, 1927). pp. 112–13.
6. Quotations are from *Middlemarch* ed. W. J. Harvey, (Penguin, 1965).
7. Martin Price, 'The Sublime Poet: Pictures and Powers', *Yale Review 58* (Winter 1969), p. 213.
8. *George Eliot Letters*, ed. Gordon S. Haight (New Haven: Yale University Press, 1954–55), 2, p. 324. My attention was brought to the letter in question by Darrel Mansell, Jr, 'George Eliot's Conception of "Form"', *Studies in English Literature* 5 (Autumn 1965), pp. 651–62, reprinted in George R. Creeger, *George Eliot: A Collection of Critical Essays* (Englewood Cliffs, N.J.: Prentice-Hall, 1970), pp. 66–78. In an excellent study, Mansell argues that 'the more relations the novel establishes, the more must be severed where they do not end . . . at best the conclusion can only cut off this network at some arbitrary point' (p. 77). My only quarrel with Mansell's theory of form in George Eliot (which he bases on the novelist's own essay, 'Notes on Form in Art') is that his interest in the 'relations which the novel itself sends outwards' leads him to scant the extent to which a novel like *Middlemarch* tries to master its internal dynamic in quasi-conventional resolutions.

13 The Decomposition of the Elephants: Double-Reading *Daniel Deronda**

CYNTHIA CHASE

Cynthia Chase is best known for her application of Derridean and de Manian deconstructive theory to readings of individual texts. Unlike Hillis Miller and Jonathan Arac, however, she argues that George Eliot, at least in *Daniel Deronda*, does not co-operate with the deconstruction of the conventions of nineteenth-century realistic fiction but endeavours to defeat deconstructive thinking. This is apparent, she argues, in the fact that realism and the idealistic aims of the narrative are at odds and that the novel refuses to acknowledge this, as the absence of circumcision from the text indicates (see Introduction, pp. 12–13).

In the seventh and penultimate volume of George Eliot's final, elephantine novel, the narration is interrupted by a long letter that the titular hero receives from a subordinate character: 'My dear Deronda', writes Hans Meyrick,

> In return for your sketch of Italian movements and your view of the world's affairs generally, I may say that here at home the most judicious opinion going as to the effects of present causes is that 'time will show.' As to the present causes of past effects, it is now seen that the late swindling telegrams account for the last year's cattle plague – which is a refutation of philosophy falsely so called, and justifies the compensation to the farmers.[1]

With this resounding fatuity, Meyrick's letter opens no less than an interpretation of the novel, for it calls attention to the issue of causality, the problem that comes to light in the anomalous plotting of Deronda's story. Meyrick's flippant sentences describe the figural logic covertly at

* Reprinted from Publications of the Modern Language Association (*PMLA*), 93 (1978), pp. 215–27.

work in the text. Focusing attention on the narrative process, these lines suggest that the novel presents itself to be read in two conflicting ways: not only as a history of the effects of causes but also as a story of 'the present causes of past effects'. *Daniel Deronda* calls for a double reading, and a close reading of Meyrick's letter offers a starting point for this procedure.[2] It sets the reader on the traces of the rhetorical principles by which the text is constructed, principles at odds with the meanings indicated by *Deronda*'s narrator and dissimulated by the novel's narrative mode. In short, the letter functions as a deconstruction of the novel.

Meyrick's 'bird-dance' (as Deronda calls it) in no way furthers the novel's plot, unlike other letters included in the text, each of which marks a turning point in the story.[3] In this it rather invites comparison with the passages of commentary incorporated by the narrator, despite the contrast between Meyrick's frivolous, self-parodic tone and the narrator's more sober style. The contrast in tone is not merely superficial. Meyrick's letter proposes an interpretation of the novel that is substantially and radically at odds with the explanations of its narrator. Aberrant as interpretation and superfluous to the plot, the letter raises a question as to its ostensible function in the novel. That is, what significance does it have for the narrator, that privileged character linked in profound complicity with the hero of the novel? The narrator's view emerges clearly in the passage that follows the inserted letter and describes Deronda's reactions. Deronda takes Meyrick's parodic mode to indicate a basic incapacity for authentic feeling, a failure to deserve to be taken seriously as a lover. 'Hans Meyrick's nature was not one in which love could strike the deep roots that turn disappointment into sorrow: it was too restless, too readily excitable by novelty, too ready to turn itself into imaginative material, and wear its grief as a fantastic costume' (chapter 32, pp. 709–10). This negative judgment reflects the fundamental strategy of the narrator and indicates one of the main ostensible meanings of the novel: seriousness and idealism triumph over parody and the ironic spirit. Meyrick's letter functions to exemplify the spirit and the style that the hero transcends.

The triumph of idealism over irony is written into the very structure of the novel's double plot, which presents us with Deronda and Gwendolen as rival protagonists. The distinction that the style of the letter helps to establish between Meyrick and Deronda is in one sense a subtler version of the opposition between Gwendolen and Deronda. From the reader's point of view, one of the erring heroine's more admirable and interesting qualities is her satirical spirit, her critical eye. This is also the admirable and interesting quality of the 'English part' of *Daniel Deronda*, which the scheme of the narrative subordinates to the more idealistic and moralistic 'Jewish part'.[4] The narrator's parable presents not merely Deronda's triumph and Gwendolen's defeat but the triumph of one mode of narration over another. Superior value is ascribed to the seriousness that distinguishes both Deronda as a character and the narrative mode employed to relate his activities, which contrasts with the more satiric mode of the Gwendolen plot and with the ironic mode of Meyrick's letter.[5] Meyrick's letter may be readily understood as a negative example in a broad esthetic and moral judgment inscribed in the story as the intention of its narrator.

The narrator's strategy is to offer in Meyrick's letter a more or less satirical view of the characters' situation and then to arrange the context in a way that deprives this view of any validity.[6] This is achieved in part by Deronda's reflections on Meyrick's superficiality but also by the plot itself, for when Deronda receives the letter, he has just learned of his Jewish birth, which gives him a basis for intimacy with Mirah that Meyrick the Gentile cannot hope to share; in this light, Meyrick's hope of winning Mirah, the main theme of the letter, appears ridiculously unfounded, 'the unusually persistent bird-dance of an extravagant fancy', as the narrator allows Deronda to observe. The tactic is to bracket the letter's ironic mode with a dramatic irony at the level of the action.

The presentation of Meyrick's letter is thus a focus for the devaluation of ironic discourse. Viewing it in these terms, even before examining the text more closely to see just what is said that must be so energetically discredited, one can anticipate a good deal of what is at stake. It is not merely coincidence that Deronda's interpretation of Meyrick closely resembles the description of the Romantic ironist in Kierkegaard's *The Concept of Irony*, a polemical Hegelian account of the ironic 'moment'. Irony, for Kierkegaard, is properly seen as a crucial but transitory moment in both classical and Christian history. In insisting on subordinating irony to the value systems inherent in the idea of history and the conventions of discourse, Kierkegaard is recognizing the threat to history and to discourse itself that an absolute irony must pose. Meyrick's whimsical missive to Deronda, while it can hardly be said to muster an absolute irony, employs an ironic mode of a sort that subverts rather than serves the establishment of meaning and value. As we shall see, it offers a deconstruction of the narrator's story and, by implication, of story in general – both of history, with its system of assumptions about teleological and representational structures, and of discourse, with its intrinsic need to constitute meaning through sequence and reference.

Daniel Deronda, of course, is not merely a fictional 'history'; it is patently about history. It focuses on the causes at work in the personal destinies of Deronda and Gwendolen and finally on the 'cause' taken up by Deronda as his destined mission. The novel claims for its hero the possibility of a genuine historical role. The narrator seeks to portray a subtle heroism, consisting in imaginative empathy with a historical destiny, the achievement of a distinctively historical imagination. In the context of this invocation of historical consciousness, Meyrick's flippant allusions to Judaic tradition are strikingly discordant. His letter shows a comparable flippancy about certain elementary conventions of writing, such as consistency and continuity. These he violates by his digressive style, continually interrupted by fanciful comments on his epistolary manner. The whole of Meyrick's letter is a tissue of allusions, a complex parroting of the diction, themes, and rhetorical strategies of various conventional texts. Far more than simply posing the dilemma of irony and history, these allusions render a strikingly exact account of discursive structures. A close reading of this curious 'bird-dance' offers, therefore, a favorable beginning for a double reading of *Daniel Deronda*.

The opening paragraph of Meyrick's letter ostensibly has no real subject matter. It presents itself as badinage. Its covert topic, however, is the plotting of *Daniel Deronda*. 'Here at home', we read, 'the most judicious opinion going as to the effects of present causes is that "time will show."' This purports to be a satire of the conventional wisdom. In the process it satirizes, too, the traditional temporality that the realistic novel is supposed to imitate. (It should perhaps be stressed that this reading of the letter is not concerned merely with the meanings that the character Hans Meyrick might conceivably have intended, any more than this reading of the novel is concerned merely with the meanings that could plausibly be ascribed to the intentions of the narrator. The text generates a much wider range of significations.)

Narrative operates, indeed, by flattering our 'judicious opinion': to read a sequence of events as a narrative is to expect that sequence to become intelligible. By the almost irresistible pressure of this expectation, the temporal sequence is conflated with a causal sequence; *post hoc* is interpreted as *propter hoc*. A novel evokes the passage of time, which is itself presented to show the 'effects' of 'causes' and thereby to reveal the events' significance. The formulation in Meyrick's letter satirizes this assumption as a kind of mental sloth, a withholding of judgment that is an evasion of interpretive effort. It would not be irrelevant to refer this criticism to Deronda's attitude toward learning his parentage, which he postpones indefinitely until he receives his mother's summons. What the narrator would wish us to interpret as a 'wise passiveness', the text of the letter ironizes as the banal creed of 'time will show.' The remainder of the passage suggests that the passive trustfulness of protagonist and reader – their trust in the revelatory power of sheer sequence – is fundamentally misplaced.

In opening an ironic perspective on the overt time scheme of the conventional novel, Meyrick satirizes the norm that Eliot's novel was criticized for violating. Some readers of *Daniel Deronda* have judged that it fails adequately to render the sense of duration and the flow of time that would make the action of the novel plausible and significant. Henry James's Pulcheria echoes this opinion when she characterizes the 'current' of the story as being rather 'a series of lakes'.[7] The 'time will show' passage identifies such objections as symptoms of a banal conception of novelistic time. The most radical critique in the passage, however, aims neither at the censure of the narrator's strategy nor at the ostensible strategy itself. Rather, the passage exposes *Deronda*'s peculiar plot as a systematic disruption of narrative principles and temporal structures. In its second sentence Meyrick's letter suggests that the novel discloses not 'the effects of . . . causes' but 'the present causes of past effects'.

The phrase describes exactly the decisive episode that has just taken place before Deronda's receipt of Meyrick's letter: the revelation of his Jewish birth. In this sense, Meyrick's letter is no mere digression from the crucial action that occupies the preceding and following chapters (51 and 53), the confrontation between the hero and his mother. Rather, it names the distortion of causality that the reader senses in this turn of the plot. What a reader feels, on the basis of the narrative presentation, is that it is *because* Deronda has developed a strong affinity for Judaism that he turns out to be of Jewish parentage. Generations of readers have registered discomfort at the disclosure of the Princess Halm-Eberstein, and generations of critics have objected to it as an awkward implausibility or a graceless admixture of romance elements. Meyrick's letter, however, names what is vitally at issue: not a violation of genre conventions or of *vraisemblance* but a deconstruction of the concept of cause.

Deronda's decisive encounter in the preceding chapter involves a revelation of origin. Origin, cause and identity are linked in the plot structure to which the letter alludes. The question of Deronda's identity, posed and left suspended, receives an ostensibly definitive answer with the disclosure of his origins. Up to this point, Deronda has been identified by his qualities or attributes, in terms, that is, of his character. With the revelation of his parentage, this identity conferred by character is seconded by an identity conferred by origin, and the latter is presented, implicitly, as the cause of the former – as the cause of Deronda's character. This presentation conforms with the conventional logic of cause and effect and exploits the myth of origin, the view of origin as having a unique generative power.

This causative force is also strongly emphasized in the Princess Halm-Eberstein's account of Deronda's family history. The power of genetic heritage proves itself all the more impressively in resurfacing in the third generation after a deliberate suppression in the second. Deronda's mother tells him: 'I have been forced to obey my dead father. I have been forced to tell you that you are a Jew, and deliver to you what he commanded me to deliver' (p. 693). 'I have after all been the instrument my father wanted. . . . His yoke has been on me whether I loved it or not. You are the grandson he wanted' (p. 726). Deronda accedes to this interpretation of the workings of origin, and the narrator in no way discredits the genealogical myth that marks these passages. Full weight is put on the metaphor of birth as destiny. Chapters 51 and 53 emphatically affirm the identification between origin and cause.

The sequence of events in the plot as a whole, however, presents Deronda's revealed origins in a different perspective. The account of Deronda's situation has made it increasingly obvious to the reader that the progression of the hero's destiny – or, that is to say, the progression of the story – positively requires a revelation that he is of Jewish birth. For Deronda's *bildungsroman* to proceed, his character must crystallize, and this must come about through a recognition of his destiny, which has remained obscure to him, according to the narrator's account, largely because of his ignorance of his origins. The suspenseful stress on Deronda's relationship with Mordecai and with Mirah orients his history in their direction, and Mordecai explicitly stresses his faith that Deronda is a Jew. Thus the reader comes upon Deronda's Jewish parentage as an inevitable inference to be drawn not simply from the presentation of Deronda's qualities and his empathy with the Jews but above all from the patent strategy and direction of the narrative. The revelation of Deronda's origins therefore appears as an effect of narrative requirements. The supposed cause of his character and vocation (according to the chapters recounting the disclosure), Deronda's origin presents itself (in the light of the rest of the text) rather as the effect of the account of his vocation: his origin is the effect of its effects.

The decisive episode of 'the Deronda plot' thus presents itself to be read in two conflicting ways. On the one hand, the narrator's account emphatically affirms its causal character. On the other hand, the plot and the overall strategy of the novel conspicuously call attention to its status as the effect of tactical requirements. The contradiction cannot be reduced to the simple distinction between the event of Deronda's birth, a genuine origin that took place in the past, and the disclosure of his birth, a retrospective account that takes place in the present. It is not the event of Deronda's birth as a Jew that is decisive for his story, but the knowledge of affirmation of it. This disclosure, as far as the plot is concerned, is the event with causative powers; yet it appears, too, as a mere effect of the account of Deronda's emerging vocation. Meyrick's inverted phrase names the contradiction that characterizes this narrative structure. It is a chiasmus or a metalepsis, a reversal of the temporal status of effect and cause: cause is relocated in the present and effect in the past. In naming Deronda's revealed Jewish parentage as the 'present cause' of his demonstrated vocation for Jewishness, its 'past effects', Meyrick's letter is naming the cause as an effect of its effects, and the effects as the cause of their cause, and is therein identifying the contradictory relationship between the claims of the realistic fiction and the narrative strategy actually employed.

Meyrick's metalepsis also describes the operation establishing Deronda's identity as a Jew. The account in the chapters on Deronda's meeting with his mother grounds itself on the principle that identity in the sense of origin precedes and causes identity in the sense of character and attributes. The account implicit in the narrative structure, however, presents character and attributes as preceding and causing the inference of origin. This goes far toward undermining the authority of the notion of identity, as well as of origin and of cause, for attributes carry the authority of identity only insofar as they belong to a system involving causality, in which behavior is causally related to identity. Meyrick's deconstructed causality, in which 'present causes' match 'past effects', describes, as we have seen, the sequence establishing the origin and identity of the hero of the novel. Since Deronda is the character whose consciousness coincides most closely with that of the narrator, and who thus represents the exemplary subject, the deconstruction of his identity has radical implications for the concept of the subject in general. The origin of the subject appears as the effect of a narrative requirement, the requirement that an ostensible cause with the authority and mystique of an origin be retrospectively posited to confirm and account for the established direction of the action. Like the concepts of cause and of identity, then, the concept of the subject is the product of a metalepsis, a rhetorical operation, an aberrant reversal or substitution of rhetorical properties.

Meyrick's letter explicitly associates the issue of Jewish identity with the identity principle of formal logic, parodically formulated as substitution of properties. He has been talking with Mordecai, Meyrick writes, 'and agreeing with him in the general principle, that whatever is best is for that reason Jewish. I never held it my *forte* to be a severe reasoner, but I can see that if whatever is best is A and B happens to be best, B must be A, however little you might have expected it beforehand.' One recognizes here the premises and procedure of the novel: if whatever is best is Jewish and Deronda happens to be best, Deronda must be Jewish, however unexpected or scandalous this may appear for the hero of a Victorian novel. The subversiveness of Meyrick's formulation lies partly in its linking of the blank, unresonant, significance-free and reference-free language of logical principles with the resonant, specific, value- and affect-charged topic of a hero and his possible identity as a Jew. The connection suggests on the one hand the constructed, artificial, non-'organic' status of the hero's story and on the other hand the preposterous character of the purportedly value-free principle. It is invoked here, of course, in reference to a property that reduces the statement to nonsense – namely, the enigmatic property of Jewishness, which properly speaking cannot exist as the logical consequence of a deductive process.

The deconstructive force of the passage has to do with its reduction of the question of human identity to the application of a logical principle: if $b = A$ and $B = b$, then $B = A$ (since A cannot at the same time equal b and not equal B, which equals b). The metaphysical issue of the identity of the subject and the humanistic issue of the identity of a person are reconstrued as a strictly logical, rhetorical issue, a question of the function of linguistic terms. A defining feature of fiction, especially of the realistic novel, is the presentation of all issues in terms of relationships among fictional characters, or fictive persons – in terms, that is, of the phenomenology of subjectivity. The choice of this context is in itself a defense of the subject as the locus of meaning and value, against an alternative account treating these as the valueless products of the operations of language itself. As discussion of the narrative structure of *Daniel Deronda* has suggested, the latter account of meaning is also inscribed in the novel (covered over by the version of the fictive subject functioning as narrator). Meyrick's formulation contributes to this account by reversing the recuperative, defensive, constructive process involved in establishing a phenomenological context. In renaming the novel's central issue as a matter of a substitution of terms, Meyrick's deconstructive gesture reconceives the significant action of human subjects as the purposeless play of signifiers.

Meyrick's letter marks what classical rhetoric called a parabasis, a shifting of attention from the level of operation of the narrator, the reconstruction of the sequence of events in an imaginary human life, to the level of operation of the text or narrative as such, the construction of a discourse and a history. The letter's phrasing plays on obscuring the distinction between the two levels of operation: 'As to the present causes of past effects', writes Meyrick, 'it is now seen that the late swindling telegrams account for the last year's cattle plague.' The sentence exploits the ambiguity of 'account for', which seems to mean both 'to render an account of' and 'to cause'. The telegrams are said not merely to explain or offer an account of the cattle plague but to produce it, to stand as the cause of which the plague is the effect. This proposes the notion that writing, in the present, causes a material event in the past (as the present requirements of writing Deronda's story seem the 'swindle' that produces the physical event of his birth as a Jew). Meyrick's play on words calls attention to an assumption inherent in narrative: an action that can be accounted for, one about which a narrative can be recounted, has by the same token an adequate and comprehensible cause, since (so the reasoning implies) to account for something consists, above all, in identifying its cause. Meyrick's metalepsis or chiasmus carries this a step further to point out the sense in which the account of an action *is* its cause. Questioning the meaning of 'accounting for' an event, the sentence is not only deconstructing the concept of causality but also putting in question the representation function of narrative. Narrative structure presents what are ostensibly fundamental properties of reality (or metaphysical categories) such as causality (or the origin of the subject, or identity) as the products of its own operations, the effect of a play of signs. Thus, far from representing the truth of the human situation, the subject's origin and destiny in a history, narrative represents with authority nothing more than its own structural operations.

Causality, the subject, identity, representation and origin are deconstructed or put in question by the reading of the novel proposed in the first half of the second sentence of Meyrick's letter. The second half of the sentence comments on the inherent preposterousness of this situation. Referring to the reversal of cause and effect, the sentence continues: 'which is a refutation of philosophy, falsely so called, and justifies the compensation to the farmers'. This satirizes the pretension to a victory over philosophy, or the claim that irony triumphs over discourse. At the moment that deconstruction claims to achieve a 'refutation' of causality or of the subject or whatever, the argument deconstructs itself in turn, ironized through the very process of making its pretension explicit. This does not happen, one should stress, as a result of a general principle or a belief that radical skepticism must be skeptical of itself. What is involved is not a mental attitude (such as the determination to view all assertions ironically) but a tropological operation, a reversal of rhetorical properties, such as the metalepsis reversing the order of cause and effect and renaming 'cause' the effect of an effect, and 'effect' the cause of the cause. The deconstructive operation, while it consists in pointing out that the concept of causality amounts to an aberrant and arbitrary ordering of rhetorical elements, is itself no more than an equally aberrant reordering of these elements, the performance of another tropological operation. It is for this specific reason that a deconstruction is not a refutation, or that a deconstructive 'refutation' can claim for itself no more authority than the refuted concept. The text's ironization of the 'refutation of philosophy falsely so called' is referring to this specific state of affairs.

However, Meyrick's satirical sentence refers as well to a state of affairs quite different from the dilemma of rhetoricity: he invokes 'swindling telegrams', 'last year's cattle plague', and 'the compensation to the farmers'.[8] These allusions satirize the deconstructive pretension to neutrality, the pretension, precisely, to constitute merely a tropological operation, free of motive and affect, just the way deconstruction has been described above. It is indeed a tropological operation that is involved, but it does not have the privilege of taking place in a neutral context empty of reference or value judgments. Rhetoric inevitably presents itself not only as trope but also as persuasion, so that deconstructive discourse inevitably lapses into a covert attempt at 'refutation', into a dogmatic or exhortative mode. Meyrick's sentence suggests that the motive and goal of 'the refutation of philosophy falsely so called' is none other than a justification of the 'compensation to the farmers', and this makes the point: the deconstructive project takes place in a context of accusation and excuse, of blame and defense, and cannot avoid the motive of self-justification.

Like the 'refutation of philosophy', which involves a cattle plague and compensation to the farmers, the deconstructive account of cause and identity inscribed in *Daniel Deronda* involves a troublesome referent and a justificatory impulse. It involves, namely, the hero's Jewishness. The narrative is relentlessly referential. In a sense the novel's principal issue is the scandal of the referent. Consideration of this issue can begin with an observation of how the specific kind of identity in question disturbs the coherence of Deronda's story. Not only the disclosure of Deronda's parentage but the preceding part of the story as well reveal themselves to be based on unwarranted shifts of rhetorical categories.[9]

The earliest episode indicating Deronda's vocation might be thought to be his rescue of Mirah. The rescue of a maiden in distress, specifically a Jewish maiden, allegorically prefigures Deronda's destiny as a savior of the Jews. The question of Deronda's own Jewishness, however, first becomes explicit in his meeting with Mordecai. Mordecai's identification of Deronda as a Jew and Deronda's acceptance of their resultant relationship mark the first step in the establishment of Deronda's Jewish identity. However, the account of this development involves a radical contradiction, which is perhaps most conspicuous in the scene where Deronda, rowing down the river to seek Mordecai, emerges out of the sunset to encounter the waiting Mordecai on Blackfriars Bridge. The narrator stresses that Mordecai has foreseen precisely this scene, that his inner vision of the 'prefigured friend' prefigured the external sight of Deronda floating into view against a glowing sky. Thus, on the one hand, Mordecai's identification of Deronda is presented as a recognition, and for this reason his assertion of a claim on him has authority and appeal. On the other hand, Deronda's assumption of the identity of Mordecai's prefigured friend is shown to be a consequence of Mordecai's act of claiming him. He becomes what Mordecai claims he is.

If one imitates the deconstructive gesture of Meyrick's letter and reads the 'Deronda plot' as a set of formulas about the identity principle, one recognizes that two different conceptions of the functioning of language are being exploited in the narrator's account. First, the account claims that an identity is recognized, that Mordecai's words on this occasion state the recognized fact. To recognize or know is

> . . . a transitive function that assumes the prior existence of an entity to be known, and that predicates the ability of knowing by way of

> properties. It does not itself predicate these attributes but receives them, so to speak, from the entity itself. . . . To the extent that it is verbal, it is *properly* denominative and constative. . . . Knowledge depends on this non-coercive possibility.
>
> (DE MAN, 'Action and Identity', p. 18)

In presenting Mordecai's identification of Deronda as a recognition, the text makes use of this cognitive, or constative, concept of language. The possibility of Mordecai's recognizing Deronda as his 'prefigured friend' depends, however, on the possibility of an inner representation prefiguring an external sight. This second notion conflicts with the constative concept of language, as is made especially clear by the explicit description of Mordecai's inner representation as a *'coercive type'*: '. . . there are persons whose yearnings, conceptions – nay, travelled conclusions – continually take the form of images which have a foreshadowing power: the deed they would do starts up before them in complete shape, making a coercive type' (p. 527). The power, the coercive function, of Mordecai's identification of Deronda is emphasized in subsequent passages describing Deronda's acceptance of the identity assigned him. This aspect of the account makes use of a concept of identity as a principle actively posited rather than known or recognized, the product of an assertion rather than a matter of fact. Such a notion, that identity is the product of a coercive speech act, deconstructs the identity principle and the constative concept of language grounded upon it. Thus the narration of Deronda's relationship with Mordecai both stresses the authority of recognition or knowledge and undermines the basis of this authority. The contradiction here resembles the one involved in the disclosure of Deronda's birth, which both stresses the causative power of origin and draws attention to the questionable status of cause.

The account of Deronda's relationship with Mordecai includes more than their encounter at Blackfriars Bridge, for the narrator tries to lend their relationship the plausibility and certainty of a gradual process, as well as the impact and authority of a decisive event. The part of the narrative describing Deronda's increasing responsiveness to Mordecai's idea also plays upon two conflicting notions of how language functions. The narrator describes Deronda's development of a Jewish identity in response to Mordecai's assertions but seeks to account for it not as a challenge to the concepts of cognition and constitution but rather as an authentic cognitive process. Mordecai and Deronda, it is suggested, are engaged in a kind of reading, a hermeneutic practice, in which the interpreter and the text (or Mordecai and Deronda) stand in a certain mutual relation. At the same time, however (as if in default of this hermeneutic model, which is hazy at best), the narrative is playing upon the notion of an act of naming, a speech act with the type of authority and validity characteristic of the performative mode. A performative utterance in and of itself accomplishes an action or brings about a situation, rather than describes or interprets it. In addressing Deronda as if he were a Jew, Mordecai is '*doing something* rather than merely *saying* something'.[10] Mordecai's speech, which so often resembles a litany, has a performative quality, and his influence on Deronda evokes the idea of a conversion. The ritual of conversion involves a speech act that changes the identity of the person who is the object of the ritual.

It is striking, however, that conversion precisely *does not* apply in regard to Jewish identity, which is inherited, historical and finally, here, genetic. For the establishment of identity as a Jew, what is required is not merely a performative but an actual performance, an act or event, not just a speech act. Such an act is remotely invoked by the romance elements in the 'Deronda plot', most notably the kind of magical metamorphosis found in fairy tales.[11] In fairy tales a ritual word and gesture produce not merely conversion (a change of spiritual status or of an inner state) but physical transformation. This would be the effect required of Mordecai's influence, were his relationship with Deronda to establish fully Deronda's identity as a Jew. Such an effect exceeds the limits of realistic narrative. To be a Jew (and this is emphasized by the narrator, who never suggests that Deronda might simply 'embrace' the Jewish 'faith') is to have been born a Jew, not merely to take up the spiritual and cultural tradition of Judaism. Thus the establishment of Deronda's identity must shift from his relationship with Mordecai to the revelation of his mother. One discovers, then, that the presentation of Deronda's Jewishness requires several shifts of ground. From the notion of the cognitive and constative function of language the account must shift to the notion of its performative function. From this it must make a further shift of ground to the notion of an actual, non-linguistic act or fact.

With this last shift to the act or the fact, the narrative goes aground. Insistence on the hero's specifically Jewish identity not only puts in question the authority of the discourse but effectively disrupts its coherence. The text's insistent reference leads relentlessly to the referent – to *la chose*, in fact: the hero's phallus, which must have been circumcized, given what we are told of his history.[12] In the period in which Deronda's story takes place, male babies were not routinely circumcized. Circumcision was ritual procedure practiced by Jews, so that evidence of circumcision amounted to evidence of Jewish origin. For Deronda not to have known he was Jewish until his mother told him means, in these terms, 'that he never looked down',[13] an idea that exceeds, as much as does magical metamorphosis, the generous limits of realism. Deronda must have known, but he did not: otherwise, of course, there could be no story. The plot can function only if *la chose*, Deronda's circumcized penis, is disregarded; yet the novel's realism and referentiality function precisely to draw attention to it. Acknowledgment of the fact or act would prevent the construction of the narrative, as it also, in fact, prevents the completion of the deconstruction. It persists as a residue of the deconstructive process. The hero's circumcized phallus, proof of origin and identity, is more than an exemplary metonymy, though it is certainly that. It is distinctively significant, not as a rhetorical structure, but as a referent – one that produces embarrassment, a sense of discomfort that is not intellectual and that is more than a sense of esthetic incongruity.

The mere emphasis on Jewishness, quite apart from any reference to circumcision, was enough to produce discomfort in many Victorian readers of *Daniel Deronda*. It led them to object to the construction of the plot, pointing out what constitutes, in fact, its metaleptic structure. One must recall just how common such a plot structure was in nineteenth-century English novels, which frequently dealt with the establishment of the hero's identity and presented the decisive evidence in a dramatic disclosure late in the story, amply prepared by incontrovertible circumstantial evidence developed in the earlier part of the novel. Few readers saw fit to object to this construction in, say, *Oliver Twist*, though the establishment of Oliver's identity is marked by the same implausibility or artificiality as Deronda's. Oliver's inheritance of his father's name and property turns on the fulfillment of a condition in his will (on conformity, that is, to a written text) that includes the stipulation 'that in his minority he should never have stained his name with any public act of dishonour, meanness, cowardice, or wrong.' That Oliver is his father's son is the effect, then, of his being, 'in effect', 'his father's son', which is to say good, or virtuous with the virtues of the middle class. The metalepsis is as patent here as in *Deronda*, but the impact is altogether different when the evidence reveals, not that the hero's parentage is 'good', but that it is Jewish. It is the specific referent in *Daniel Deronda* that generates its deconstructive effects, by calling attention to the metaleptic structure, which otherwise might not give rise to comment. The scandal of the referent calls attention to the scandal of metalepsis or, more generally, of rhetoricity. The glaring referent highlights the narrative structure as a strictly groundless construct. While it would be misleadingly reassuring to suggest that this is the real reason for readers' objection to 'the Jewish part', it would be equally mistaken to suppose that the objection has nothing to do with rhetoricity.

For many of Eliot's contemporary readers, being a Jew, like having sexual organs, was something to which as little attention as possible should be called. Both terms involved in the notion of a circumcized penis would produce embarrassment. For the men of Eliot's day, sexual identity and Jewish identity did have a kind of structural similarity. Each claimed, on the one hand, an irreducible physical element and, on the other, an enormous burden of cultural, spiritual, and historical significations. Each involved two extremes, unlike, for example, identity as a member of the middle class, the sort of identity more typically in question for a novel's hero (as for Oliver Twist). The physical element was necessary but not sufficient, while the cultural dimension was significant but, strictly speaking, not sufficient. The authority of the physical element as the basis of identity was undermined by the importance of the cultural element and vice versa.[14]

This mutually canceling effect comes into play in *Daniel Deronda* when the narrator stresses both the hero's vocational affinity for Jewishness and his Jewish genealogy. Deronda's demonstrated empathy with Judaic tradition makes the disclosure of his Jewish birth seem either superfluous or implausibly neat, while the asserted fact of his genetic heritage makes his intellectual and emotional affinity seem at once superfluous and inadequate and casts doubt on its authenticity as free choice. The deconstructive effect of the Jewish referent is not merely to call attention to the groundlessness or rhetoricity of the narrative structure. It operates in a more precise and far-reaching way as well. Thus the referentiality of the identity at issue, Jewishness, suspends the principle of identity between two modes: the performative mode, which would define it as a form of activity, and the constative mode, which would define it as a matter of knowledge. Like the affirmation of the hero's Jewishness, which must stop short of acknowledging his circumcision, affirmations of a performative and of a constative concept of identity must stop short of asserting the fact or the act. Full affirmation of the constative mode would mean portraying Deronda's self-identification as real knowledge (as opposed to acceptance of another's word, whether Mordecai's or the Princess Halm-Eberstein's). Full affirmation of the performative mode would mean portraying Deronda's self-identification as a real action, such as the attempt to restore Jewish nationhood, which he is about to undertake at the novel's close. Both possibilities are excluded from the narrator's account. Both the origin of Deronda's history (the fact of his birth) and its goal (the act of restoration) are excluded from his history proper. Deronda's parentage is introduced not as the testimony of the narrator but as the account of the Princess Halm-Eberstein, and his birth is located in a past prior to the time of the novel. Similarly, Deronda's activity in Palestine is introduced not as an actuality but as an eventuality subsequent to the novel's time.

To put it another way, the text brackets the decisive assertion in a story within a story and banishes the decisive performance to a fictive future beyond the story's end. This exclusion of knowledge and action from the realistic narrative proper signifies an acknowledgment of their constitutionally fictional status and with that an acknowledgment of the limited possibilities of language. It is implicitly acknowledged that 'the possibility for language to perform is just as fictional as the possibility for language to assert' (de Man, 'Action and Identity', p. 27).

Thus there emerges in *Daniel Deronda* an account of the determining connections between the referential function of language and its constative and performative functions. Its inexorable referentiality prohibits the narrative from claiming authority either as a genuine fact or as a genuine act, for the referent itself constitutes the fact and the act and remains extralinguistic, necessarily excluded from the discourse that inevitably refers to it. Circumcision stands as an emblem for the fact or act that is at once the proof that the text requires and the referent that it excludes. The 'all-presupposing fact' has a peculiar double status. It signifies a proposition that carries authority neither as knowledge nor as performance, alluded to in the epigraph to chapter 1 as the novel's point of departure, which cannot be made fully explicit: '. . . whether our prologue be in heaven or on earth, it is but a fraction of that all-presupposing fact with which our story sets out.' This formula also names the text's fractionally presented referent the fact of the hero's Jewish identity, affirmed in an account that omits to acknowledge its signifying mark.

The unacknowledged mark is the circumcized phallus emblematizing the powers of constatation, performance and reference. It is the exemplary signifier, and it commemorates a fiat allowing the possibility of signification. It is a sign that stands for a story, told to account for the origin of Jewish identity: the story, namely, of Abraham and Isaac and of Jehovah's intervention to prevent the completion of an act of autocastration. An account that would link the possibility of signification with the possibility of origin and of identity must invoke a divine power. *Deus ex machina* cuts short the cutting off of the race: so the mark of circumcision signifies. Divine dispensation grants genealogy, history and signifying power, as Jehovah intervenes before the actual obliteration: it suffices that the possibility of obliteration should be admitted and the process instituted or prepared. The story told here in terms of a divine fiat relates how it is that, while the conditions of truth or authentic meaning (such as causality) are disclosed to be without authority, that disclosure in truth never carries authority itself (since, as we have observed, the disclosure takes place as a rhetorical reversal like the reversals that constitute the conditions of truth). Divine fiat allows the destruction of discourse to stand as mere deconstruction, a 'refutation' as fictitious as the truth of history or philosophy that it refutes. Circumcision marks this account of the institution of signification. As a mark that tells too much of the conditions of history or too much of the limits cutting off signification or storytelling, circumcision is a sign that the story must evade or exclude or cut out: narrative must cut out or cut around the cutting short of the cutting off of narrative. In this circumcisive outlining, *Daniel Deronda* affirms a history that elicits deconstruction.

A distinctive aspect of *Daniel Deronda*'s deconstructive mode is signaled by the peculiar status of its referent as the exemplary signifier that refers to the story of the institution of signification. 'That all-presupposing fact from which our story sets out' is a reference to another story, a story conceived as an account of the conditions of storytelling. The chapter containing Hans Meyrick's letter presents an excellent example of this operation. It opens with an epigraph quoted from La Rochefoucauld, which offers a statement exactly coinciding with the narrator's (and Deronda's) evaluation of the difference between Mordecai's character and Deronda's. The quoted passage sounds the theme of love and irony, authenticity and inauthenticity, and represents the traditional moral and esthetic judgment with which the narrator's account aligns itself, so that for the narrator the epigraph functions to lend the authority of a classical precedent to that judgment. The aphorism also, through its form, seeks an effect similar to that which the narrator seeks in presenting certain dubious elements of the Deronda plot (such as Mordecai's second sight): an effect of surprise resolving into conviction. Thus La Rochefoucauld's aphorism takes the form of two symmetrical pseudoparadoxes: 'La même fermeté qui sert à résister à l'amour sert aussi à le rendre violent et durable; et les personnes faibles qui sont toujours agitées des passions n'en sont presque jamais véritablement remplies.' The aphorism exemplifies a classical rhetorical mode that compels conviction by means of its symmetrical metaphorical assertions.[15] The category of 'fermeté' seems to account for both resistance to love and the durability of love. The category of 'faiblesse' seems to account for both 'agitation' and shallowness. A truth that reveals itself as a rhetorical structure, La Rochefoucauld's aphorism resembles the narrative structure of *Daniel Deronda*. The authority of a prior text is being invoked to ratify not only the message but also the rhetorical usage favored by the narrator. By the same token, however, the epigraph stands as a *pretext* for the deconstructive operation in Meyrick's letter, which indeed proposes a reading of the entire narrative as a deconstruction of La Rochefoucauld's aphorism: an extended critical commentary on its precepts, its rhetorical mode, and their attendant metaphysical claims.[16] Thus the text of *Daniel Deronda* presents as its point of departure a prior text, a rhetorical and syntactic structure, rather than the dilemmas of subjectivity. The starting point of the novel's discourse is, not the subject, but written language.[17] The signifying process performed by the text is one of allusion or citation in which the signifier points toward a referent constituted as another exemplary signifier. The citational mode testifies to the partial or fictive cutting off from meaning: the circumscribed sign reaches a meaning in the form of a further sign.

The text of Meyrick's letter offers explicit emblems for the citational mode of the novel, in addition to the implicit emblem of circumcision.

The letter places the novel under the rival signs of Hesperus and Hyperion: 'Meanwhile I am consoling myself for your absence by finding my advantage in it – shining like Hesperus when Hyperion has departed.' If Hyperion is the god of an art envisaged as the light of truth, Hesperus is the god of an art conceived as a process of forging of forgery. The citational (or deconstructive) text of *Daniel Deronda* is a consummate forgery passing as an authentic work, and the rival lovers, Deronda and Meyrick, along with the rival gods, Hyperion and Hesperus, personify the two kinds of reading elicited by the narrative: the reading carried out by the narrator and the deconstructive reading proposed by passages such as Meyrick's letter.

However, it can be misleading to think of the two readings in personified or personifying terms, since they constitute a single discontinuous process that moves away from personification, abandoning the notion of the subject for the notion of linguistic operation, reconstruing the narrative's starting point as a text rather than as a subject. More apposite than the rivalry of Hesperus and Hyperion is Meyrick's allegory of the 'mystery' and the 'basis':

> I leave it to him to settle our basis, never yet having seen a basis which is not a world-supporting elephant, more or less powerful and expensive to keep. My means will not allow me to keep a private elephant. I go into mystery instead, as cheaper and more lasting – a sort of gas which is likely to be continually supplied by the decomposition of the elephants.

Instead of a symmetrical confrontation between opposites of the same status, such as Hesperus/Hyperion, one may think of *Daniel Deronda*'s aporia as an asymmetrical obstruction: composition/decomposition (taking the latter term in its material sense, which is *not* the opposite of composition), or a single word for the single process or text: (de) composition. I cut short the process here – as Meyrick writes, 'without comment or digression'.[18]

Notes

1. George Eliot, *Daniel Deronda* (Harmondsworth: Penguin, 1967), p. 704 (Book 7, chapter 52). All page references are to this edition of the novel.
2. In this rereading of Eliot's last novel. I follow the hint of Henry James's Theodora, that in *Daniel Deronda* the 'mass is for the detail and each detail is for the mass,' and ask the question of whether, and how, the detail and the mass are 'for' each other in this text. Theodora defends the novel in James's '*Daniel Deronda*: A Conversation', originally published in *The Atlantic Monthly*

in 1876 and republished in Gordon Haight's valuable collection, *A Century of George Eliot Criticism* (Boston: Houghton, 1965). I am indebted to previous critics of *Deronda* for analyzing the meanings of the novel enforced by its narrator and pointing out the contradictions and insufficiencies of this narration. Important studies include David Kaufmann's *George Eliot and Judaism* (New York: Haskell, 1970): F. R. Leavis' *The Great Tradition* (London: Chatto and Windus, 1948) and his introduction to the edition of the novel (New York: Harper, 1961); Barbara Hardy's *The Novels of George Eliot: A Study in Form* (London: Athlone, 1959) and her introduction to the Penguin edition (cited in note 1); and W. J. Harvey's *The Art of George Eliot* (New York: Oxford University Press, 1961). Felicia Bonaparte's *Will and Destiny: Morality and Tragedy in George Eliot's Novels* (New York: New York University Press, 1975) has a pertinent chapter on 'loose threads in the causal web'.

3. These other notes or letters are Deronda's note to Gwendolen, accompanying her redeemed necklace; Lush's message to Gwendolen; Gwendolen's note summoning Herr Klesmer; the notes exchanged between Grandcourt and Gwendolen during their second courtship; Lydia Glasher's letter to Gwendolen, accompanying the poisoned diamonds; the Princess Halm-Eberstein's summons to Deronda; and Gwendolen's final missive to Deronda on his wedding day. In contrast with these decisive missives, the gratuitous, purposeless character of Meyrick's letter stands out sharply. The gratuitous character of order is also one of its explicit topics.
4. The distinction between two plots is a sort of fiction that begs a great many questions, and actually to distinguish 'narrative modes' in the novel, with the intention of relating them to the separate plots, would be a complicated task, if not impossible. Nevertheless, this broad division has been registered almost unanimously by readers of the novel who, preferring 'the English part', have deplored its subordination to 'the Jewish part'. There is more in this than a mere objection to what have been described as the novel's occasional sentimentalities or moralism; there is more also than Victorian readers' anti-Semitic objections to the glorification of Jewishness. As I shall argue, the supremacy of 'the Jewish part' challenges fundamental tenets of belief about the structure and validity of language.
5. Meyrick practices, not just a narrative mode alien to the narrator's, but a non-narrative art: he is a painter. Deronda's imaginative sympathy with the *histories* of the novel's heroines contrasts with Meyrick's enthusiasm for their appearance as paintings – Gwendolen as a 'Van Dyke duchess', Mirah as a Berenice (see chapter 37). Both the rivalry between language and painting and the conflict between different narrative modes appear also in *Middlemarch.* Will Ladislaw speaks up for the 'fuller image' of language, the 'true seeing [which] is within', in objection to the painted images of Dorothea as a 'perfect young Madonna' enthusiastically composed by his friend Adolf Naumann, a German painter (chapter 19). But Ladislaw's easy and playful use of language resembles Meyrick's and contrasts with that of Casaubon, who searches for origins and causes, tracing the history of myths. Both Meyrick and Deronda, then, are revisions of the ambivalent and incompletely realized figure of Ladislaw. The different distribution of allegiances and values among these characters in *Middlemarch* and in *Daniel Deronda* could be the starting point for

a study of the distinctive ways that these two texts exploit the functions of narrative.

6. The discrediting of Meyrick's letter is only one instance among many in which this strategy is employed; see, e.g., the beginning of chapter 41 (p.568), which portrays Deronda's rehearsal to himself of the commonsensical view of his encounter with Mordecai. This is identified as 'the answer Sir Hugo would have given', an observation that partially discredits it, since Sir Hugo's limited judgment has been documented. In the novel's larger scheme, the English side as a whole comes to occupy this role. Since 'English' characters' judgments are ironized, their criticism of, or disbelief in, the Deronda plot implicitly ratifies that plot's implausibilities.

7. HENRY JAMES, *'Daniel Deronda*: A Conversation', in Haight. See also J. Hillis Miller on flowing water as one of the recurrent metaphors that tend to appear in expressions of the classic assumptions about narrative and history ('Narrative and History', *English Literary History* (*ELH*), 41, 1974, p. 460).

8. Meyrick's next sentence continues the satire of formal critical discourse, with its pretensions to neutrality and exactness: 'My own idea that a murrain will shortly break out in the commercial class, and that the cause will subsequently disclose itself in the ready sale of all rejected pictures, has been called an unsound use of analogy' (p. 704). The critical mind responds to Meyrick's nonsensical and mischievous fantasy by decrying merely his 'unsound use of analogy' – an incongruous understatement parodying the whitened diction distinctive of philosophy and criticism (and deconstructive criticism).

9. The narrative is a series of 'unwarranted substitutions leading to ontological claims based on misinterpreted systems of relationship'; see Paul de Man 'Action and Identity in Nietzsche', *Yale French Studies*, 52 (1975), p. 20. De Man is describing Nietzsche's deconstructive account of our knowledge of entities, which resembles the issue involved in *Daniel Deronda* to the extent that both pose the question of the identity principle.

10. J. L. AUSTIN, *Philosophical Papers* (Oxford: Oxford University Press, 1961), p. 223. Austin introduces a distinction between the constative, or descriptive, function of language and another, 'performative' function. In its ordinary usage, language includes, in addition to statements, such performative utterances as 'I apologize' or 'I name this ship the *Queen Elizabeth*', assertions in which 'in saying what I do, I actually perform that action.' Another example would be the act of baptizing, which confers a name and a religious identification on the person baptized. Conversion to Christianity can be affected by such a performative utterance. Mordecai's talks with Deronda partly function in this way, but they cannot confer Jewish identity.

11. The narrator stresses Mirah's 'transformation' after her fairy-tale rescue and her adoption by the Meyricks (see chapter 32).

12. Deronda did not go to live with Sir Hugo Mallinger until he was two years old.

13. STEVEN MARCUS, *Representations: Essays on Literature and Society* (New York: Random, 1976), p. 212, note:

It is only when he is a grown man, having been to Eton and Cambridge, that he discovers that he is a Jew. What this has to mean – given the conventions of medical practice at the time – is that he never looked down. In order for the plot of *Daniel Deronda* to work, Deronda's circumcised penis must be invisible, or non-existent – which is one more demonstration in detail of why the plot does not in fact work.

14. Discovery of identity generally does involve both physical lineage and a spiritual, cultural, even financial patrimony, and the importance of one or the other factor may vary from case to case, but neither is so extreme or decisive as both are in *Daniel Deronda*.
15. In Book 2, chapter 1, of *The Mill on the Floss*, the narrator criticizes the delusory effects of metaphor (see J. Hillis Miller, 'Optic and Semiotic in *Middlemarch*', in *The Worlds of Victorian Fiction*, ed. Jerome H. Buckley (Cambridge Mass.: Harvard University Press, 1975). It is interesting that the passage aims at delusory metaphors as the basis of our sense of control or authority: the narrator is satirizing, specifically, the school authorities' control over Tom Tulliver. In *Daniel Deronda*, Meyrick's letter resists the narrator's authority to impose metaphors. The letter closes with a satirical citation literalizing a biblical metaphor: 'But while her brother's life lasts I suspect she would not listen to a lover, even one whose "hair is like a flock of goats on Mt. Gilead" – and I flatter myself that few heads would bear that trying comparison better than mine.'
16. The relation between the aphorism and the novel, that is, may be construed as an example of how metaphorical structure is deconstructed by narrative structure, or vice versa (since the conspicuous rhetoricity of the aphorism evokes a deconstruction of the narrative's rhetorical premises).
17. De Man, 'Nietzsche's Theory of Rhetoric', *Symposium* (Spring 1974), p. 40: 'The self which was at first the center of the language as its empirical referent now becomes the language of the center as fiction, as metaphor of the self. What was originally a simply referential text now becomes the text of a text, the figure of a figure.' The narrative of the metamorphosis of the text should not be understood any more literally than the personification of two kinds of text.
18. See Meyrick's letter, p. 708: 'Excuse the brevity of this letter. You are not used to more from me than a bare statement of facts without comment or digression. One fact I have omitted. . . .'

14 *Daniel Deronda* and Circumcision*

K. M. Newton

The book from which this essay is drawn argues – against the relativism implicit in Stanley Fish's contention that criticism is split into 'interpretive communities' divided by irreconcilable critical principles and strategies – that all critical schools have sufficient in common to engage in legitimate and productive debate. Thus Cynthia Chase's deconstructive reading of *Daniel Deronda* can in turn be deconstructed by a critical approach which uses historical and intentionalist arguments. Circumcision is a presence in the novel, not an absence, though unmentioned and unmentionable, and functions as a sign open to various interpretations (see Introduction, pp. 13–14).

In a footnote to an essay first published in 1975, Steven Marcus remarked that a graduate student of his, Lennard Davis, had noticed something interesting about *Daniel Deronda*:

> Mr Davis has discovered a detail – or a missing detail – in *Daniel Deronda* that throws the whole central plot of the novel out of kilter. Deronda's identity is a mystery to himself and has always been. It is only when he is a grown man, having been to Eton and Cambridge, that he discovers that he is a Jew. What this has to mean – given the conventions of medical practice at the time – is that he never looked down. In order for the plot of *Daniel Deronda* to work, Deronda's

* Reprinted from K. M. Newton, *In Defence of Literary Interpretation: Theory and Practice* (London: Macmillan Press, 1986), pp. 197–211 (footnotes renumbered from the original).

> circumcised penis must be invisible, or non-existent – which is one more demonstration in detail of why the plot does not in fact work. Yet this peculiarity of circumstance – which, I think it should be remarked, has never been noticed before – is, I have been arguing, characteristic in several senses of both George Eliot and the culture she was representing[1].

This 'detail' has been used as a central element in a deconstructive reading of the novel by Cynthia Chase.

Chase argues that the novel demands not only a spiritual conversion on the part of Deronda, but also a physical transformation of the type found in fairy tales. It is not enough for Deronda to 'take up the spiritual and cultural tradition of Judaism', since the narrator makes it clear that to be a Jew is to be born a Jew. But *Daniel Deronda* employs a discourse that cannot accommodate such a transformation. Chase writes:

> Insistence on the hero's specifically Jewish identity not only puts in question the authority of the discourse but effectively disrupts its coherence. The text's insistent reference leads relentlessly to the referent – to *la chose*, in fact: the hero's phallus, which must have been circumcized, given what we are told of his history. In the period in which Deronda's story takes place, male babies were not routinely circumcized. Circumcision was a ritual procedure practiced by Jews, so that evidence of circumcision amounted to evidence of Jewish origin. For Deronda not to have known he was Jewish until his mother told him means, in these terms, 'that he never looked down', an idea that exceeds, as much as does magical metamorphosis, the generous limits of realism. Deronda must have known, but he did not: otherwise, of course, there could be no story. The plot can function only if *la chose*, Deronda's circumcized penis, is disregarded; yet the novel's realism and referentiality function precisely to draw attention to it.[2]

Chase goes on to use this 'detail' and her interpretation of it to make a number of deconstructionist points concerning rhetoric and signification in the novel.

In the passage I have quoted from Chase she uses conventional historical discourse: 'In the period in which Deronda's story takes place, male babies were not routinely circumcized.' She is seeking to validate her interpretation by reference to history, and in doing so she introduces into her interpretation empirical considerations, which require to be supported by evidence and to submit to testing. Since 'Deronda's circumcized penis', Chase claims, 'is disregarded', then the question of the author's intentionality is also introduced, even though elsewhere Chase denies that intention is important for her interpretation: her reading is not 'concerned merely with meanings that could plausibly be ascribed to the intentions of the narrator. The text generates a much wider range of significance.'[3] But for circumcision to be disregarded in the novel the author must have known about circumcision as a Jewish practice and chosen to ignore it for the purposes of the story.

Chase's use of historical discourse and her implicit assumption about the author's intention opens up her interpretation to legitimate consideration by critics interested in historical and intentional matters, either to support it or to call it into question. It is not only critics who practise historical and intentional interpretation who might feel that Chase's reading gives them the opportunity to enter into critical dialogue and debate. Critics who employ philosophical discourse in literary interpretation might be interested in the use she makes of philosophical terminology associated with J. L. Austin, since her reading might be questionable if her understanding of Austin was not defensible from a philosophical point of view.

The question Chase's interpretation raises from the viewpoint of a critic interested in history and authorial intention is whether or not she is right to assume that only Jews would have been circumcised in nineteenth-century England and that George Eliot knew this but was compelled to disregard this knowledge for the purpose of making her plot work. There are, however, several other points connected with the question of intention that need to be considered before we discuss further the historical aspect of this question.

It could be argued that the fact that the matter of circumcision has been noticed only recently and apparently not troubled readers for nearly a hundred years[4] indicates that this is no more an internal contradiction in the novel than the inconsistent time schemes are an internal contradiction in *Othello*. Yet George Eliot's commitment to realism and the great pains she took in her work to create an authentic and accurate representation of the world, to the smallest 'detail', one feels tempted to say, suggest that it would have been unlikely that she would have thought nothing of infringing realism by disregarding a documentary fact about Jews to serve her literary purposes. Chase is right to believe that, if George Eliot departed from realism in this instance, this is a clear disruption of the coherence of the novel's realistic discourse. Another defence of George Eliot might be that she could have simply forgotten that Jews were circumcised. Given her deep interest in and knowledge of Judaism and Jewish culture, this seems extremely unlikely. It might also be claimed that, bearing in mind Victorian ignorance in such matters, Deronda need not know that he is circumcised, but this can hardly be reconciled with the interest he develops in and the study he makes of Judaism. A final possibility that needs to be considered is that we cannot know for certain that he was circumcised, but this would seem to be contradicted by the fact that he was 'little more than two years old' (p. 697)[5] when his mother chose to separate him from Jewish life and gave him to Sir Hugo. Chase's position can only be seriously challenged, I believe, by the view that George Eliot intended circumcision to be realistically present in the novel even though it is not mentioned in so many words. I shall argue that it is possible not only to accommodate Deronda's circumcision in a realistic interpretation of the novel but also to use this 'detail' to overcome some of the traditional objections that have been made to the 'Deronda plot'.

The first point to make in supporting this position is that direct reference is not necessary for some element to be seen as present in a literary text. Critics, for example, have not been deterred from discussing such matters as incest in *The Mill on the Floss* or the physical relationship between Dorothea and Casaubon in *Middlemarch* despite the fact that they are not explicitly referred to in the text.[6] But the claim that circumcision is included in the realism of *Daniel Deronda* is fundamentally different in its nature, since it is based on logic and not interpretative speculation. In terms of realism circumcision is logically entailed by the fact that Deronda is a Jew and is brought up in a Jewish family until he is two years old. There is no need for it to be mentioned directly, since it is included in Deronda's Jewishness. A weakness of Chase's argument that circumcision is disregarded and deconstructs the novel's claim to realism is that her interpretation itself disregards the impossibility of circumcision being referred to openly in a Victorian novel. Readers of novels are well aware that they, as theorist of narrative Seymour Chatman puts it, 'must fill in gaps with essential or likely events, traits and objects which for various reasons have gone unmentioned'.[7] Circumcision has the same status in this context as sexual organs. As Chase herself remarks, both sexual organs and circumcision would be likely to create embarrassment among Victorian readers. But, though no embarrassing reference may be made to sexual organs in Victorian novels, even a Victorian reader would assume that characters, being human, possessed them, and would know, without having to be told by the author, that these unmentionables performed a signifying function – for example, in defining the characters' sexual identity, in determining the nature of relationships between them, in accounting for any children they might have. I would suggest that circumcision signifies in a similar way in *Daniel Deronda*.

It might be objected by those who see George Eliot as a typical narrow-minded Victorian that she would never have contemplated even an indirect allusion to circumcision. This view is hard to justify. Deronda is explicitly said to be two years old before he is given to Sir Hugo. For Chase this is conclusive proof that Deronda would have been circumcised and that the novel, therefore, disregards it. But she ignores the obvious point that it is George Eliot who supplies this piece of information. If circumcision is irreconcilable with the realism of the plot, as both Marcus and Chase claim, then George Eliot could easily have arranged matters so that Deronda was handed over to Sir Hugo almost immediately after birth, or at least been vague as to when he was handed over. The fact that she provides information which makes it virtually certain that he would have been circumcised does not suggest that circumcision is disregarded; on the contrary, it suggests that she intends it to be present in the novel as a signifier though she cannot mention it explicitly.

But the most serious objection to my position is the claim by Chase that in the period in which the novel is set circumcision is an unmistakable sign of Jewishness and that therefore Deronda must know he is a Jew even though the plot is based on his lacking such knowledge. I now return to the historical question. Chase refers to the fact that circumcision was not 'routinely' practised in Victorian England. But, though it was not 'routine', is there evidence to suggest that it was fairly common for non-Jews to be circumcised? If there is, Chase's interpretation of the novel is clearly vulnerable and my argument is strengthened, since circumcision need not be an unambiguous sign of Jewishness. I shall try to demonstrate that such evidence exists.

It is clear from nineteenth-century medical books that circumcision was a standard treatment for the common condition in infants of congenital phimosis, the contraction of the preputial orifice. I shall quote some representative comments:

> In all common cases of natural phimosis, the best modern operators in this metropolis, and many excellent surgeons abroad, prefer circumcision.[8]
>
> In all cases [of phimosis] I prefer circumcision as the simplest and speediest operation, and as leaving the most satisfactory result.[9]
>
> Another common condition is a prepuce much too long. . . . Such prepuces always call for circumcision.[10]

George Eliot's own physician, Sir James Paget, something of an authority on this area of medicine, also believed that phimosis 'frequently requires operation in children, especially if the orifice of the prepuce be very narrow',[11] though Paget believed that surgery was too often resorted to in such cases. Paget was also a friend of George Eliot and George Henry Lewes and a copy of the first edition of the book I have quoted from, published in 1875, with a dedication to Lewes, is to be found among their books in Dr Williams's Library.[12]

There is also some evidence that even in the nineteenth century circumcision was performed for hygienic reasons, though I have not been able to find conclusive evidence for this. P. C. Remondino in his admittedly bizarre *History of Circumcision* maintains that 'the physician class' in the United States, France and England thoroughly practise circumcision as a hygienic precaution with every male child in their own families, and he goes on to say more generally, 'The practice is now much more prevalent than is supposed, as there are many Christian families where males are regularly circumcised soon after birth, who simply do so as a hygienic measure.'[13]

Several of the writers whom I have quoted mention that phimosis could encourage masturbation, which was almost universally condemned during this period, and clearly this would be an additional reason for circumcising infants. One physician provides a particularly graphic example of a case that requires circumcision:

> The body of the penis was well developed, but the glans was very small and pointed, tightly imprisoned in the contracted foreskin . . . upon touching the orifice of the urethra he was slightly convulsed, and had a regular orgasm. . . . As excessive venery is a fruitful source of physical prostation and nervous exhaustion, sometimes producing paralysis, I . . . recommended circumcision as a means of relieving the irritated and imprisoned penis.[14]

Even Paget, comparatively objective on the subject of masturbation, believed it could have a bad effect on the young: 'Practised frequently by the very young, that is, at any time before or at the beginning of puberty, masturbation is very likely to produce exhaustion, effeminacy, over-sensitiveness and nervousness.' In fact, he is sorry that he cannot find it particularly injurious to health: 'I wish that I could say something worse of so nasty a practice; an uncleanliness, a filthiness, forbidden by GOD, an unmanliness despised by men.'[15] But the general medical view was that it could be a serious health hazard as well as being immoral, and it was believed that it could be inhibited by circumcision:

> I will take it for granted that the above given causes of irritation, phimosis, worms, etc., have been removed. If these simpler measures fail, the child must be most carefully watched, the hands kept fastened outside the cot, blistering fluid . . . applied if needful to the prepuce and glans, and to the inside of the thighs. This failing, the child should be circumcised without anaesthetic. This step acts as a warning which is long remembered; furthermore, it leads to hardening and diminished sensibility of the glans. It may be relied upon as curative, if it be supplemented by careful judicious watching.[16]

Remondino, who agrees with one Dr Vanier that the prepuce is 'the principle [*sic*] cause of masturbation',[17] believes that the discouraging of masturbation is a major benefit of circumcision. And Alex Comfort, who has made a study of attitudes to masturbation in the nineteenth century, states that circumcision was increasingly used to combat it: 'The eighteenth and early nineteenth century, believing masturbation to be a harmful as well as a sinful practice, attempted to cure it, but from 1850 to 1879 surgical measures become increasingly popular.'[18]

A common theory of the origin of circumcision is that it was designed to diminish interest in sex and thus to remove a barrier to concentration on religion. Renaissance medical writers had believed the foreskin contributed greatly to sexual pleasure. Fallopius noted that the male organ 'is not of itself lubricate if it has no foreskin, and yet in the venereal act it requires notable lubricity', and Alex Comfort writes of Sinibaldi, 'The seat of male pleasure . . . Sinibaldi holds to be the foreskin.'[19] Sir James Paget expressed similar views:

> The function of the prepuce in the act of copulation is explicable on the principle that, other things being equal, the force of a reflex act is directly proportionate to the force of the incident impression which it follows . . . the energy of the secretion and expulsion of the seminal fluid, during copulation, will (other things being equal) be proportionate to the quantity of highly excitable surface which is stimulated in the act. The mucous membrane of the prepuce, naturally reverted during copulation, supplies a large extent of highly-excitable surface.

This passage from Paget is quoted in what Steven Marcus, in *The Other Victorians*, regards as one of the most significant books of the Victorian era: William Acton's *The Functions and Disorders of the Reproductive Organs*, first published in 1857. Acton goes on to comment,

> Admitting, as I do, that this distinguished physiologist is right in the abstract, I am still of the opinion that the prepuce in man (at least in civilized life) is the cause of much mischief, and that we could well spare that organ. As offering an additional surface for the excitement of the reflex action, this fold of membrane, in the present state of society, aggravates an instinct rather than supplies a want. The tenor of all I daily observe shows that, in the unmarried, it additionally excites the sexual desires, which it is our object to repress. In the act of sexual congress, its existence may, I grant, give additional pleasure; and, as age advances, it may be necessary to copulation. Without it, there may be difficulty in exciting the flagging powers; but in the present state of society, all tends to prove that we require restraint, not excitement.[20]

Although Acton does not state directly that it would be a good thing if infants were circumcised, this seems the obvious implication of his remarks. He also sees the foreskin as a danger to health generally, since it 'predisposes to many forms of syphilis', and in the case of a narrow foreskin 'is often the cause of emissions, masturbation, or undue excitement of the sexual desires, which it becomes very difficult for the sufferer to endure'.[21] It would therefore seem clear that, in the period in which the novel is set, circumcision would not have been identified solely with Jews since it would commonly have been performed in cases of phimosis, and also to combat masturbation, and, possibly, for hygienic reasons or to diminish interest in sex generally.

How does this historical investigation of circumcision affect the interpretation of *Daniel Deronda*? A recurrent theme in George Eliot's fiction is the tension between sign and meaning; all signs need to be interpreted and even what may appear to be the most obvious sign can be misinterpreted: 'Signs are small measurable things, but interpretations are illimitable' (*Middlemarch*, chapter 3). This theme is also present in *Daniel Deronda*, particularly in connection with Deronda: 'Both Emperor and Rabbi were wrong in their trust of outward signs: poverty and poor clothes are no sign of inspiration, said Deronda to his inward objector, but they have gone with it in some remarkable cases' (p. 571). Deronda, who is subject to 'oppressive scepticism' (p. 685), is represented as being aware that signs do not possess immanent meaning and that an individual's desires shape his reading of signs. The main role circumcision plays in the novel, I suggest, is as an ambiguous sign. In Chase's interpretation, in contrast – somewhat ironically since deconstruction normally emphasises the polysemic possibilities of the signifier – circumcision functions as an unambiguous sign of Jewishness.

There is nothing in Deronda's life up until his chance encounter with Mirah to connect him with Jews, apart from circumcision. Since, as I have tried to show, circumcision could be performed for other reasons, Deronda has no reason to believe it to be a sign of Jewishness. Not that this possibility would have been welcome to someone of his upbringing, as he possesses some popular prejudices about Jews: 'Deronda could not escape (who can?) knowing ugly stories of Jewish characteristics and occupations' (p. 246). But obviously circumcision could be a sign of Jewishness, and this could account for the personal element in his fear that Mirah may be related to 'vulgar' Jews: 'In his anxiety about Mirah's relatives, he had lately been thinking of vulgar Jews with a sort of personal alarm' (p. 415).

But Deronda believes that the strongest probability is that Sir Hugo Mallinger is his father. It is the sudden realisation that he could be Sir Hugo's illegitimate son which makes him aware of the ambiguity of signs when he is compelled to make 'a new mental survey of familiar facts' (p. 205). Even if Sir Hugo is his father, circumcision could still be a sign of Jewishness if his mother was Jewish, though it would be unlikely that Sir Hugo would have consented to a Jewish rite being performed for a son who was to be brought up as a Christian. It could simply be a sign without significant meaning – that he suffered from phimosis as an infant or that his doctor believed in circumcision as a health safeguard. But, and no doubt this would be the most worrying possibility, it could also be a sexual sign. It could have been carried out for distasteful reasons.

Deronda's first doubt about his identity occurs in the context of sexual excess and licence: his question to his tutor about why popes and cardinals had so many nephews. He then thinks it almost certain that he was the product of such excess. What therefore could his having been circumcised signify in such a context? As I suggested above, circumcision not only was a means of discouraging masturbation but was also seen, in the Victorian period and earlier, as diminishing sexual desire in general. Deronda's circumcision, therefore, could be interpreted as a sign that it was feared that he might inherit the excessive sexual desires of one or both of his parents, and that this step was taken to lessen the possibility that such inherited desires might lead to masturbation or illicit sexual indulgence. William Acton, for example, believed that children could inherit strong sexual passions from their parents:

> but I feel certain that very young children may inherit a disposition to affections of these organs, which causes them to rub themselves and incidentally to excite abnormal sensations and partial erections. . . . Early voluptuous ideas . . . are also, I think, traceable to the brain; and I believe, heritable, like many other qualities, from parents who have not held the animal passions in any sort of check.[22]

Circumcision, then, offers many possibilities for ambiguity of meaning in Deronda's situation, and several of his characteristics can be interpreted as understandable reponses to this ambiguity: his apprehensiveness at the thought of 'vulgar' Jews, as I have already mentioned, and his dread at finding out the truth about his parentage. But, most important, his anxiety about his identity is made psychologically credible since this sign could mean both so much and so little.

If circumcision is seen as part of the theme of the ambiguity of signs, this also helps to dispose of a difficulty that has often been said to undermine the credibility of the plot. The fact that Deronda turns out to be a Jew and so is able to fulfil the role that Mordecai has created for him seems too contrived and convenient to be reconcilable with the novel's realism. As Chase puts it, Deronda's transformation into a Jew is a 'magical metamorphosis' that 'exceeds the limits of realistic narrative'.[23] Chase's view that normal causality is inverted in the novel seems attractive. The root of the problem, however, is in Deronda's attitude to Mordecai's claim that he is a Jew. There is no difficulty in accounting for Mordecai's belief in it, since he possesses the visionary expectation that someone will come to carry on his work. Deronda must also have something of the physical appearance of a Jew. We are told he is dark, for example, but again the signs are ambiguous since his face is 'not more distinctly oriental than many a type seen among what we call the Latin races' (p. 553). If there is no evidence whatever to support Mordecai's belief that Deronda is a Jew, it is difficult to understand, from a realistic standpoint, why he should resolve to fulfil Mordecai's idealistic hopes if he can, since he must be Jewish by race to do so. That he should then turn out to be a Jew seems to be the product of the author's will and not a credible working out of events.

In a book I published on George Eliot's fiction a few years ago, I attempted to qualify objections to this aspect of the novel by arguing that Deronda was in effect gambling that Mordecai might be right and that this could be related to the gambling theme which embraces the activities and behaviour of many of the characters. However, I felt compelled to add, somewhat defensively, that 'Deronda has more than his fair share of luck in the novel'.[24] I now believe that this interpretation can be greatly strengthened and the realism of this part of the novel defended if circumcision is taken into account as an ambiguous sign. If Deronda is circumcised, he must be aware that he has something in common with the Jews, and, since he does not know for sure the truth about his parentage, there is a reasonable chance that he might be a Jew. There is a suggestion that he is not totally surprised by Mordecai's claim that he is a Jew. He does not dismiss it as absurd or bizarre: 'The claim hung, too, on a supposition which might be – nay, probably was – in discordance with the full fact: the supposition that he, Deronda, was of Jewish blood. Was there ever a more hypothetic appeal?'(p. 570). To say only that Mordecai 'might be' or 'probably' was wrong is odd if there is nothing whatever to connect Deronda with Jews. And the only possible personal link he could have had with Jews before Mirah encouraged his interest in them is circumcision. But circumcision is not proof that he is a Jew, much as he would like to be one after encountering Mordecai's idealism; it is only a possibility. Deronda is well aware how easily desire influences interpretation, and he must prepare both himself and Mordecai in case it is proved he is not a Jew. It will be clear, however, that, if Deronda knows he is circumcised, then the gamble I originally believed to be rather a long shot emerges as a much safer bet. His willingness to comply with Mordecai's 'hypothetic' belief, at least provisionally, and his turning out actually to be a Jew are reasonable and probable and therefore easily reconcilable with realistic narrative. Consequently, the plot of the Deronda side of the novel is much more defensible.

The fact that there is nothing to show that Deronda is a Jew until more than half way through the novel and that it is only proved conclusively in chapter 51 indicates that those who read the book for the first time without prior warning would think of circumcision too late, if it occurred to them at all, for it to have any serious influence on their response and interpretation. Thus it would be only during re-reading that this matter and its implications would be likely to occur to the reader. It might be argued that this is evidence that George Eliot could not have intended circumcision to play any role in the novel. But it is not unusual for novels to be constructed in such a way that clues to the working out of events are unlikely to be noticed on a first reading, and I am not thinking only of detective stories but also of such a novel as Jane Austen's *Emma*. I have already suggested that there are indications that Deronda believes it possible he might be Jewish before he has any reason for thinking so, apart from circumcision, and it seems to me that a number of clues that Deronda is circumcised occur in chapter 16, in which he first fears he is illegitimate. If these clues are picked up, then the chapter and the events that follow from it make more sense.

I used to be of the opinion that this chapter illustrated the dramatic inferiority of the Deronda side of the novel since it failed to make Deronda's crisis of identity convincing. His sense of estrangement on becoming aware that he is probably Sir Hugo's illegitimate son seemed excessive since, apart from not disclosing the secret of his birth, Sir Hugo's treatment of him leaves nothing to be desired. He is loved by Sir Hugo, educated by him at Eton and Cambridge, allowed to choose without constraint what he wants to do with his life. As T. S. Eliot remarked of Hamlet, Deronda's emotional disturbance seems 'in excess of the facts as they appear'.[25] I now believe that the fundamental sense of difference which Deronda experiences and the language in which it is expressed can be justified if his fear that he is illegitimate is accompanied by the knowledge that he is circumcised, and I shall suggest that certain connotations of the language of this chapter make this interpretation possible.

The narrator states that, though only thirteen, Deronda's knowledge went beyond that of a child: 'Having read Shakespeare as well as a great deal of history, he could have talked with the wisdom of a bookish child about men who were born out of wedlock and were held unfortunate in consequence. . . . But he had never brought such knowledge into any association with his own lot' (p. 205). If the young Deronda is knowledgeable about illegitimacy, there is no reason why he should not know something about the practice of circumcision. His sudden realisation that he might be illegitimate would then connect with his awareness that he is circumcised, which until then he had no reason to think significant, and create the fear that he might be different in some fundamental way from Sir Hugo and his class. Circumcision becomes a sign of difference, and, though he cannot be sure of its meaning, it fills him with dread.

The imagery used to describe Deronda's state of mind gives some justification for this interpretation:

> If his father had been wicked – Daniel inwardly used strong words, for he was feeling the injury done him as a maimed boy feels the crushed limb which for others is merely reckoned in an average of accidents – if his father had done any wrong, he wished it might never be spoken of to him: it was already a cutting thought that such knowledge might be in other minds.
>
> (p. 209)

This imagery of being maimed and wounded is used several times. Other examples are: 'he would never bring himself near even a silent admission of the sore that had opened in him' (p. 210); 'A surprise that came to him before his first vacation, strengthened the silent consciousness of a grief within, which might be compared in some ways with Byron's susceptibility about his deformed foot' (p. 213); and, perhaps most strikingly, 'The sense of an entailed disadvantage – the deformed foot doubtfully hidden by the shoe, makes a restlessly active spiritual yeast, and easily turns a self-centred, unloving nature into an Ishmaelite' (p. 215). Although Deronda's nature is of 'the rarer sort' that resists such distortion, the reference to 'Ishmaelite', with its connotation of both Jew and outcast, provides a clue to his situation, and at this point in the novel, especially in the context of imagery of maiming, injury and deformity, the only characteristic that could connect Deronda with Jewishness is circumcision.

Chase's general view of the novel, that the 'triumph of idealism over irony is written into the very structure of the novel's double plot',[26] is fundamentally conventional and has been shared by almost all critics. Clearly, as Chase implies, such idealism is suspect if it is dependent on disregarding circumcision. But, if circumcision is seen as indirectly present, one can take a different view of the relation between idealism and irony in the novel. Although idealism is not subverted, irony is still allowed its place. Indeed, in a novel in which Romantic preoccupations are so much in evidence, one should not be surprised by the incorporation into the narrative structure of Romantic irony, in which idealistic commitment and irony or scepticism coexist without the one being transcended by the other. Circumcision is relevant to this since it casts an ironical light on Deronda's Jewishness and on the concept of cause which assumes that there is equilibrium or logical relation between cause and effect. The exalted role Mordecai envisages for Deronda as the bearer of 'the sacred inheritance of the Jew' (p. 558), and Deronda's identification with it, are dependent on Deronda's being a Jew by race, yet the only attribute that associates him with Jewishness is circumcision, and even that sign is ambiguous; and the deep-seated human desire for causal order and proportion, both in the world and in narrative, is mocked by the disequilibrium that exists between the triviality of this sign and the magnitude of the consequences that follow from it.

There can, of course, be no conclusive proof that George Eliot intended circumcision to be a signifying presence in the novel, unless documentary evidence is discovered.[27] But clearly the novel itself raises the subject and critics must decide which of the three attitudes that it is possible to have towards it is most defensible: namely, that it is a signifying presence, a signifying absence, or performs no signifying function at all. My argument that it is a signifying presence undermines the still-common view that George Eliot's fiction embodies Victorian high-mindedness and seriousness and accepts the constraints that operated upon the imagination of the novelist during her period. It is difficult to reconcile this image of her with my claim that she intended such a matter as circumcision to be indirectly signified in *Daniel Deronda* and provided clues to its presence. But such an image is now surely indefensible, since much recent criticism has convincingly demonstrated, from various perspectives, that her imagination functioned more indirectly and allusively than previous critics believed.

Notes

1. Steven Marcus, 'Human Nature, Social Orders, and 19th Century Systems of Explanation: Starting in with George Eliot', *Salmagundi*, 28 (1975) p. 41.
2. Cynthia Chase, 'The Decomposition of the Elephants: Double-Reading *Daniel Deronda*', Publications of the Modern Language Association (*PMLA*), 93 (1978) 222-3.
3. Ibid., p. 217.
4. It is possible, however, that Henry James is covertly alluding to this missing 'detail' when, in '*Daniel Deronda*: A Conversation', Pulcheria makes what might seem, on the face of it, a rather distasteful remark: 'I am sure he had a nose, and I hold that the author has shown great pusillanimity in her treatment of it. She has quite shirked it.' See *A Century of George Eliot Criticism*, ed. Gordon S. Haight (London, 1966), p. 100.
5. Quotations and page numbers are from *Daniel Deronda*, ed. Barbara Hardy (Harmondsworth, 1966).
6. See Tony Tanner, *Adultery in the Novel: Contract and Transgression* (Baltimore and London, 1979), pp. 66-72; and A. L. French, 'A Note on *Middlemarch*', *Nineteenth-Century Fiction*, 26 (1971-72), pp. 339-47.
7. Seymour Chatman, *Story and Discourse: Narrative Structure in Fiction and Film* (Ithaca, New York and London, 1978), p. 28. As Chatman also points out,

signification in a novel must function in terms of norms. If a male character has been born into a Jewish family, the assumption must be that he has been circumcised, unless it is made clear that he is not, even though Jewish infants with a family history of bleeding could be exempted. One must assume the norm unless the text provides evidence to the contrary.

8. SAMUEL COOPER, *Practice of Surgery* (London, 1826), pp. 577-8.
9. JOHN ERICHSEN, *The Science and Art of Surgery* (London, 1853), p. 910.
10. W. H. A. JACOBSON, *The Diseases of the Male Organs of Generation* (London, 1893), p. 622.
11. SIR JAMES PAGET, *Clinical Lectures and Essays*, ed. Howard Marsh (London, 1879), p. 71.
12. See WILLIAM BAKER, *The George Eliot – George Henry Lewes Library: An Annotated Catalogue of their Books at Dr Williams's Library*, London (New York and London, 1977), p. 153.
13. P. C. REMONDINO, *History of Circumcision* (Philadelphia and London, 1891), p. iv.
14. LEWIS A. SAYRE, *Lectures on Orthopaedic Surgery and Diseases of the Joints* (London, 1876), pp. 14–15.
15. PAGET, *Clinical Lectures*, pp. 291, 292.
16. JACOBSON, *Diseases of the Male Organs*, p. 458.
17. REMONDINO, *History of Circumcision*, p. 224.
18. ALEX COMFORT, *The Anxiety Makers: Some Curious Preoccupations of the Medical Profession* (London, 1967), p. 95.
19. IBID., pp. 17, 26.
20. WILLIAM ACTON, *The Functions and Disorders of the Reproductive Organs in Youth, in Adult Age, and in Advanced Life* (London, 1858), pp. 23–4.
21. IBID., p. 24.
22. IBID., p. 55.
23. CHASE, in *PMLA*, 93, p. 222.
24. K. M. NEWTON, *George Eliot: Romantic Humanist: A Study of the Philosophical Structure of her Novels* (London, 1981), p. 196.
25. T. S. ELIOT, 'Hamlet and his Problems', in *The Sacred Wood: Essays on Poetry and Criticism* (London, 1960), p. 101.
26. CHASE, in *PMLA*, 93, p. 215.
27. However, since the article that forms the basis of this chapter was published in *Essays in Criticism* in 1981, another article has appeared which argues that the apocalyptic symbolism of the novel suggests that circumcision is intended to be included. See Mary Wilson Carpenter, 'The Apocalypse of the Old Testament: *Daniel Deronda* and the Interpretation of Interpretation', *PMLA*, 99 (1984), pp. 56–71.

Notes on Authors

JONATHAN ARAC, a critic in the forefront of contemporary American post-structuralist criticism, is Professor of English and Comparative Literature at Columbia University. Among his books are *Commissioned Spirits* (1979) and *Critical Genealogies* (1987).

CYNTHIA CHASE, one of the major practitioners of the form of deconstructive criticism associated with Paul de Man, is Assistant Professor of English at Cornell University. She is the author of *Decomposing Figures: Rhetorical Readings in the Romantic Tradition* (1986).

TERRY EAGLETON is the best-known British Marxist critic and theorist. He is a Fellow of Linacre College, Oxford. His books include: *Myths of Power: A Marxist Study of the Brontës* (1975); *Criticism and Ideology* (1976); *Walter Benjamin, or Towards a Revolutionary Criticism* (1981); *The Rape of Clarissa* (1982); *Literary Theory: An Introduction* (1983); *The Function of Criticism* (1984); *William Shakespeare* (1986); *The Ideology of the Aesthetic* (1990).

CATHERINE GALLAGHER, one of the leading New Historicist critics working on nineteenth-century fiction, is Associate Professor of English at the University of California, Berkeley. She is the author of *The Industrial Reformation of English Fiction* (1985).

SANDRA M. GILBERT and SUSAN GUBAR are probably the major feminist critics working in the field of women's writing. Gilbert is Professor of English at Princeton and Gubar is Professor of English at Indiana University, Bloomington. Their books include *The Madwoman in the Attic* (1979); *The Norton Anthology of Literature by Women* (1985); *No Man's Land: The Place of the Woman Writer in the Twentieth Century* (1988).

MARY JACOBUS is a leading post-structuralist feminist critic. She is Professor of English at Cornell University. Among her books are *Tradition and Experiment in Wordsworth* (1976) and *Reading Woman* (1986).

DAVID LODGE, until recently Professor of English at the University of Birmingham, has endeavoured in his criticism to combine Anglo-American formalism with more theoretical approaches, such as structuralism and Bakhtinian dialogic criticism. He is the author of *Language of Fiction* (1966); *The Novelist at the Crossroads* (1971); *The Modes of Modern Writing* (1977); *Working with Structuralism* (1981); *After Bakhtin* (1990).

COLIN MACCABE has made a significant contribution to British post-structuralist criticism. He currently combines his post of Head of Production at the British Film Institute with that of Professor of English at the University of Pittsburgh. Among his books are *James Joyce and the Revolution of the Word* (1979) and *Theoretical Essays: Film, Linguistics, Literature* (1985).

D. A. MILLER is a critic whose work aims to reconcile American and European traditions in criticism of the novel. Professor of English at the University of California, Berkeley, he is the author of *Narrative and Its Discontents* (1981) and *The Novel and the Police* (1988). His more recent criticism shows a move towards New Historicism.

J. HILLIS MILLER, originally associated with phenomenological criticism, has been a major figure in deconstructive criticism since the early 1970s. Formerly at Yale, he is now Professor of English and Comparative Literature at the University of California, Irvine. His books include *Charles Dickens: The World of his Novels* (1958); *The Disappearance of God* (1963); *Poets of Reality* (1965); *The Form of Victorian Fiction* (1968); *Thomas Hardy: Distance and Desire* (1970); *Fiction and Repetition* (1982); *The Linguistic Moment* (1985); *The Ethics of Reading* (1987).

K. M. NEWTON is Senior Lecturer in English at the University of Dundee. Among his books are *George Eliot: Romantic Humanist* (1981); *In Defence of Literary Interpretation* (1986); *Interpreting the Text* (1990).

DIANNE F. SADOFF is Associate Professor of English at Colby College, Waterville, Maine. She is the author of a psychoanalytic study of nineteenth-century fiction, *Monsters of Affection* (1982).

Further Reading

I have divided the books and articles listed here into five broad categories, which reflect, I believe, the main tendencies in criticism of George Eliot's work over the past twenty years or so, followed by a final section for collections and general studies of interest. I have marked with an asterisk those studies which seem to me to have made a particularly significant contribution to modern criticism of her work.

(1) Language, realism, narration

BELSEY, CATHERINE *Critical Practice*. London: Methuen, 1980. (Argues that George Eliot is a writer of 'classic realist texts'.)

BERSANI, LEO *A Future for Astyanax: Character and Desire in Literature*. London: Marion Boyars, 1978. (Critique of realism in *Middlemarch*. Discussed in Introduction.)

CHRIST, CAROL 'Aggression and Providential Death in George Eliot's Fiction'. *Novel*, 9 (Winter 1976), pp. 130–40. (Critique of realism. Discussed in Introduction.)

CLARK-BEATTIE, ROSEMARY '*Middlemarch's* Dialogic Style'. *Journal of Narrative Technique*, 15 (1985), pp. 199–218. (Bakhtinian approach.)

CLAYTON, JAY 'Visionary Power and Narrative Form: Wordsworth and *Adam Bede*'. *English Literary History*, 46 (1979), pp. 645–72.

DALE, PETER 'Symbolic Representation and the Means of Revolution in *Daniel Deronda*'. *Victorian Newsletter*, 59 (1981), pp. 25–30.

EDWARDS, MICHAEL 'George Eliot and Negative Form'. *Critical Quarterly*, 17 (1975), pp. 171–9.

ERMATH, ELIZABETH D. *Realism and Consensus in the English Novel*. Princeton: Princeton University Press, 1983.

GARRETT, PETER K. *The Victorian Multiplot Novel: Studies in Dialogical Form*. New Haven: Yale University Press, 1980. (Bakhtinian approach.)

GINSBURG, MICHAEL PELED 'Pseudonyms, Epigraphs and Narrative Voice:

Middlemarch and the Problem of Authorship'. *English Literary History*, 47 (1980), pp. 542–58.

HENBERG, M. C. 'George Eliot's Moral Realism'. *Philosophy and Literature*, 3 (1979), pp. 20–38.

HERTZ, NEIL 'Recognizing Casaubon'. *Glyph: Textual Studies*, Vol. 6. Baltimore: Johns Hopkins University Press, 1979, pp. 22–41. (Deconstructive reading.)

KENDRICK, WALTER M. 'Balzac and British Realism: Mid-Victorian Theories of the Novel'. *Victorian Studies*, 20 (1976), pp. 5–24.

KERMODE, FRANK 'Lawrence and the Apocalyptic Types'. *Critical Quarterly*, 10 (1968), pp. 14–38. (Discusses *Middlemarch* in relation to typology.)

KNOEPLMACHER, U. C. *George Eliot's Early Novels: The Limits of Realism*. Berkeley: University of California Press, 1971.

LEVINE, GEORGE *The Realistic Imagination: English Fiction from Frankenstein to Lady Chatterley*. Chicago: Chicago University Press, 1981.

MCGOWAN, JOHN P. 'The Turn of George Eliot's Realism'. *Nineteenth-Century Fiction*, 35 (1980), pp. 171–92.

MILLER, J. HILLIS *The Form of Victorian Fiction*. Notre Dame, Indiana University of Notre Dame Press, 1968.

* —— 'Narrative and History'. *English Literary History*, 41 (1974), pp. 455–73. (Pioneering deconstructive reading of *Middlemarch*. Discussed in Introduction.)

* —— 'Optic and Semiotic in *Middlemarch*', in Jerome H. Buckley, (ed.) *The Worlds of Victorian Fiction*. Cambridge, Mass.: Harvard University Press, 1975. (Deconstructive reading. Discussed in Introduction.)

—— 'The Two Rhetorics: George Eliot's Bestiary', in G. Douglas Atkins and Michael L. Johnson, (eds) *Writing and Reading Differently: Deconstruction and the Teaching and Composition of Literature*. Lawrence, Kansas: University Press of Kansas, 1985, pp. 101–14. (Deconstructive reading of *The Mill on the Floss*.)

NEWTON, K. M. 'The Role of the Narrator in George Eliot's Novels'. *Journal of Narrative Technique*, 3 (1973), pp. 97–107.

SHEETS, ROBIN '*Felix Holt*: Language, the Bible, and the Problematic of Language'. *Nineteenth-Century Fiction*, 37 (1982), pp. 146–69.

SWANN, BRIAN '*Middlemarch*: Realism and Symbolic Form'. *English Literary History*, 39 (1972), pp. 279–308.

(2) Ideology, history, politics

BAMBER, LINDA 'Self-Defeating Politics in George Eliot's *Felix Holt*'. *Victorian Studies*, 18 (1975), pp. 419–35.

* EAGLETON, TERRY *Criticism and Ideology: A Study in Marxist Literary Theory*. London: New Left Books, 1976. (Contains Marxist critique of her fiction. Discussed in Introduction.)

* GALLAGHER, CATHERINE *The Industrial Reformation of English Fiction: Social Discourse and Narrative Form, 1832–1867*. Chicago: University of Chicago Press, 1985. (New Historicist reading of *Felix Holt*, part of which is included in this collection.)

—— 'George Eliot and *Daniel Deronda*: The Prostitute and the Jewish Question', in Ruth Bernard Yeazell, (ed.) *Sex Politics, and Science in the Nineteenth-Century Novel*. Baltimore: Johns Hopkins University Press, 1986.

GOODE, JOHN *'Adam Bede'*, in Barbara Hardy, (ed.) *Critical Essays on George Eliot*. London: Routledge & Kegan Paul, 1970. (Marxist reading. Discussed in Introduction.)

MARCUS, STEVEN 'Human Nature, Social Orders, and 19th Century Systems of Explanation: Starting in with George Eliot'. *Salmagundi*, 28 (1975), pp. 20–42.

PYKETT, LYN 'Typology and the End(s) of History in *Daniel Deronda*'. *Literature and History*, 9 (1983), pp. 62–73.

—— 'George Eliot and Arnold: The Narrator's Voice and Ideology in *Felix Holt the Radical*'. *Literature and History*, 11 (1985), pp. 229–40.

WIDDOWSON, PETER, STIGANT, PAUL, BROOKER, PETER 'History and Literary "Value": The Case of *Adam Bede* and *Salem Chapel*'. *Literature and History*, 5 (1979), pp. 2–39.

* WILLIAMS, RAYMOND *The Country and the City*. London: Chatto & Windus, 1973. (Contains critique of *Adam Bede*. Discussed in Introduction.)

(3) Feminism

AUERBACH, NINA 'The Power of Hunger: Demonism and Maggie Tulliver'. *Nineteenth-Century Fiction*, 30 (1975), pp. 150–71.

AUSTEN, ZELDA 'Why Feminist Critics are Angry with George Eliot'. *College English*, 37 (1967), pp. 549–61. (Discussed in Introduction.)

BEER, GILLIAN *George Eliot*. Brighton: Harvester Press, 1986. (Defends George Eliot against feminist attacks. Discussed in Introduction.)

BELSEY, CATHERINE 'Re-Reading the Great Tradition', in Widdowson, Peter, (ed.) *Re-Reading English*. London: Methuen, 1982. (Combines feminism with politics. Discussed in Introduction.)

BLAKE, KATHLEEN *'Middlemarch* and the Woman Question'. *Nineteenth-Century Fiction*, 31 (1976), pp. 285–312.

* GILBERT, SANDRA M. and GUBAR, SUSAN *The Madwoman in the Attic: The Woman Writer and the Nineteenth-Century Imagination*. New Haven: Yale University Press, 1979. ('The Lifted Veil' and *Middlemarch* are considered at length. Discussed in Introduction.)

GOODE, JOHN '"The Affections Clad with Knowledge": Woman's Duty and the Public Life'. *Literature and History*, 9 (1983), pp. 38–51.

HOMANS, MARGARET 'Eliot, Wordsworth, and the Scenes of the Sisters' Instruction'. *Critical Inquiry*, 8 (1981), pp. 223–41.

JACOBUS, MARY *Reading Woman: Essays in Feminist Criticism*. London: Methuen, 1986. (As well as essay included in this collection, contains chapter on 'The Lifted Veil' which combines feminism and psychoanalysis.)

LEVINE, GEORGE 'Repression and Vocation in George Eliot: A Review Essay'. *Women and Literature*, 7 (1979), pp. 3–13.

MILLER, NANCY K. 'Emphasis Added: Plots and Plausibilities in Women's Fiction'. *Publications of the Modern Language Association (PMLA)*, 96 (1981), pp. 36–48.

NESTOR, PAULINE *Female Friendships and Communities: Charlotte Brontë, George Eliot, Elizabeth Gaskell*. Oxford: Clarendon Press, 1985. (Argues that George Eliot's depiction of the female temperament is anti-feminist.)

NEWTON, JUDITH LOWDER *Women, Power, and Subversion: Social Strategies in British Fiction, 1778–1860*. Athens: University of Georgia Press, 1981. (Combines feminism with politics. Discusses *The Mill on the Floss*.)

SHOWALTER, ELAINE *A Literature of Their Own: British Women Novelists from Brontë to Lessing*. Princeton: Princeton University Press, 1977.

—— 'The Greening of Sister George'. *Nineteenth-Century Fiction*, 35 (1980), pp. 292–311.

WEED, ELIZABETH '*The Mill on the Floss* or the Liquidation of Maggie Tulliver'. *Genre*, 11 (1978), pp. 427–44.

WILT, JUDITH '"He Would Come Back": The Fathers of Daughters in *Daniel Deronda*'. *Nineteenth-Century Literature*, 42 (1987), pp. 313–38.

ZIMMERMAN, BONNIE '*Felix Holt* and the True Power of Womanhood'. *English Literary History*, 46 (1979), pp. 432–51.

(4) Psychoanalytic criticism

CHASE, KAREN *Eros and Psyche: The Representation of Personality in Charlotte Brontë, Dickens and George Eliot*. London: Methuen, 1984.

EMERY, LAURA COMER *George Eliot's Creative Conflict: The Other Side of Silence*. Berkeley: University of California Press, 1976.

KUCICH, JOHN 'George Eliot and Objects: Meaning and Matter in *The Mill on the Floss*'. *Dickens Studies Annual*, 12 (1983), pp. 319–37.

—— 'Repression and Dialectical Inwardness in *Middlemarch*'. *Mosaic*, 18 (1985), pp. 45–63.

REDINGER, RUBY V. *George Eliot: The Emergent Self*. London: The Bodley Head, 1976; New York: Alfred A. Knopf, 1977. (Psychoanalytically influenced biography.)

(5) Studies of the intellectual and cultural context of her fiction

ASHTON, ROSEMARY 'The Intellectual "Medium" of *Middlemarch*'. *Review of English Studies*, 30 (1979), pp. 154–68.

—— *The German Idea: Four English Writers and the Reception of German Thought*. Cambridge: Cambridge University Press, 1980.

BAKER, WILLIAM *George Eliot and Judaism*. Salzburg: Universität Salzburg, 1975.

BEER, GILLIAN *Darwin's Plots: Evolutionary Narrative in Darwin, George Eliot and Nineteenth-Century Fiction*. London: Routledge & Kegan Paul, 1983.

* BONAPARTE, FELICIA *The Triptych and the Cross: The Central Myths of George Eliot's Poetic Imagination* (New York: New York University Press,1979). (Discusses *Romola* as an attempt to combine novel and epic.)

CARPENTER, MARY WILSON *George Eliot and the Landscape of Time: Narrative Form and Protestant Apocalyptic History*. Chapel Hill, NC: University of North Carolina Press, 1986.

COLLINS, K. K. 'G. H. Lewes Revised: George Eliot and the Moral Sense'. *Victorian Studies*, 21 (1978), pp. 463–92.

DALE, PETER 'George Eliot's "Brother Jacob": Fable and the Physiology of Common Life'. *Philological Quarterly*, 64 (1985), pp. 17–35. (One of the few studies of this short story.)

GRAVER, SUZANNE *George Eliot and Community: A Study in Social Theory and Fictional Form*. Berkeley: University of California Press, 1984.

GREENBERG, ROBERT A. 'Plexuses and Ganglia: Scientific Allusion in *Middlemarch*'. *Nineteenth-Century Fiction*, 30 (1975), pp. 33–52.

LEVINE, GEORGE 'George Eliot's Hypothesis of Reality'. *Nineteenth-Century Fiction*, 35 (1980), pp. 1–28.

MASON, MICHAEL YORK '*Middlemarch* and Science: Problems of Life and Mind'. *Review of English Studies*, 22 (1971), pp. 151–69. (Probably the first article to argue that G. H. Lewes's thinking had a crucial influence on her fiction.)

MYERS, WILLIAM *The Teaching of George Eliot*. Leicester: Leicester University Press, 1984.

NEWTON, K. M. 'George Eliot, George Henry Lewes and Darwinism'. *Durham University Journal*, 66 (1973–74), pp. 278–93.

—— 'Historical Prototypes in *Middlemarch*'. *English Studies*, 56 (1975), pp. 403–8.

—— *George Eliot, Romantic Humanist: A Study of the Philosophical Structure of her Novels*. London: Macmillan Press, 1981.

SHAFFER, E. S. *'Kubla Khan' and 'The Fall of Jerusalem': The Mythological School in Biblical Criticism and Secular Literature*. Cambridge: Cambridge University Press, 1975. (Discusses *Daniel Deronda* in relation to Biblical criticism.)

SHUTTLEWORTH, SALLY *George Eliot and Nineteenth-Century Science: The Make-Believe of a Beginning*. Cambridge: Cambridge University Press, 1984.

STONE, DONALD D. *The Romantic Impulse in Victorian Fiction*. Cambridge, Mass.: Harvard University Press, 1980.

VOGELER, MARTHA S. 'George Eliot and the Positivists'. *Nineteenth-Century Fiction*, 35 (1980), pp. 406–31.

WELSH, ALEXANDER *George Eliot and Blackmail*. Cambridge, Mass.: Harvard University Press, 1985. (Study of the novels in relation to the 'information culture' of the nineteenth century.)

WIESENFARTH, JOSEPH *George Eliot's Mythmaking*. Heidelberg: Carl Winter, 1977.

—— '*Middlemarch*: The Language of Art'. *PMLA*, 97 (1982), pp. 363–77.

WITEMEYER, HUGH *George Eliot and the Visual Arts*. New Haven: Yale University Press, 1979.

WRIGHT, T. R. 'George Eliot and Positivism: A Reassessment'. *Modern Language Review*, 76 (1981), pp. 257–82.

(6) Collections and general studies

ADAM, IAN (ed.) *This Particular Web: Essays on 'Middlemarch'*. Toronto: University of Toronto Press, 1975.

BLOOM, HAROLD (ed.) *Modern Critical Views: George Eliot*. New York: Chelsea House Publishers, 1986.

—— *Modern Critical Interpretations: George Eliot's 'Middlemarch'*: New York: Chelsea House Publishers, 1987.

BUCKLEY, JEROME (ed.) *The Worlds of Victorian Fiction*. Cambridge, Mass.: Harvard University Press, 1975.

DENTITH, SIMON *George Eliot*. Brighton: Harvester Press, 1986.

KNOEPFLMACHER, U. C. and LEVINE, GEORGE (eds) *Nineteenth-Century Fiction* (special issue: George Eliot, 1880–1980), 35 (1980), pp. 253–455.

MCSWEENEY, KERRY *Middlemarch*. London: George Allen and Unwin, 1984.

SMITH, ANNE (ed.) *George Eliot: Centenary Essays and an Unpublished Fragment*. London: Vision Press, 1980.

Index